MAGIC MISOPROSTOL

Reproductive Justice and Abortion Liberation in Latin America

Cordelia Freeman

First published in Great Britain in 2025 by

Bristol University Press
University of Bristol
1–9 Old Park Hill
Bristol
BS2 8BB
UK
t: +44 (0)117 374 6645
e: bup-info@bristol.ac.uk

Details of international sales and distribution partners are available at bristoluniversitypress.co.uk

© Cordelia Freeman 2025

The digital PDF and ePub versions of this title are available open access and distributed under the terms of the Creative Commons Attribution-NonCommercial-NoDerivatives 4.0 International licence (https://creativecommons.org/licenses/by-nc-nd/4.0/) which permits reproduction and distribution for non-commercial use without further permission provided the original work is attributed.

British Library Cataloguing in Publication Data
A catalogue record for this book is available from the British Library

ISBN 978-1-5292-3687-3 paperback
ISBN 978-1-5292-3688-0 ePub
ISBN 978-1-5292-3689-7 OA PDF

The right of Cordelia Freeman to be identified as author of this work has been asserted by her in accordance with the Copyright, Designs and Patents Act 1988.

All rights reserved: no part of this publication may be reproduced, stored in a retrieval system, or transmitted in any form or by any means, electronic, mechanical, photocopying, recording, or otherwise without the prior permission of Bristol University Press.

Every reasonable effort has been made to obtain permission to reproduce copyrighted material. If, however, anyone knows of an oversight, please contact the publisher.

The statements and opinions contained within this publication are solely those of the author and not of the University of Bristol or Bristol University Press. The University of Bristol and Bristol University Press disclaim responsibility for any injury to persons or property resulting from any material published in this publication.

Bristol University Press works to counter discrimination on grounds of gender, race, disability, age and sexuality.

Cover design: Hayes Design and Advertising
Front cover image: Getty/Silvana Flores

For all those fighting for reproductive justice,
for everyone, everywhere.

Contents

Acknowledgements		vi
Introduction		1
1	From the Favelas of Brazil to the WHO: The Biography of Misoprostol	22
2	Supporting Misoprostol Abortions: The 'Accompaniers' Facilitating Access	50
3	The Mobilities of Misoprostol: Pharmaceuticals on the Move	79
4	Misoprostol and the Law: Manipulating the Margins	103
5	Misoprostol and Its Relations: In Search of a Gold Standard	133
For Abortion Liberation: A Conclusion		155
References		167
Index		192

Acknowledgements

This book would never have been possible without the generosity of my research participants. I am incredibly grateful for the time given to me by all the people I spoke to in the process of researching misoprostol and accompaniment practices. So thank you, to every one of you, for your expertise, enthusiasm, relentless pursuit of reproductive justice, and care for all people who take control of their own reproductive lives. *La lucha continua.*

The research would also not have been possible without the generous support of two funders, which offered me the resources to conduct fieldwork and the time to think and write. This work was supported by the Wellcome Trust [217311/A/19/Z] and Economic and Social Research Council [ES/T009640/1].

Thank you to Bristol University Press, and my editor Zoë Forbes in particular, for supporting my vision for this book and for shepherding it through the process.

I also wish to thank all the colleagues I have worked with while conducting this research, from the School of Geography at the University of Nottingham, where this research began, to the Department of Geography at the University of Exeter, where I now work. I have so appreciated co-teaching with colleagues, having our 'book club' of fellow book writers, and learning so much from you all.

I have also had the great privilege of co-writing with brilliant colleagues who have taught me so much about abortion theory, praxis, and politics. Thank you to Sydney Calkin, Francecsa Moore, Raquel Drovetta, Agustina Rúa, Olivia Engle, Deirdre Duffy, Rishita Nandagiri, and Julieta Chaparro-Buitrago. And to Sandra Rodríguez, for being such a big part of this abortion project over the last few years and always making me question what I thought I knew. Thank you.

This book is just one output from my work on abortion in Latin America over the past few years, and I am so grateful to the fantastic organizations that I have worked with on creative and engaged projects. Thank you to Fondo MARIA, Gabriela Jáuregui and Eréndira Derbez for your work on the graphic novel *Será Deseada*, which can be downloaded for free on the Fondo MARIA website; Women on Web for the Find Your Abortion Project;

and the Colectiva por la Libre Información para las Mujeres in Peru for all the work on the investigative journalism podcast *Las Públicas* as well as the short documentary *Mientras Todo Iba Pasando*. I warmly encourage readers to visit these resources, which provide a rich and empathetic understanding of abortion in Latin America.

Lastly, to my family, with love. To my parents and siblings, George for always supporting me and being so understanding through the whole book writing process, and our wonderful children, S and H. I am so proud of how confidently you assert your bodily autonomy, but sometimes you do just have to put your shoes on.

Introduction

On a spring morning in November 2022, I walked through the quiet streets of a Buenos Aires suburb to interview an abortion *acompañante*. I arrived at a small health clinic and was taken through the back to the garden where a tiny lean-to housed a desk with a computer and a couple of chairs. Before I could sit down, the phone rang and I could overhear a young woman explain that she was pregnant and was desperate not to be. The *acompañante* answered her questions with reassuring confidence and swiftly set up the next steps of the process to help the woman obtain the safe abortion she clearly desired. '*Tienes un don*' [You have a gift], I told her afterwards. She laughed it off; this process I overheard was second nature to her and is how she spends her days. She is a proud *acompañante*, someone who accompanies others through an abortion, most commonly with the medication misoprostol, alone or in combination with mifepristone. This was a window onto the abortion accompaniment process that I was researching and has come to form the central pillar of this book.

Magic Misoprostol tells the story of the abortion pill misoprostol and how it came to play such an important role in the reproductive lives of people all around the world. This medication has been called 'magic' due to its efficacy for safe and cheap self-managed abortions, which has resulted in the transformation of abortion access in Latin America. Misoprostol began its life as a stomach ulcer medication, but because of its stark warning – not to be used by pregnant women! – women in Brazil who were seeking ways to end their pregnancies began experimenting with it. Over time, they developed an effective regimen and the pill, as well as knowledge of how to take it, spread across the region. This book covers this experimentation process, the activist groups supporting people to have abortions with misoprostol, the politics of moving the pills in clandestine contexts, how the use of misoprostol plays with the law, and how misoprostol has far-reaching relations with other technologies. This book argues that misoprostol and the people who have mobilized it in Latin America have transformed abortion safety, knowledge, and practices, with global effects. Latin America has been the key context for this activism and knowledge making, but with ramifications that have changed abortion access across the world.

Misoprostol is a prostaglandin, a hormone-like compound that can have various effects and, importantly in this case, provokes uterine contractions. When used with the right dosage and at the right time, these contractions can expel and terminate a pregnancy. The discovery of these abortifacient properties of misoprostol has led to a fundamental reshaping of abortion access and safety across Latin America and the world. This is not an equally accessible panacea as the medication is not available to all people in all places, but Latin America has higher rates of access than other parts of the world. Despite the region having some of the most restrictive abortion laws, the expansion of knowledge about and use of misoprostol has brought safe abortions to millions of people seeking to end their pregnancies (De Zordo, 2016; Fernández Vázquez and Szwarc, 2018). As one interviewee in Mexico told me: 'Women have abortions. I mean, of course, you know that it is our daily routine, right?' *Magic Misoprostol* charts this story, from the rearticulation of misoprostol as an abortifacient to its commonplace, safe, and effective use to terminate pregnancies, in order to explore reproductive justice, mobility, and scientific knowledge and, ultimately, to set out a vision for abortion liberation.

The magic of misoprostol

The title of this book was born out of hearing how my interview participants spoke about misoprostol. An *acompañante* in Peru wondered aloud, 'misoprostol has done magic with women's reproductive health, hasn't it?'; another in Argentina told me about how 'revolutionary' medical abortion has been; and a doctor in Peru called misoprostol 'fabulous' and 'extraordinary'. One interviewee in Peru passionately declared that 'pills are the solution to abortions in the whole world'. It is not just me who has found this – 'thank God misoprostol exists today!' exclaimed a male obstetrician-gynaecologist cited by De Zordo (2016, 20), while Belfrage (2023, 11) found that *acompañantes* 'venerated misoprostol, imbuing it with agentic powers' and Fernández Vázquez and Szwarc (2018) call it 'revolutionary'. The wonder of the magic of misoprostol is clearly widespread.

But the title of this book is tongue in cheek. Misoprostol *has* been extraordinary and revolutionary, but it would not have been if it were not for the women who first experimented with it to provoke their own abortions in the 1980s, or the abortion providers who found ways to transport the pills across borders in the early 2000s, or the *acompañantes* today who provide supportive and empathetic care for those using misoprostol. The magic of misoprostol, then, is in the love and care of a 'constellation of actors' (Berro Pizzarossa and Nandagiri, 2021, 23) who have transformed its potential across decades and continents. Could we call misoprostol magic were it not for the tireless work and care of those seeking reproductive autonomy for themselves and others?

The ability to terminate a pregnancy with medications has been hailed as the most significant development in reproductive technology since the contraceptive pill (Winikoff and Sheldon, 2012), but I am wary of a 'technological fix' approach when the chemical effects of misoprostol are not the solution by themselves. Reifying misoprostol alone ignores the processes involved in bringing the medication to those who need it and the relationships that are crucial to creating its efficacy (Suh, 2021; Krauss, 2023). It is *how* misoprostol is used that has allowed it to become a tool to bring about political agency (Vacarezza, 2021). The actors and processes that have developed the use of misoprostol as an abortifacient have opened up access to abortions, but also altered what an abortion can look like, taking the practice outside medicalized and legal frameworks. This is the magic of misoprostol that I focus on.

When misoprostol is taken up by feminist actors in tandem with empathetic care, accessible information, and autonomy, the results of access to misoprostol really have been transformative. Since the expansion of the use of abortion pills in Latin America since the 1980s, maternal mortality and morbidity have both fallen significantly (Jelinska and Yanow, 2018). It is no longer the case that abortions need to be performed by a medical professional in order to be safe, and people who have used abortion pills have found them to be their preferred method to terminate their pregnancy. Abortions with pills are viewed as simpler, cheaper, more private, easier to fit into daily lives, and more 'natural' than a procedural (surgical) abortion (Lafaurie et al, 2005; Ramos et al, 2014; Wainwright et al, 2016). Once viewed as an act of desperation or 'a last and dangerous resort of the marginalised and vulnerable', self-managed abortion is now recognized as a safe and viable option for those seeking to end a pregnancy (Erdman et al, 2018, 14). Now, millions of people have abortions using misoprostol every year in Latin America and across the world. While misoprostol on its own is not inherently magical, this book uses misoprostol as a starting point from which to explore knowledge making, feminist activism, reproductive justice, and abortion liberation in Latin America.

What is an abortion?

The question 'what is an abortion?' may seem like a straightforward one. We typically use it to refer to the purposeful termination of a pregnancy. But the mechanics of that are often misunderstood, thanks in no small part to the creation of misinformation by anti-abortion actors. Broadly speaking, there are two ways in which an abortion is performed: procedural and medical.

A procedural abortion, also known as a surgical abortion, is a simple and quick healthcare procedure typically performed through either vacuum aspiration or dilation and extraction. A vacuum aspiration takes place with local or general anaesthetic during a procedure lasting 5–10 minutes, whereby a tube is inserted into the womb through the cervix and suction is applied to extract the contents (Orr, 2017). The dilation and extraction method is generally used beyond 15 weeks of gestation under local or general anaesthetic; during a 10–20 minute procedure, forceps are inserted into the dilated cervix to extract the pregnancy (Orr, 2017).

It is these types of procedure that are what many people think of when they think of an abortion. However, the meaning of an abortion has been changed by the advent of medication that terminates a pregnancy. A medical (or medication) abortion involves taking pills that end a pregnancy and provoke its expulsion. Taking the medication mifepristone followed by misoprostol gives the highest rates of efficacy (95–98 per cent effective), but misoprostol can be taken alone when mifepristone is not available (75–90 per cent effective; Singh et al, 2018). These pills are safe and, since 2005, the World Health Organization has recognized misoprostol as an essential medicine and in 2018 listed misoprostol alone as a recognized method of medical abortion (Assis, 2020).

The development of medical abortions since the 1980s has led to a shift in who 'performs' an abortion, with it now being highly common for the person to access pills through a healthcare or non-healthcare setting and then take the pills and complete the abortion alone. Therefore, the person who takes the pills is their own 'provider', and people who support the process – whether through sharing information, procuring the pills, or guiding them through the process – can be seen as the 'support team' (Jelinska and Yanow, 2018). The process of taking pills outside a clinical context is called 'self-managed abortion', which is not a 'less unsafe' last resort, but has proven to be a safe and effective option across the world (Erdman et al, 2018; Jelinska and Yanow, 2018).

The conceptualization of a 'safe abortion' has, therefore, been disrupted through the introduction of abortion pills. A presumption that abortions are safe if accessed through a trusted medical context but unsafe if accessed through any other, particularly any illegal, way no longer stands. Fears of 'illegal abortions' consisting of shadowy back streets, coat hangers, and knitting needles are not completely unfounded, but these are far less common now that knowledge of and access to abortion pills, primarily misoprostol, have expanded. Despite the proven safety and efficacy of abortion, including medical abortion, it is unique in being such a highly legislated healthcare procedure. This has been termed 'abortion exceptionalism' to highlight how abortion is regulated in an exceptional and overly stringent way compared to other procedures of comparable safety and complexity (Joffe and Schroeder, 2021). Such over-regulation, argues Millar (2023), is a mode of stigma-in-action that positions abortion as a moral issue rather than a medical one and exacerbates fears of its riskiness or complexity.

Abortion in Latin America

Abortions are highly common in Latin America. Latin America and the Caribbean has the world's highest estimated abortion rate at 44 abortions per 1,000 women (Singh et al, 2018). The majority of scholarship on abortion in the region has centred on abortion as either a legal issue or as a public health issue. But still, the issue of religion looms large, and I am frequently asked about the role of Catholicism in abortion law and public sentiment. Catholic doctrine has certainly influenced the culture of abortion in Latin America. Despite numbers of self-declared Catholics falling, the Church and anti-abortion movements are highly organized, resourced, and influential in political sectors, resulting in the Catholic Church playing an outsized role in abortion politics in the region (Marcus-Delgado, 2019). Since the 1990s, ultra-conservative Catholic groups such as Opus Dei and the Legionaries of Christ have successfully swayed law and policy on sexual and family issues, including abortion (Blofield and Ewig, 2017). But Catholicism isn't the whole story, as evangelicalism has grown across the region, with many of these groups being as fiercely anti-abortion as hardline Catholics.

The presumption that Catholicism alone explains anti-abortion sentiment in Latin America can also be challenged by figures that show that Catholic women access abortions at a rate higher than most other groups (Morgan and Roberts, 2012), and by the existence of organizations such as Catholics for Choice, which advocates for a reproductive justice approach and respect for people's decisions about their own lives. Neither is Catholic doctrine reflected in public opinion on abortion, including by those who identify as Catholics, as the majority of populations do support abortions in at least some circumstances. Religion does, therefore, play a role in understanding the landscape of abortion in Latin America, but it is a more complex picture than Catholicism alone and Catholic practice itself is far from monolithic (Morgan and Roberts, 2012).

Since I began research for this book in 2019, and certainly since I began researching abortion in Latin America in 2013, the legal developments with regard to abortion in the region have been astonishing.[1] As recently as 2020, 97 per cent of Latin Americans lived in countries where access to abortion was highly restricted (Taylor, 2022). There were small pockets of legal abortion access 'on demand' in Cuba, Uruguay, and Mexico City, but otherwise the picture was bleak (Encarnación, 2022). However, the advent

---

[1] Abortion laws are now shifting at such a fast pace that this may no longer be the accurate state of abortion laws in Latin America. For a reliable and promptly updated source of current abortion laws, please see the website of the Center for Reproductive Rights: https://reproductiverights.org/maps/worlds-abortion-laws/

of the *marea verde* (green tide/wave) has led to a sweep of reforms, including the legalization of abortion in the first 14 weeks of pregnancy in Argentina in 2020 and in the first 24 weeks in Colombia in 2022, and the nationwide decriminalization of abortion in Mexico in 2023.

Historically, the early 20th century and even the 19th century was a time for progressive action regarding abortion in Latin America. Nicaragua's 1891 penal code permitted abortions to save a woman's life, and the law remained until 2006 (Marcus-Delgado, 2019). Argentina became a world leader in decriminalizing abortion after rape in 1922, and Chile, Brazil, Mexico, and Uruguay all followed in the 1930s (Molina, 2022). Most countries introduced 'therapeutic abortion' reforms that would allow for abortions in 'exceptional circumstances' such as if the pregnant person would otherwise die, with only three countries – Chile, the Dominican Republic, and El Salvador – refusing abortions even in those circumstances (Marcus-Delgado, 2019). The 1960s then saw demands for safe and legal abortion from feminist groups but, apart from the legalization of abortion in Cuba, no significant progress was made (Nolan, 2022). The Latin American feminist movement of the 1970s to the 1990s took bodily autonomy as a central focus, but the dominance of military dictatorships and repressive 'democracies' forced the movement into an oppositional position and stymied feminist political progress (Rivera Berruz, 2023). This situation remained until the region's 'pink tide' (1998–2018), when a swathe of Left-wing governments came to power and six Latin American countries took steps to decriminalize abortion (Molina, 2022). The *marea verde* then ushered in the wave of reforms that have changed the landscape since 2020.

That is not to say Latin America is a legal paradise of abortion. Central America and the Caribbean still have particularly harsh laws, and the Dominican Republic, El Salvador, Haiti, Honduras, Nicaragua, and Suriname criminalize abortion in all circumstances (Marcus-Delgado, 2019). These countries have even moved backwards with Nicaragua, Honduras, and El Salvador all revoking abortions that had been allowed under certain circumstances (Marcus-Delgado, 2019; Taylor, 2022). The consequence of these laws is that it makes safe abortions harder to access and results in the fear of prosecution as well as active persecution of those who have accessed abortions or who present with 'unexplained' miscarriages (Bergallo et al, 2018). The Honduran state, for instance, is actively pursuing the criminalization of women who access reproductive healthcare services and are subsequently forced into a brutal legal system that presumes their guilt in an illegal abortion (García et al, 2020). The majority of these women are young, single domestic workers who are recommended by legal advisors to plead guilty as the 'best option' to avoid a worse conviction (García et al, 2020). Similarly, as Oberman (2018) shows in El Salvador, it is poor, innocent women who are prosecuted and convicted of abortion-related crimes there, including homicide, when presenting at a hospital with a miscarriage. The situation in El Salvador is intensified by the successful recruitment of doctors into law enforcement efforts, reporting anyone who they think may have induced their own abortion. Despite this depressing picture, these countries with hyper-restrictive abortion laws are increasingly becoming outliers (Taylor, 2023).

Even with the broad move towards more progressive abortion laws, abortion politics and discourse can still be fierce. Abortion is viewed as a dramatic battleground and the procedure is debated far more than any other medical issue, resulting in hostility around abortion even where it is legal (Marcus-Delgado, 2019). While other sexual and reproductive rights issues provoke debate, abortion has been a key node for counter-mobilization, and neoconservative and religious groups have forged alliances to prevent progressive change (Barbieri et al, 2021). In response, feminist and other groups have highlighted the public health crisis that has resulted from a lack of legal access to abortion.

Despite all of the strides made, which are detailed in this book, there are still huge disparities in who is able to access a safe abortion. The adage that 'rich women have abortions, poor women die' still rings true far too often. As one interviewee who supports people with access to abortions in Peru explained:

> So what's the problem here? The money. Because if I have money and I go to a clinic and I say, 'I'm pregnant, I've taken antibiotics, I feel sick', 'ah, well, I don't think it [the foetus] is moving anymore', the doctor sedates you and that's it. Nothing happens and you leave happy. But if you're poor, really, where do you go? If you're poor, you take whatever concoctions they give you.

The abortion case-fatality rate is 22 per 100,000 in Latin America and the Caribbean, which is higher than most locations in the global North but significantly lower than in Africa (141 per 100,000) and Asia (62 per 100,000; Singh et al, 2018). The mortality rate has reduced notably, as even in 2015 Latin America had the world's highest number of maternal deaths per capita from unsafe abortion procedures (Taylor, 2022). This reduction and these geographical differences are likely due to high rates of access to misoprostol in Latin America, which has decreased the number of people attempting abortions through unsafe methods (De Zordo, 2016). Nevertheless, it is poor and Indigenous women who are most likely to suffer from severe abortion restrictions or access to a safe abortion, even where abortions are legally available (Wurtz, 2012).

Even with deaths from unsafe abortion reducing due to more availability and knowledge of how to use misoprostol, abortion remains a public health issue in Latin America. State inaction on this and the continuation of the situation whereby people die due to lack of access to safe abortions led my co-authors and I to use the term 'states of uncare' to refer to 'a context where state-led systems of care and care policies are orientated toward restricting abortion and where those who access abortion and those who facilitate it face reprisals' (Duffy et al, 2023, 610). Situations whereby an 11-year-old girl in Argentina attempted suicide twice and experienced a forced C-section after being raped by her grandmother's boyfriend and an 11-year-old girl in Paraguay experienced a forced C-section after being raped by her stepfather exist because of the denial of abortion by these states of uncare (Marcus-Delgado 2019; Encarnación, 2022). These brutal examples are not inevitable, and they exist in sharp contrast to the ordinariness of the millions of safe abortions that take place every year in Latin America.

The inescapable context that underpins this situation of abortion in Latin America is that of patriarchal control, machismo, and marianismo. Abortion is not an isolated issue, and these patriarchal structures and sociocultural understandings reinforce gendered violence across the region, including gender-based violence, femicide, and atrocities that have been committed during civil wars and under military dictatorships (Wilson, 2014). For Hernandez (2002), machismo is a phenomenon that creates a gendered division between men and women in Latin America and solidifies the rights of men over women. Machismo may look slightly different between Latin American countries, and has been defined in many ways, but can be broadly understood as expectations of the dominance of men, the norm of violence, the cult of virility, and of the oppression of women (Hernandez, 2002). Its female counterpart, marianismo, refers to the cultural expectation that women are submissive, self-sacrificing, and derive their power from marriage and motherhood (González, 2005). These phenomena provide a framework for understanding gendered violence and how it can become codified through law, policy, and healthcare, including regarding abortion. As Rita Segato (2021) argues, male violence against women is born out of a desire for power, rather than sex, in a male hierarchy that can be understood as 'mafia-like'. It is this patriarchal desire for power over women, and expectations of compulsory motherhood, that shape the landscape of abortion in Latin America. Reproductive decisions, including whether to have an abortion, are inevitably constrained in the context of patriarchal social order and social, economic, and cultural conditions that force 'choice' (Correa and Petchesky, 1994).

These religious, legal, political, and public health discourses are important to understand the landscape of abortion in Latin America, but they are not the focus of this book. Instead, *Magic Misoprostol* is an examination of how people have made safe abortions a reality, regardless of any state's position on the procedure. By using the abortion pill misoprostol as a starting point, this book explores the biography of the pill, how accompaniment groups have made it into an affective abortion technology, how the pills and information about them move, how they relate to the law, and the relationships between misoprostol and other reproductive technologies. This chapter now explains three bodies of literature that run through the book: reproductive justice, mobilities, and the geographies of scientific knowledge.

Reproductive justice

Reproductive justice is a framework developed by Black feminist activists and scholars in the United States, such as Loretta Ross, Rickie Solinger, and Dorothy Roberts, as a way to move beyond an individualized, 'pro-choice' framing of reproduction. It instead focuses on three tenets: the right to have children, the right not to have children, and the right to parent in safe environments and with dignity. Reproductive justice is 'a political movement that splices *reproductive rights* with *social justice* to achieve *reproductive justice*' (Ross and Solinger, 2017, 9, emphasis in original) and refuses to view reproduction as an issue of individuals. In response to liberal feminist calls for reproductive rights that centre on individuals' rights, 'choice', and privacy, reproductive justice emphasizes the collective.

The collective is important, because as Ross and Solinger (2017) note, the denial of an individual's sexual and reproductive dignity harms the whole community. Reproductive justice is, therefore, 'the struggle for the collective conditions for sustaining life and persisting over time amid life-negating structural forces, and not just the right to have or not have children' (Murphy, 2017, 142). This entails expanding the scope of what reproductive health encompasses to include community needs and institutional structures and to address the social contexts of reproductive rights, including historical and contemporary oppression that creates racial, economic, and sexual inequities (Gurr, 2014). Reproductive justice also importantly refuses to stay rooted in isolated, specific reproductive access issues and instead considers the life arc to bring in issues such as clean water, labour rights, and education as well as access to reproductive concerns such as contraception, sex education, and abortion.

So how can this framework, which developed in a specific context in the United States, help us to understand the politics of reproduction in Latin America? While reproductive justice initially focused predominantly on women of colour, primarily Black women, it has expanded and been taken up by scholars working on topics such as fat women and trans men who have been, or have attempted to become, pregnant (LaMarre et al, 2020), work on reproductive justice and disability (Jarman, 2015), and trans rights (Radi, 2020). As Ross (2017, 306) argues, reproductive justice 'thrives in the borderlands of ambiguity, and its incompleteness offers amazing flexibility and adaptability to allow multiple interpretations that invite elaboration and clarification'. Therefore, while structural oppression in the United States is not articulated in the same way as in Latin America, a reproductive justice approach examines how the state dictates who can, should, and cannot have children and under what conditions, with a particular focus on how certain racialized communities become targets of reproductive punishment (Ross, 2017).

Laura Briggs (2022) makes the case that reproductive justice has always been transnational. For instance, she explains how Loretta Ross, one of the movements' best-known thinkers, went to meetings in El Salvador, Mexico, Nicaragua, Cuba, Brazil, and Chile in the 1980s and 1990s, when reproductive justice was being articulated as a concept. While the concerns of reproductive justice were formalized in the US context, this happened through global alliances and its tenets have now spread around the world (Briggs, 2022). Nevertheless, Latin American feminists have been sceptical of ideas that travel south from the United States and Europe and have responded by developing theories that account for the dynamics of travelling and the differences within the Latin American context (Rivera Berruz, 2023). Reproductive justice is one example of an approach that has been rearticulated as it has travelled from its origin in the United States to Latin America.

In its travels, the concept of reproductive justice has resonated with many people and groups across Latin America (Nolan, 2022). Academics have used reproductive justice in Latin American contexts to develop understandings of the Zika virus (Stern, 2016), forced sterilizations (Vasquez Del Aguila, 2022), midwifery (Borboleta et al, 2022), abortion (Ruiz, 2023), birth control (Colón Warren, 2023), trans activism (Fernández Romero, 2020), and legal change (Algora, 2021). But beyond academia, activists, lawyers, bioethicists, and physicians caring for sexual and reproductive health have found it to be helpful in providing a vision of social transformation that includes the legalization of abortion but also goes far beyond it (Arguedas-Ramírez and Wenner, 2023).

This is not to say that reproductive justice has been accepted by all. Lynn Morgan (2015) discusses her experience of presenting her work to academic anthropologists in Argentina, where she made a case for favouring reproductive justice over reproductive rights. This was met with disdain from the audience, who argued that '[w]e have fought long and hard for the government to grant us the rights we deserve, and we are not giving up now' (Morgan, 2015, 137). Between 2003 and 2013, an explicit human rights framing had led to positive change on a variety of social issues beyond abortion, and the language of rights was, therefore, seen by Argentine activists as a winning strategy and the topic of reproduction was not one they were willing to give up in favour of reproductive justice. The context of Argentina as a post-dictatorship state meant that a human rights framing has assumed a prominence and is respected by the government, which allows activists to put direct pressure on political actors to change laws.

The Argentine feminist anthropologists pushed back against reproductive justice because of the ways that race, class, and gender discrimination intersect differently in the US context compared with Argentina, because Argentine feminists have long taken a broad approach to reproduction that already encompasses issues such as class, racism, and environmental degradation, and because reproductive justice wasn't seen as necessary when rights language was already being used effectively to bring about change (Morgan, 2015). Morgan had underestimated the powerful symbolism of rights frameworks for feminists in Argentina and this example shows how reproductive justice has not been universally taken up in Latin America. However, since 2015, an increasing number of academics and activist groups have begun using the term as it becomes rearticulated in the Latin American context.

Another concept that has been used to understand the politics of reproduction in Latin America is that of reproductive governance. Developed by Morgan and Roberts (2012), this broadly encapsulates the process through which institutions and actors exercise control over reproductive lives at the individual and population levels. These actors include the state, religious groups, non-governmental organizations, and social movements, and the forms of control can include law, financial incentives, moral claims, and direct coercion. Reproductive governance has, therefore, provided a powerful way to capture the ways in which seemingly individual reproductive decisions are enmeshed within nation-state political agendas and economic policies (Singer, 2022). Importantly, Morgan (2019) notes that as reproductive governance has developed in scholarship on Latin America, it is increasingly going beyond specific reproductive issues to address reproductive justice. It is for this reason that in this book I specifically use reproductive justice rather than reproductive governance.

Reproductive justice and governance encompass multiple facets of reproductive lives and beyond, and abortion is just one aspect, albeit a centrally important one (Thomsen, 2015). While my research centres on misoprostol as a technology of abortion, abortion cannot be disentangled from sex education, contraception, teen parenthood, sexual and gender-based violence, incest, environmental health, welfare provision, and violence and discrimination from healthcare professionals. This book explores the ways that '[m]isoprostol has changed the landscape of reproductive justice as a technological discovery' (Assis, 2020, 128) by taking an intersectional perspective on the structural factors that determine access to abortions, critiquing the limits of legal approaches, and analysing strategies make reproductive justice a reality. While reproductive justice as a US-formulated framework should not be imposed on the Latin American context, I seek to be part of a conversation among scholars working in Latin America who have found it a useful way to articulate the struggles, experiences, and hopes for reproductive lives in the region.

Mobilities

Mobilities scholarship has emerged from interdisciplinary work on movement, migration, and transport to consider inequalities and the politics of mobilities. In this book, I particularly draw on Mimi Sheller's work on mobility justice to interrogate what moves, what doesn't move, and how actors can intervene in mobilities, and to further develop the concept of 'abortion mobilities'. I use mobilities in a multi-scalar way, incorporating the chemical effects of misoprostol within the body and the transportation of misoprostol within urban areas, but also the movement of pills and the knowledge of how to use them at the global scale.

Mimi Sheller's *Mobility Justice* (2018a) is part careful theoretical detailing of mobilities scholarship and part manifesto for a more just future. As she details, mobilities research 'focuses not simply on movement per se, but on the power of discourses, practices, and infrastructures of mobility in creating the effects of both movement and stasis, demobilization and remobilization, voluntary and involuntary movement' (Sheller, 2018a, 11). Mobility justice as a concept provides a way of understanding how power and inequality govern movement, whether of people, resources, or information. This governance creates uneven mobilities as communities are differently controlled, tracked, and surveilled along lines of gender, race, ethnicity, class, caste, nationality, age, sexuality, and disability (Sheller, 2018a).

Mobility justice is an inherently embodied concept then. Some bodies move through space more easily, while others will face restrictions (Sheller, 2018b). Sheller (2011) explains how gender has been a particular focus of such research, exploring the overt curtailment of women's movement and the overlooking of women's needs as well as the racialized mobility regime 'in which racialized minorities cannot exercise full freedom of mobility, being constantly impeded by police stops, searches, arrests, police shootings, and imprisonment without due process and protection of the law' (Sheller, 2018a, 65). Nonetheless, Sheller (2018a) emphasizes that a mobility justice approach goes beyond just the movement of bodies and is equally attentive to the governance of the global circulations of things.

A mobility justice approach pertains to abortion in the 'disciplining of mobile subjects' (Sheller, 2018a, 66), which has governed people's access to safe abortions. This is through both forced mobility and immobility, which can be interdependent, as 'some people's freedom of mobility impacts and depends on others' coerced mobilities, slowed mobilities, uprootings, and re-routings' (Sheller, 2018a, 96). We can see this in the economic privilege of who has been able to access an abortion with a trusted doctor or at home, compared to those who navigate unsafe spaces or experience extended journeys in search of abortion pills. Sheller has also been critical of previous work that has been overly focused on the urban scale, and she stresses that 'we urgently need to connect these scales of the body, street, city, nation, and planet into one overarching theory of mobility justice' (Sheller, 2018b, 31). The mobilities of people, pills, and knowledge detailed in this book cut across such scales.

Abortion mobilities can be defined as the 'movement—or lack of movement—of people, information, and things across space that facilitate or constrain abortion access at different scales' (Engle, 2022, 2). This fits within a broader 'reproductive mobilities' literature that has explored how spatial and temporal mobilities underpin much of reproduction from fertility and abortion travel to detention and deportation, across multiple scales (Frohlick et al, 2019; Speier et al, 2020). Abortion mobilities provides a new perspective on this work as, generally, mobility to facilitate reproduction has been examined more than the prevention of reproduction (Murray and Khan, 2020). While the movement of people for abortions has been included in abortion mobilities work (Pheterson and Azize, 2005; Gilmartin and White, 2011; Side, 2016, 2020; Freeman, 2017; Sethna and Davis, 2019; Murray and Khan, 2020), the movement of abortion pills has received particular attention more recently (Calkin, 2019; Calkin and Freeman, 2019; Freeman, 2020). Sydney Calkin's (2021; 2023) work, in particular, has shown how the 'unruly' mobility of abortion pills creates particular challenges for states attempting to govern their use. But the movement of pills also offers up opportunity for those seeking to end their pregnancies, as the pills can move to those who need them rather than people needing to move for a procedural abortion (Calkin et al, 2022).

Abortion mobilities scholarship has also included work on the mobilities of information and activism about abortion (Calkin et al, 2022). Abortion hotlines, for example, are one strategy that have been deployed across Latin America to provide accurate and accessible information about abortion at a relatively low cost (Drovetta, 2015). Hotline phone numbers even have their own mobility, with the information shared through stickers, leaflets, and graffiti across spaces such as public toilets, trains, and walls (Bloomer et al, 2020). An abortion mobilities focus has, therefore, interrogated the governance of the movement of people, pills, and ideas and the forms of activism that politically reimagine abortion access (Calkin et al, 2022).

One key focus of this abortion research has been scale. For instance, Calkin (2019) uses scale as a way to analyse the changes that have taken place in access to abortion, such as mobile clinics and telemedicine. She uses the idea of 'scale jumping' to explain how state forms of power can be creatively challenged, one example being the Women on Waves' 'abortion boat', which leaves one country's jurisdiction and travels outwards into international waters to defy their abortion laws (Calkin, 2019). In my own work, a colleague and I have expanded the scales of abortion mobilities research even further to detail the intertwined multi-scalar effects of misoprostol from the bloodstream of the person taking the pills as well as the global political regime governing misoprostol (Freeman and Rodríguez, 2024a).

This book, then, uses mobility justice and current abortion mobilities scholarship to explore what moves, what doesn't move, and how actors have intervened in mobilities. This comes most clearly to the fore in Chapter 3, but mobilities as a broad framework helps us to explain the discovery of misoprostol as an abortifacient in the 1980s as well as activist mobilization and the relationship between misoprostol and other reproductive technologies.

The geographies of scientific knowledge

Understanding the story of how misoprostol went from being a stomach ulcer drug to an abortion pill used by millions of people around the world necessitates a foundation in the geographies of scientific knowledge. The key areas of thought that underpin this are science and technology studies (STS) scholarship, Latin American feminist and decolonial thought, and work on pharmaceuticals.

STS as an interdisciplinary set of literatures has challenged traditional ideas of linear progress in scientific knowledges (Knopes, 2019). Within STS scholarship, it is particularly feminist and postcolonial approaches that have provided a basis for exploring the value-laden and spatially contingent underpinnings of science and knowledge (Tsing, 2005; Harding, 2009; Harding, 2014). Postcolonial STS approaches have shown that a deep understanding of science must examine how it has been co-constituted with colonialism (Subramaniam et al, 2016), with 'a striking emphasis on the "situatedness" of technoscience', a focus on the 'contact zones' of empire, [and a] re-emphasis of the local in how it is at the centre, not the periphery of knowledge making (Anderson, 2002, 651).

Feminist STS, meanwhile, has explored the unequal benefits of scientific knowledge and the inequities in the production of that knowledge (Subramaniam et al, 2016). Both feminist and postcolonial STS materialized from social justice movements in the 1960s and 1970s that critiqued the assumption that science is objective, value-free, or equitable (Subramaniam et al, 2016). Despite their similarities in taking seriously 'other' ways of knowing, both have at times ignored the key concerns of the other; feminist STS too often sidelines race and colonialism, while postcolonial STS does not always account for gender (Subramaniam et al, 2016). However, both feminist and postcolonial STS, despite their internal differences, 'decenter and parochialize dominant ways of thinking about the production of scientific and technological knowledge and their familiar philosophic assumptions' (Harding, 2009, 418).

The global South has been neglected by STS scholars despite the centrality of critiques of northern science and work on the power imbalances of northern technologies in postcolonial contexts (Rajão et al, 2014). Social science STS scholarship from Latin America is relatively new (Kreimer, 2007), but the breadth of research from Latin America is rapidly increasing (Medina et al, 2014; Kreimer and Vessuri, 2018). As such, Latin American scholars have contributed important work on 'centre-periphery' relations in scientific research, Indigenous knowledges, and inclusion, including gender inclusion (Kreimer and Vessuri, 2018). Together, this work has helped to critique the localities and centres of scientific knowledge making. The South is not just a site for the extraction of materials, labour, or data – it is a centre of theory making, practice, and innovation in its own right (Harding, 2016).

Latin American decolonial and feminist thought is deeply intwined with these STS approaches. Much of this focuses on the importance of thought produced in Abya Yala (Latin America) and the violent legacies of colonialism. These legacies go beyond colonialism as the domination of land and peoples, but must include how the production of knowledge about the 'othered' cultures dominated and how this knowledge fed back into ideas of evolution and progress in the colonial metropoles (Curiel et al, 2016). Maria Lugones' work on the coloniality of gender, for example, shows how the colonization of the Americas executed 'a hierarchical, dichotomous distinction between human and non-human [that] was imposed on the colonized in the service of Western man. It was accompanied by other dichotomous hierarchical distinctions, among them that between men and women' (Lugones, 2010, 743). Lugones (2007) has been a critical voice in decolonial feminism, drawing together intersectional perspectives from Black and women of colour feminists in the United States with theories of modernity from Latin American thinkers such as Aníbal Quijano. In her work on multiple relations of power, Lugones has traced the particular gender system that was imposed on Latin America through colonialism and served to eradicate communities and knowledges. These gendered effects were part of the Western cultural and ideological matrix that was imposed on Indigenous people through colonialism and oppressed communities in numerous ways (Cusicanqui, 2010). Scientific development was also central to the colonial project, which required scientific and technical achievements in areas such as oceanography, metallurgy, and cartography (Harding, 2017). The extractive nature of colonial and postcolonial knowledge production, which has involved manipulation and lack of Indigenous representation, has meant that these scientific 'developments' have often been fraught with suspicion and conflict (Schwartz Marin and Fiske, 2022).

By drawing on historically undervalued knowledges and experiences, decolonial feminism offers important critiques of Western feminism as well as key perspectives that had been marginalized. Latin American feminists began to discuss the creation of knowledge from outside Europe and North America, developing decolonial feminism, which incorporates views of Afro-Caribbean, Indigenous, peasant, and academic feminists (Montanaro, 2017). These feminisms provide a way to challenge the Eurocentric, ethnocentric, and universalizing nature of hegemonic feminisms, often through vindicating ancestral knowledges from Abya Yala (Montanaro, 2017). Across Latin America, we have seen the increasing attention paid to Indigenous thought and Indigenous feminism, which highlight concerns that diverge from those of urban feminists but still share complementary interests such as racism, sexism, and economic exploitation (Hernández Castillo, 2010). Indigenous feminist thought has critiqued liberal feminism and its frequent emphasis on the individual rights of women, which does not represent the central tenets of Indigenous women's struggle (Bastian Duarte, 2012). These ideas are, therefore, key to the geographies of scientific knowledge in Latin America, rooted in colonialism as the process of producing knowledge about the 'other' and the extraction of raw materials, labour, and knowledge (Soto Laveaga, 2009; Curiel et al, 2016). In response, Latin American decolonial thought argues for scientific pluralism that can encompass multiple ontologies and epistemologies, an idea that sits at odds with positivist scientific approaches (Harding, 2016).

The geographies of scientific knowledge that inform my research also necessarily derive from work on medicines and pharmaceuticals. Medical anthropologists, for instance, have long examined medicines from their conception to their use. Whyte et al (2002) have been particularly influential here with their work on the social lives of medicines and the materialities of pharmaceuticals as they are developed, manufactured, marketed, prescribed, and used. A 'biography of pharmaceuticals' approach emphasizes how medicines are products of human society but also *producers* of it (Van der Geest et al, 1996). This intersects with the work of Andrew Barry (2005) and 'informed' materials, whereby chemicals must be understood through their far-reaching relations beyond the laboratory into regulatory, legal, and economic realms. This body of scholarship has moved pharmaceutical thinking beyond just the object to include the process through which medicines come to be and the effects they go on to have (Hardon and Sanabria, 2017). After all, '[t]here can be no pharmaceuticals without that work: bare molecules do not become pharmaceuticals without ties to health concerns, scientific knowledge, appropriate regulation, effective marketing, and receptive prescribers and publics' (Greene and Sismondo, 2015, 2). The socialization approach to medicines underpins my research into misoprostol as an object, but one that is part of the 'living labyrinth' of chemical infrastructures (Hardon and Sanabria, 2017).

To understand the political significance of misoprostol, it is important to cover the legitimization of science in global North spaces that has posited the global South as a space of experimentation rather than knowledge making (Harding, 2014; Liboiron, 2021). This book sits in conversation with other work on material and knowledge extraction, such as the use of Mexican wild yam in the large-scale production of contraceptive pills, that puts the protagonists at the heart of the story about global science and the politics of knowledge (Soto Laveaga, 2009). The global South and North are of course not isolated from one another (Rajão et al, 2014), and this book seeks to show the connections of scientific knowledge, materials, and solidarities that span global abortion networks. Scholarship on the geographies of scientific knowledge underpins my research on how misoprostol has been studied, experimented with, and suppressed. This emphasizes the tensions between knowledge developed by poor, Indigenous, and Black women in Latin America and 'legitimate' scientific knowledge determined by Western science. *Magic Misoprostol* contributes to critical, decolonial scholarship on how knowledge is made and made to be forgotten through engaging with knowledges 'constructed *from* the territories and bodies in struggle' (Gago and Mason-Deese, 2019, 208, emphasis in original). Throughout the story of misoprostol, it is Latin American people with the capacity to gestate who have been at the forefront of creating and sharing knowledge on its capacities and use.

Talking about abortion

This book draws on three years of ethnographic research on the mobilities of abortion in Latin America. With a pilot grant funded by the Wellcome Trust in 2019 and then a larger one from the Economic and Social Research Council in 2020, I began exploring the people, things, and knowledges that move to facilitate abortion access across the region, but as I began the research, the importance of misoprostol became evident, and the focus of my project shifted towards it. I then spent the following years talking to people about misoprostol.

This book draws on 64 interviews with abortion activists and providers, predominantly in Mexico, Peru, and Argentina but also in countries such as Colombia, Costa Rica, and Venezuela. The majority were conducted by me alone, with some of the Peru interviews conducted by Sandra Rodríguez, who worked with me on part of the project and was vital to its success. The interviews were a mix of online during the most severe parts of the COVID-19 pandemic and in-person when travel restrictions allowed. The in-person interviews took place in a range of locations where participants felt comfortable; these included cafes, offices, and health facilities. Sixty-three of the interviews were in Spanish, with one in English, and all translations (and potential translation errors) are my own.

The interviews are weighted towards the Peruvian context, which comes through in the empirical examples, but the other interviews as well as secondary literature are intertwined to broaden the geographical focus of the book. The goal of this book is to explore misoprostol and activism around it at the regional level of Latin America, and the trade-off is that there is not always the scope to consistently explain national or more local complexities. I encourage readers to engage with the rich literature included in the references list that does do this more context-specific work so effectively.

When I tell people I research abortion, I am often met with remarks about how difficult it must be to find participants or how challenging it must be to deal with the stigma. This has been far from my experience. Through existing contacts and 'cold emailing', I got in touch with people who in some way work on the topic of abortion access, whether through being an abortion *acompañante*, working for an abortion-related organization, or working in abortion healthcare. Those who agreed to an interview were keen to share their experiences and thoughts and also to ask me about other strategies of creating routes to abortion access that I may have gleaned through my research. I was often seen as a knowledge sharer, with the interview being a place for the interviewee to gather knowledge, not just pass it one-way to me. Some participants did talk to me about feeling over-researched as people around the world had begun taking note of Latin America's *marea verde*, and one *acompañante* group explicitly declined to be interviewed as they felt that European academics conducting research in Latin America are overly extractive.

While I did not collect demographic data on the participants, the ways in which they spoke about themselves showed some general trends. There was a large age span, from the early twenties until roughly the sixties, though the majority were on the younger end of the spectrum, particularly those who saw themselves as activists or *acompañantes*, while the older participants were more likely to be health professionals who supported pathways to abortion access. The participants were also more likely to be university educated than the general population and most lived in major cities. While I cannot comment more generally on their socioeconomic status or how they defined their ethnicity, some reflected on their status as middle class and only a small number explicitly defined themselves as being part of an Indigenous community.

Some of those who agreed to be interviewed were very clear that they wanted me to use their names as part of their activist practice, whereas most required confidentiality. The book therefore uses a combination of real names, pseudonyms, and descriptors. The rich material that came out of the interviews comes to the fore in the subsequent chapters to understand the strategies and techniques employed by individuals and groups to provide safe and effective autonomous abortions. I therefore use interview quotes from multiple perspectives and, at times, at length to give space to the voices of my participants. These accounts centre the experiences of the communities affected by the restriction of abortion and the activists and providers working to provide safe and effective abortion care where that has been denied by the state.

In the spirit of feminist research, I have no desire to claim objectivity on abortion. Misoprostol has been proven to be safe and effective, and strategies by abortion activists in Latin America have been proven to save lives, makes lives liveable, and engender solidarity. This book, therefore, serves to showcase this evidence gathered through years of rigorous in-depth data collection. In the words of Gago and Mason-Deese (2019, 202): 'It is not an issue of throwing out the notion of objectivity, but rather reformulating …: Feminist objectivity is situated knowledge.' The aim of the book is to present the struggles, work, activism, and care around self-managed abortions with misoprostol in Latin America to an English-speaking audience in order generate solidarity with a wariness of salvationist feminism. The fight for bodily autonomy connects us across the world.

Outline of the book

This book focuses on differing aspects of the life of misoprostol that together provide a rich understanding of how it has transformed abortion access in Latin America, with global ramifications. The first chapter explores the biography of misoprostol from its initial 'discovery' as an abortifacient when women with unwanted pregnancies in Brazil began experimenting with it to its current standing as a widely used and accepted technology of abortion. This is a tale of scientific understanding that forces us to rethink our conceptions of 'science' and who takes part in (re)making knowledges of pharmaceuticals. The chapter draws on interviews with abortion activists and providers who tell their part in the process of understanding the properties of misoprostol, developing an effective regimen so that it successfully leads to an abortion, and sharing that knowledge with people who desire an abortion.

The second chapter provides a detailed look at *acompañantes* (accompaniers), who have been fundamental to making misoprostol 'magic'. This chapter details the political vision of *acompañamiento*, which, instead of replicating a medical model of service provision, entails a commitment to provide safe, effective, and holistic abortion care outside medical contexts in ways that value autonomy and collectivism. The chapter explores what this approach means in practice, the complex and shifting relationships between *acompañantes* and healthcare professionals, the motivations that led people to become *acompañantes,* and how *acompañantes* have created informal and formal networks to generate and build knowledge around this form of abortion care. This develops reproductive justice scholarship in particular by exploring how *acompañantes* fight for the right not to have children and take an intersectional approach to provide support for poor, Indigenous, and rural women who face the greatest barriers to safe healthcare.

The third chapter uses a mobilities lens to examine how misoprostol as a (non-)reproductive object travels between spaces to those that need it. The chapter pays attention to the people, places, and strategies that enable misoprostol to move to those needing it. It first focuses on four sites where misoprostol is procured – pharmacies, the black market, laboratories, and networks – then details some of the mobility strategies enacted by activists, from postal systems to abortion robots, how misoprostol is paid for and how the movement of pills has shifted the spaces where abortions take place. The mobility of misoprostol is deeply uneven but in fighting for reproductive justice, activists and *acompañantes* have democratized and enabled access to misoprostol across Latin America.

The fourth chapter deals with the legal aspects of misoprostol and the strategies that activists have used to harness the marginality of misoprostol to support abortion access at the edges of the law. It sets out the challenges and opportunities of changing abortion laws in Latin America along with the 'prefigurative politics' approaches that *acompañantes* have developed when the law does not serve them. It then details how, through using specific language, employing code words, and writing 'scripts' for abortion seekers to use, *acompañantes* ensure that self-managed abortions remain hidden from legal authorities and medical professionals. Next, this chapter explores the use of 'healthcare' as a way to morally legitimize abortion care even where it is criminalized. It then discusses the legal threats and harassment faced by activists. It ends with an exploration of how states can use 'strategic ignorance' to look away from the issue of abortion, but more recently have begun to legalize abortion as a new strategy of reproductive governance.

The fifth chapter takes a relational approach to place misoprostol in context with other reproductive technologies to show that it does not exist in isolation. These other 'technologies' can be: knowledges, such as ancestral understandings of the abortifacient properties of plants that have been used in 'hybrid' ways with misoprostol; the 'other' abortion medication, mifepristone; or additional medications, such as methotrexate, letrozole, and ulipristal acetate, which have been experimented with in combination with misoprostol in order to enhance its efficacy. Misoprostol is also entangled with the politics of its 'other uses', for managing miscarriages, for preventing and treating postpartum haemorrhage, and for labour induction, which both expand and restrict access to the medication; and it is entangled with procedural abortions, which are not in opposition to medical abortions – instead, the two technologies can support bodily autonomy and reproductive justice.

The concluding chapter reflects back on the key themes explored in the book through a proposal of abortion liberation. This refers to the full separation of abortion from the state, with autonomy given to pregnant people to manage their reproductive lives in the ways that work best for them. While Western understandings of abortion centre on it being highly medicalized (that is, only to be performed by a medical professional), liberation allows for the conceptualization of other practices and understandings. Misoprostol and the people who have mobilized it in Latin America have transformed abortion safety, knowledge, and practices with implications that have spread and can continue to ripple across the globe. As we can see from practices in Latin America, another abortion world is possible.

1

From the Favelas of Brazil to the WHO: The Biography of Misoprostol

The biography of misoprostol tells a story of self-experimentation, reproductive autonomy, and a questioning of the meaning of science and knowledge. Misoprostol was designed in the 1970s by Searle as a treatment for gastrointestinal issues, and by the 1980s, it was commonly sold in Brazil and other countries around the world. Given the illegality of abortion in Brazil at that time, people wishing to end their pregnancies would use a range of methods, including plants and surgical techniques. In this context, women began noticing a stark warning on misoprostol packaging – a heavily pregnant cartoon woman with a red line across and a warning that the medication can cause miscarriages and, therefore, must not be used by pregnant women. This warning of toxicity served as an advertisement to women desiring an abortion and so they began to self-experiment with misoprostol and, in doing so, eventually developed an effective and safe way to end pregnancies.

This chapter details this story and provides a feminist and decolonial analysis of what counts as 'science' and 'knowledge' as this abortion medication spread across Latin America but also back into the laboratories of the global North. Misoprostol is now used in medical spaces across the world for abortions, but also other obstetric purposes, and is classed as an essential medicine by the World Health Organization (WHO). This chapter also explores the role of *acompañantes* – the individuals and groups who facilitate safe, feminist, empathetic abortion care across Latin America – in creating an effective regime of using misoprostol for abortions and then disseminating this information among people seeking to end their pregnancies. The biography of misoprostol, the 'pharmaceutical outlaw' (MacDonald, 2021, 377) that has a 'double life' (De Zordo, 2016), is, therefore, a tale of resistance, the reclamation of scientific knowledge, and the fight for bodily autonomy in a context that criminalizes it.

A stomach ulcer drug becomes an abortifacient

In 1973, the pharmaceutical company Searle developed a new medication for the treatment of stomach ulcers and gave it the name misoprostol. Its development came after it was found that this family of prostaglandins, the E series, inhibited the secretion of acid and could, therefore, prevent ulceration and damage in the gastric organs (Walt, 1992). It was marketed for the treatment of non-steroidal anti-inflammatory drug (NSAID)-related ulcers in particular, as these medications reduce the production of prostaglandin, the hormone that neutralizes stomach acid through increasing the production of stomach mucus. Misoprostol was no stomach ulcer wonder drug, however, as it is not more effective than other medications available and has a higher risk of side effects, most notably diarrhoea and abdominal pain (Walt, 1992; Hawkey et al, 1998). Nevertheless, certain advantages – such as being stable at room temperature, being cheap and readily accessible, and being orally active – meant that misoprostol became a commonly used medication (Ho and Ngai, 1999).

G.D. Searle & Co, the pharmaceutical company that synthesized misoprostol, was formed in 1888 as the Searle and Hereth Co and went on to spearhead numerous pharmaceutical 'firsts', including the first oral contraceptive, the first motion sickness medication, and the first bulk laxative as well as the sugar substitute aspartame (Watkins, 1998). The Searle and Hereth Co became G.D. Searle & Co in 1908 and then in 1985 was acquired by Monsanto in a US$2.7 billion deal (Greenhouse, 1985). Monsanto reported that they saw Searle's pharmaceutical focus as a way to bring to market the drugs they were developing in their biotechnology laboratories, while Searle were keen to diversify their holdings (Greenhouse, 1985). In 2000, Monsanto/Searle completed a merger with Pharmacia & Upjohn, and in 2003, the US multinational pharmaceutical and biotechnology corporation Pfizer acquired Pharmacia and largely retired the Searle name. As will become evident, these corporations have not had an easy relationship with misoprostol's developments.

Throughout the 1980s, misoprostol began to be approved for the treatment of gastric ulcers by national drug boards, including by the US Food and Drug Administration (FDA) in 1988 (Löwy and Dias Villela Corrêa, 2020; MacDonald, 2021). It was marketed with the brand name Cytotec and was predominantly recognized under this name until generic versions of misoprostol began to be manufactured later. Cytotec was registered in Brazil in 1986, and in 1988, Biolab, a Brazilian laboratory, began marketing the drug (Barbosa and Arilha, 1993; Veldhuis et al, 2022b). That's when the next chapter for misoprostol began.

As misoprostol became more commonly prescribed and used across the country in the late 1980s, Brazilians noticed the severe warning on the packaging indicating that it must not be used by pregnant women due to the risk of it causing a miscarriage. At this time in Brazil, abortions were prohibited in almost every circumstance, but an estimated 1.4 million abortions still took place clandestinely every year (Guedes, 2000). Many of these were dangerous, with 300,000 women hospitalized annually with complications and abortion accounting for 12 per cent of maternal deaths (Guedes, 2000). There was, therefore, an enormous appetite for safe methods of ending an unwanted pregnancy, regardless of the legal situation of abortion.

Poor women, who could not gain access to safe, discrete doctors like their richer counterparts could, began to experiment with misoprostol to work out the dosage and method of ingestion that would most effectively cause uterine contractions that would expel a pregnancy. Misoprostol was relatively cheap and, due to being registered as a stomach ulcer drug, was available at pharmacies across the country (Assis, 2020). This meant that women could purchase misoprostol themselves and avoid having to use clandestine clinics, known colloquially as 'angel factories', or other methods such as the insertion of twigs or catheters or the use of teas and herbs (Costa, 1998; Guedes, 2000). This experimentation with misoprostol began to spread among women, first in Brazil and then across the Latin America region, with knowledge gradually expanding to improve the dosages and routes of administration (Veldhuis et al, 2022b).

While some medical researchers claimed that the source of knowledge of the 'side effect' of misoprostol was 'not known' (Coêlho et al, 1991), word of mouth was the primary way that people learned about misoprostol in the early days in Brazil. A 1993 study found that 84 per cent of misoprostol users had learned about the drug from friends, relatives, or colleagues and 10 per cent directly from a pharmacist (Costa and Vessey, 1993). Despite the importance of word-of-mouth knowledge sharing, these women were not alone in their experimentation, and pharmacists and drugstore workers, doctors, the media, and the manufacturer were critical in the sharing of knowledge about misoprostol (Barbosa and Arilha, 1993). Pharmacists were able to sell misoprostol without a prescription and, therefore, served as an unofficial channel to circumvent restrictive abortion legislation (Löwy and Dias Villela Corrêa, 2020). The importance of information being shared through word of mouth was likely underestimated by many professionals in a context where knowledge making about pharmaceuticals has been presumed to be largely confined to research laboratories and clinical trials.

While it is challenging to glean information on how exactly misoprostol was being administered by these women seeking to end their pregnancies, case reports do shed some light on initial regimes of misoprostol. One study from Brazil lists cases where the attempted abortion was unsuccessful and the ingested doses had been 600 and 800 micrograms of misoprostol, which is three or four tablets (González et al, 1993). However, other people who had taken a total of 1,600 or 1,800 micrograms did experience a complete abortion. This suggests that knowledge of the effective dosage was patchy, but that some people were using a sufficient amount to terminate a pregnancy.

Locating the exact time when misoprostol began to be used as an abortifacient is also challenging given its clandestinity. It has been reported as first entering Brazil in 1985 (Löwy and Dias Villela Corrêa, 2020) or 1986 (Barbosa and Arilha, 1993; Costa, 1998), and its 'misuse' for abortions was noted by medical professionals from 1988 (González et al, 1993). A 1993 study analysed manufacturer sales data of Cytotec in Brazil and found that in 1986 nearly 261,000 units were sold and just three years later, in 1989, this had risen to 581,000 (Barbosa and Arilha, 1993). Between January 1989 and August 1992, 48.9 million tablets of misoprostol were sold in Brazil alone, enough for 12.2 million complete abortions (Coêlho et al, 1993). By 1991, Cytotec was widely recognized as an abortifacient across Brazil, with an estimated one million boxes of the medication being sold (Nations et al, 1997). The steep increase in sales of misoprostol in the late 1980s appears to be consistent with the spread of information among women on how to use the medication in order to provoke an abortion. The increase in sales and the growing public awareness of the abortifacient properties of misoprostol led to attempts by the Brazilian government to regulate the use of misoprostol, but sales continued to increase. Options to terminate unwanted pregnancies had been expanded, and the maternal mortality rate from unsafe abortion fell (Assis, 2020). Brazil's status as the 'cradle' of misoprostol as an abortifacient was confirmed (De Zordo, 2016).

The adoption of misoprostol as a technology to end pregnancies did not spread evenly across the country, with knowledge appearing to be more widespread in certain locations. Ceará, a state in north-eastern Brazil, for example, was a particular hot spot for the use of misoprostol to terminate pregnancies, and a 1990 study found that 72 per cent of women admitted to hospitals with medical complications from abortion there had used Cytotec – this was compared to 34 per cent in Recife and 45 per cent in Rio de Janeiro (Barbosa and Arilha, 1993). The geographic spread of misoprostol as an abortifacient was, therefore, patchy, but awareness of it gradually grew across the region. One interviewee in Peru who was working in the field of reproductive health in the 1980s recalled the movement of misoprostol and knowledge surrounding it at Peru's border with Brazil. The borderlands were a contact zone and the use of the medication then spread into the rest of the country so that now, even though misoprostol is only registered as a stomach ulcer medication, its use for abortion and other obstetric uses is widespread, with a corresponding reduction in abortion complications. One interviewee in Argentina explained that misoprostol entered the country from Brazil and

Paraguay and that health professionals began to notice its use in the early 2000s. She stated that the first time health professionals 'heard about pills being used for abortion was from patients in low-income neighbourhoods who told them, "there's a pill", and then the doctors said "but no, what's the pill?", and they were thinking about illegal things, dangerous things, things that were not recommended.'

Another interviewee in Peru, a health worker, remarked that misoprostol 'has been around forever'. Working in a rural part of the country in the 1990s, she remembered first learning about misoprostol and how to use it from magazines in Chile that were published by a sexual and reproductive health organization. She then procured the medication in the capital, Lima, but it did not work, and then she struggled for some time to buy it again. She contrasted this with the current situation in Peru, where 'now it is super easy, and it is super cheap', and she noticed access expanding especially during the COVID-19 pandemic. Misoprostol had also been available in Mexico since the 1980s, initially as Cytotec but then with an explosion of generic brands when abortion was decriminalized in Mexico City (Belfrage, 2023). In Bolivia, meanwhile, misoprostol was first recorded as being used to terminate pregnancies in the mid-1990s even though, like in other Latin American countries, it had been available in pharmacies since the 1980s (Kimball, 2020). As this shows, just the presence of misoprostol in a country is not enough to lead to its take up as an abortifacient; knowledge of its 'other uses' and how to use it effectively is also required.

Unfortunately, little information exists on how Brazilian women were conceptualizing their use of misoprostol. Assis and Erdman (2021, 2) found that 'many of the working-class women first recorded using misoprostol in north-eastern Brazil did not associate the drug with abortion, but used it as a preventative measure against the risk of pregnancy', which is consistent with understandings of early abortion as 'menstrual regulation'. The scientific literature does give some clues to how women were experiencing their use of misoprostol, as some went to medical facilities when they started bleeding or were concerned about the amount of blood, and the studies report on whether the pregnancy was ended or not (González et al, 1993). But in the vast majority of cases, no information exists on the women who pioneered the creation of misoprostol as an abortifacient.

The medical world takes note

As early as 1983 there were published concerns about the impacts of failed prostaglandin abortions (Collins and Mahoney, 1983; Ringel et al, 1983; Hoevels-Guerich et al, 1984), but these were speculative and inconclusive based on little evidence. For example, the report by Collins and Mahoney (1983) was based on just one case report. But these did have an effect, and when the US FDA was considering the approval of misoprostol for gastric purposes, one reviewer argued that these benefits were outweighed by the abortifacient properties of the medication and warned of 'the potential for inadvertent or deliberate misuse by pregnant women' (Templeton, 1998, 937).

In 1987, the first scientific study of the use of misoprostol for obstetric purposes was published by a Brazilian researcher, followed by one from Argentine researchers in 1991, and then a boom in publications after that (Assis, 2020). The first study looking at how misoprostol was being used specifically for self-managing abortions was from Brazil in 1991 (Coêlho et al, 1991). Researchers visited 103 pharmacies in Fortaleza, in northeastern Brazil pretending to look for a solution to their or their girlfriend's unwanted pregnancy, with some pharmacies visited twice. Across 190 visits, pharmacy staff recommended misoprostol, either alone or with another medication, to terminate the pregnancy 99 times (52 per cent), showing that knowledge about it was widespread and easily accessed even as early as 1991. This was corroborated by another study in Fortaleza that asked women who were seeking emergency treatment at the hospital what they had taken (Schönhöfer, 1991). In 1988, 12 per cent of those admitted had taken misoprostol, but this rapidly jumped to 73 per cent in 1990. Schönhöfer also notes that complications were less common among those who had used misoprostol than other methods.

In the early 1990s, medical literature noted that uterine contractions that could provoke an abortion were an evident 'side effect' of misoprostol (Coêlho et al, 1991; Walt, 1992), but it was not seen as an effective technology for terminating a pregnancy. Costa and Vessey (1993, 1260) described it as showing 'some uterine effects' but noted that it was 'not effective in inducing complete abortion'. Similarly, Coêlho et al (1991) described misoprostol as being 'a weak abortifacient, but the induced bleeding justifies women to ask for medical assistance and they then can obtain access to curettage at public hospitals'. Schönhöfer (1991, 1534) likewise explained that given that 'abortion is illegal in Brazil, pregnant women often ask pharmacists to recommend drugs to induce abortion or uterine bleeding, so that they can then go to hospital for emergency curettage'. Thus, while its uterine effects were noted, it was viewed more as a 'passport' that would allow people to receive care for an incomplete miscarriage in a public health setting rather than as a method for successfully completing an abortion itself (Barbosa and Arilha, 1993, 239).

Authors were also dismissive of those who were using misoprostol for this purpose, with Coêlho et al (1993, 1263) calling them 'perverse strategies and false solutions' while González et al (1993, 59) referred to the 'misuse' of misoprostol in Brazil a 'sad fact'. Such dismissals of misoprostol in the scientific literature do not seem to have been shared by medical professionals working around abortion on the ground, however. An obstetrician who was working in Peru in the 1990s explained that there was 'mysterious literature on the topic' but that more and more studies began to describe the effects of misoprostol and she keenly read up on the literature because of the demand for it she was noticing with her patients. She found a lot of secrecy around misoprostol and was surprised that despite it being commonly used and being available for medical use, her colleagues were not discussing it or speaking about it at conferences.

The first studies of misoprostol as an abortifacient unsurprisingly began in Latin America, as that is where its use began, but medical professionals soon began to notice this spreading to other contexts. De Zordo (2016), for instance, interviewed Spanish and Italian obstetrician-gynaecologists who recalled first seeing the abortifacient potential of misoprostol in the late 1990s and early 2000s with Latin American migrants who brought the knowledge of how to use it in this way over to Europe. The move to start testing misoprostol in the global North was then swift. In 1991, the French health ministry asked the pharmaceutical company Roussel Uclaf to test misoprostol in combination with mifepristone, the latter of which was created by Roussel Uclaf and approved for abortions in 1988 (Klitsch, 1991). Preliminary results were positive, with efficacy rates of over 95 per cent. Soon after, researchers began to conduct trials with misoprostol as an abortifacient in locations including Mozambique (Bugalho et al, 1993), the United States (Creinin and Vittinghoff, 1994), the United Kingdom (El-Refaey and Templeton, 1994), and China (Sang et al, 1994). This launched the legitimization process whereby misoprostol became officially recognized as an abortifacient through research and trials of the 'polycentric communications network' of modern science (Chambers and Gillespie, 2000, 223).

The first time misoprostol appeared in the *British Medical Journal* in relation to medical abortion was in a 1992 letter to the editor written by Thong and Baird (1992). They were responding to previous correspondence about the cost of medical abortions and suggested that oral misoprostol appeared to be an effective and safe prostaglandin, costing only £1, when used in combination with mifepristone. At the time, the standard procedure had been the use of 1 milligram of gemeprost vaginal pessary, which cost £21. The same authors, along with a colleague, J.E. Norman, had published an article in *The Lancet* the previous year reporting on their study inducing abortions using mifepristone and misoprostol (Norman et al, 1991, 1233). They noted the context of experimentation in Latin America, writing that '[t]he unauthorised use of misoprostol as an abortifacient is widespread in some countries, including Brazil' and citing a paper reporting on congenital malformations seen in babies born to mothers in Ceará, Brazil, who had attempted to terminate their pregnancies using misoprostol (Fonseca et al, 1991).

Norman et al concluded, based on their findings, that misoprostol may be a highly effective method of inducing abortions. Even as early as 1992, 95 per cent of patients who had an abortion using mifepristone plus a prostaglandin would recommend this method of abortion to their friends and almost 100 per cent were satisfied with the method (Thong et al, 1992). By 1998, it was reported in the *British Journal of Obstetrics and Gynaecology* that 'the drug now forms the basis of a number of first and second trimester regimens for medical (non-surgical) evacuation of the uterus used around the world' with 'increasing interest in the use of misoprostol' (Templeton, 1998, 937).

As the years progressed, and as experimentation with misoprostol continued informally and then began more formally, more and more evidence showed that misoprostol could be used to terminate pregnancies on its own. Between 1986 and 1993, misoprostol was transformed from a stomach ulcer drug that women began experimenting with to end their unwanted pregnancies into a recognized abortifacient with trials conducted across the globe. The knowledge that began in favelas in Brazil was soon confirmed in the global scientific community (Assis and Erdman, 2021). When the correct dosage and form of administration was found, abortion efficacy rates of 88–93 per cent, with very low risk of serious complications, at just 0.2 per cent, became apparent in clinical studies (Cohen et al, 2005). The WHO recognizes misoprostol as an essential medication, and it is used to terminate millions of pregnancies every year in and beyond medical settings. The dismissal of misoprostol as a 'perverse strategy' (Coêlho et al, 1993) had been proven wrong indeed.

The medical community soon began using misoprostol for obstetric purposes, even though this had to be done 'off-label'. Off-label use of medications is generally accepted. The US FDA recognizes that 'in certain circumstances, off-label uses of approved products are appropriate, rational, and accepted medical practice', and the European Parliament explicitly permits doctors 'to use licensed medicines for indications or in doses or by routes of administration outside the recommendations given in the licence' as long as patients are informed (Ho and Nagi, 1999; Goldberg et al, 2001, 38). The registration of a drug is intended to regulate how that product can be advertised, not how it can be used in clinical practice (Dzuba et al, 2013). Off-label use of a drug does require sound scientific evidence to justify it, and by 2001, scientific studies had provided sufficient evidence for misoprostol's effective use for medical abortions in the first trimester, for cervical ripening before a procedural abortion, and for induction of labour, with some evidence of its effective use for prevention of postpartum haemorrhage (Goldberg et al, 2001).

While new discoveries in obstetrics and gynaecology tend to be taken up quickly in clinical practice, the lack of licencing proved a barrier for the uptake of misoprostol in formal use (Weeks et al, 2005). The lack of official licencing can make medical professionals wary of using medications, fearing litigation, but enough began using it that off-label use of misoprostol rapidly accounted for the majority of its use (Gemzell-Danielsson et al, 2007). By the mid-2000s, enough evidence of this off-label use was proven that evidence-based protocols and guidelines concerning its administration and usages became established (De Zordo, 2016).

Many medications are used off-label for multiple indications and it rarely causes controversy, but as the next section shows, this was not the case with misoprostol (Hale and Zinberg, 2001). Off-label use is often actively sought by drug manufacturers as this helps them to develop new markets (Joffe and Weitz, 2003) as part of attempts 'to evergreen their products by linking them to new indications' (Hardon and Sanabria, 2017, 122). But, in the case of misoprostol, this 'literally unscripted' (MacDonald, 2021, 382) use was first developed by those seeking to end their own pregnancies and then by the medical professionals who supported such experimentation. Such individual practices can be seen as an 'escape valve' to expand reproductive choices regardless of the legal situation (Shepard, 2000). The manufacturer themselves, however, were not in favour of these developments.

Misoprostol and controversy

There have been two main flashpoints when controversy around misoprostol peaked. The first was when misoprostol was initially being informally used for abortions and fears of foetal abnormalities abounded. The second was when misoprostol began to be used globally for abortions, including by healthcare professionals, and the manufacturer, Searle, publicly disavowed any connection to the abortifacient properties of the drug. These two events speak to the politics of knowledge as well as the stigma of abortion. Despite misoprostol being recognized as an essential medication, it continues to be highly contested due to how it disrupts medical and legal authority in typically medicalized domains, such as pregnancy, childbirth, and abortion (Suh, 2021).

Some of the early scientific discussions about misoprostol being used to terminate pregnancies emerged due to fears of malformations in children born after an unsuccessful attempt to end the pregnancy with misoprostol. A German doctor, Peter Schönhöfer (1991), wrote a piece for *The Lancet* arguing that misoprostol is only effective half of the time, and the other half of the time the foetus is exposed to the risk of severe malformations such as hydrocephaly, bone lesions, and widening of cranial sutures. He concluded that '[a] drug such as misoprostol cannot safely be marketed under such conditions' (Schönhöfer, 1991, 1535). These concerns largely came from the work of Fonseca et al (1991), who reported five cases of an unusual congenital malformation of the frontotemporal region of the skull after the pregnant person had taken misoprostol and suggested a causal relation between misoprostol and foetal malformations. Such fears soon reached the general public, and the Brazilian newspaper *O Globo* published an article stating 'Popular abortifacient deforms fetuses' (Löwy and Dias Villela Corrêa, 2020, 678). Doctors and the public believed the use of misoprostol would lead to 'a generation of monsters', and parents of children born with anencephaly would overhear strangers calling them 'abortion children' (Löwy and Dias Villela Corrêa, 2020, 677). As later studies showed, the causal link made by Fonseca and colleagues was unfounded, but the link persisted in medical and public minds long after.

As the controversy around misoprostol being used for abortions and the fears of it causing foetal malformations became more widely known, Searle felt the need to make a public statement. W. Wilson Downie from International Medical Operations at Searle penned a letter that was published in *The Lancet* to publicly condemn any use of misoprostol beyond the prevention and treatment of stomach ulcers (Downie, 1991). He wrote that 'the labelling for misoprostol clearly states that the product is contraindicated for use by pregnant women. Searle regards the administration of misoprostol, either alone or in combination with other drugs to interfere with the course of pregnancy, as misuse of the product' (Downie, 1991, 247). Searle have publicly acknowledged that they knew that misoprostol was being used for its 'side effects' and distanced themselves from the practice.

Misoprostol's notoriety had also reached the Brazilian government, and in 1991, the government imposed restrictions on misoprostol to curb this unofficial use (Guedes, 2000). While misoprostol had previously been available to purchase from a pharmacy without a prescription, in July 1991, the Ministry of Health introduced restrictions on how the medication could be marketed and allowed it to be sold only in pharmacies, which were ordered to keep a copy of the prescription for their records (Costa, 1998). Some states imposed even stricter regulations – for example, it was completely banned in Ceará, the state where misoprostol was first noted as being used for abortions, it was limited to hospital use only in Rio de Janeiro and Minas Gerais, and it could be sold for gastrointestinal purposes only in São Paulo (Costa, 1998). These restrictions had clear effects on access to misoprostol as units sold fell from 572,134 in 1991 to 150,207 in 1992 (Barbosa and Arilha, 1993), with sales by region in line with the severity of restrictions there (Costa, 1998). Biolab, the company producing misoprostol in Brazil, made an agreement with the Ministry of Health to reduce production in order to limit the number of pills in circulation (Barbosa and Arilha, 1993). Some groups supported these restrictions and even called for it to be entirely withdrawn from the market given its use for abortions, while others, primarily gynaecologists, argued that it needed to remain available due to its role in increasing the safety of abortions and reducing the need to use less safe methods (Assis, 2020). Of course, these measures did not prevent people from accessing misoprostol through other means. Some pharmacies continued to sell it without a prescription and a black market soon flourished, with sellers finding that government restrictions allowed them to significantly raise their prices (Costa, 1998).

Given that Searle distanced themselves from misoprostol's use for abortions in 1991, it is perhaps unsurprising that they remained unwilling to engage with this secondary use. In 1998, the US FDA reported adverse obstetric outcomes after misoprostol was used for labour induction and requested that Searle add this risk to their labelling, to outcry from the American College of Obstetricians and Gynecologists (ACOG) Committee, who pointed to evidence on how safe and effective it was (Lockwood, 2001). Then, when Searle's patent of the Cytotec brand (US Patent No 3,965,143) ended in July 2000, within a month Searle's medical director had published a 'Dear Doctor' letter underlining that misoprostol was to be used for gastrointestinal purposes only and that they could not provide information on risks when used for any other purpose. Searle specifically stated that 'the purpose of this letter is to remind you that Cytotec administration by any route is contraindicated in women who are pregnant because it can cause abortion. Cytotec is not approved for the induction of labor or abortion' (Hale and Zinberg, 2001, 59). Searle explained that this warning was needed due to the reported 'adverse outcomes'. Controversially, this letter was issued without first notifying the US FDA. As recognition of misoprostol as an abortion pill grew, so too did the danger that Searle would be targeted by the US anti-abortion lobby, and Searle sought to avoid controversy among rumours that they were facing lawsuits relating to adverse pregnancy outcomes and reports that the company had been included on a pro-life website's list of companies that support abortion (Lockwood, 2001; Alfirevic and Weeks, 2006). Charles Lockwood, Chair of the ACOG Committee on Obstetric Practice, quickly denounced Searle's letter in an editorial for *Contemporary OB/GYN*. He stated that while he knew the letter would cause widespread problems, what he

> did not realize was that, by virtue of my position at ACOG, I was about to be thrown into a political vortex fed by trial lawyers, radical consumer groups, the Pro-Life movement, Congress, and the media. Within this vortex, the truth would often be subordinated to trial-lawyer posturing, abortion politics, and anti-medical-establishment rhetoric. (Lockwood, 2001, 8)

The Searle letter had immediate consequences and some hospitals stopped using misoprostol for fear of potential legal consequences (Lockwood, 2001). But in a surprising turn of events, just weeks after Searle's letter went public, the US FDA approved the combination of misoprostol with mifepristone for early pregnancy termination (Hale and Zinberg, 2001). This put Searle in a complicated position as their patent had expired at the same time that the US government had approved it as an abortifacient. As Hale and Zinberg (2001, 60) noted, '[o]n the one hand, the company states that misoprostol is not to be administered to pregnant women, and yet the use of misoprostol with mifepristone is now required by the FDA'. This situation was then partially resolved in 2002 when Searle worked with the US FDA to issue new labelling that acknowledged at least that misoprostol could be used for the induction of labour (Lockwood, 2002). This FDA approval shifted perceptions of misoprostol and was a landmark moment in the de-medicalization of abortion care (Karlin and Joffe, 2023).

While the Searle letter controversy may appear to have been swiftly resolved, Searle's relationship to misoprostol has had serious and long-lasting consequences. Searle refused to manufacture a placebo to be used in blinded clinical trials, which has hampered its testing for life-saving treatment such as postpartum haemorrhage (Potts and Hemmerling, 2006). The stigma surrounding abortion has meant that misoprostol has been treated as a 'marginal and suspect character', rather than welcomed for its notable medical capabilities (MacDonald, 2021, 376). For example, in Africa, three of the biggest sources of maternal mortality – haemorrhage, septic abortion and pre-eclampsia – could all be reduced with easy access to misoprostol (Weeks et al, 2005). Searle's wariness of being associated with non-gastrointestinal uses of misoprostol has had serious effects.

Searle's distancing themselves from misoprostol's use for abortions has meant that those seeking to use it for that purpose have to find their own guidelines for use, rather than being able to refer to the packaging insert (Philip et al, 2004). The 200-microgram tablet size it is manufactured in is not ideal for all of its uses, and the information that comes with the pills will not be accurate for an abortion (Elati and Weeks, 2009). Still today, Pfizer's patient product information and physician prescribing information only explains the use of Cytotec for the prevention of stomach ulcers related to arthritis/pain medication, and package inserts contain inadequate storage instructions (Yanow et al, 2021). Moreover, pharmacy staff can only officially recommend dosages for gastrointestinal purposes and pharmaceutical handbooks, such as Mexico's *Diccionario de Especialidades Farmacéuticas*, cannot include obstetric information about misoprostol, so few pharmacy workers have been able to access accurate information about its other uses (Billings et al, 2009). Research on knowledge of misoprostol among pharmacy workers has found that only 15–17 per cent recommend a dosage that could potentially be effective for a complete abortion (Lara et al, 2006; 2011). Instead, in many cases, staff have been recommending ineffective dosages of misoprostol or even recommending non-abortifacient methods, such as hormonal injections. The controversial nature of abortion has meant that for some actors and in some parts of the world, misoprostol has been seen as 'too hot to handle' (MacDonald, 2021, 386).

Nevertheless, there is a silver lining to these multiple lives of misoprostol. As one abortion activist in Peru explained, because it is registered for other medical uses, 'that makes it easier for the drug to exist in pharmacies – it is restricted, but at least it does exist'. It is precisely because misoprostol has other uses that it can be manufactured and sold in restricted environments. She continued, 'it is good that misoprostol is registered with the DIGEMID, which is the General Directorate of Medicines, as a drug for other uses, right, for obstetric uses' even if its sale is restricted, as is the case in Peru, since this to some extent negates the challenges of importing it across borders. Two health professionals in Peru also celebrated the introduction of misoprostol into the country. One doctor began using it in the early 2000s and found it 'extraordinary' for the treatment of 'unsolved' problems such as haemorrhage, labour induction, and softening the cervix when performing a vacuum aspiration after an incomplete miscarriage. For him, this 'fabulous drug' was the perfect answer to a number of obstetric problems, and he noted that it was widely supported by obstetricians and gynaecologists, the Peruvian Society of Obstetrics and Gynecology, and the Ministry of Health, but crucially only for the 'other' obstetric uses, not for abortions. The other doctor said, '[misoprostol] has made my life easier, I'll tell you', particularly when performing procedural abortions on patients who had not been pregnant before. She explained that dilating the cervix is a painful experience for patients and some would 'scream', but with the use of misoprostol, the cervix ripens 'like jelly' and the dilation is much easier. She described a time when she used misoprostol: 'I am joking with the patient, we are gossiping about our lives, and when she realizes "what, it's over?"'

The global inequities in biomedicine are well documented and the Searle controversies surrounding misoprostol form part of this (Sunder Rajan, 2017). Searle's refusal to manufacture a placebo or provide usage or risk information is an example of science bending to the needs of the company, not to the people using the medication (Harding, 2014). But Searle's wariness has not prevented the use of misoprostol; the fact that it exists and is registered in countries for gastrointestinal purposes has opened up the opportunity for those seeking to end their pregnancies to 'misuse' it for that purpose. When Searle's patent ended in 2000, other pharmaceutical companies were able to manufacture and market their own generic versions of misoprostol, and when the WHO then listed it as an essential medicine, its use became registered across the world (Atukunda et al, 2015). Misoprostol's controversies, which began as soon as its use as an abortifacient was noticed by the medical community, exemplify how abortion, particularly when self-managed by poor women in the global South, becomes a point of scepticism, fear, and wariness. It was only as misoprostol was legitimized by global North science that these controversies began to wane. Greene and Sismondo (2015, 2) argue that every pharmaceutical is 'an object that mediates borders between medical science and popular belief, health and disease, and spheres of licit and illicit', and the controversies around misoprostol exemplify the veracity of that claim.

The creation of a regime

Throughout the 2000s, misoprostol was spreading across the world in both its physical form and as a new technology of abortion. But misoprostol is ineffective if not administered through a certain route or in sufficient quantity. The most common amount of misoprostol taken for an effective termination is 2,400 micrograms, or 12 pills, which can seem like a very high number for those accustomed to other medications where usually one or two pills are taken. The most frequent regimen for a misoprostol-only abortion is three doses of four 200-microgram pills, with each dose taken 3 to 12 hours apart, administered vaginally, buccally (between the cheek and gum), or sublingually (under the tongue). This '4 × 4 × 4 method' (Singer, 2022) is a specific regimen and it did not come about by accident. Brazilian and then other Latin American women became their own laboratories for self-experimenting with the number of pills, the timing, and the route that would be most effective. Individuals were experimenting on their own bodies but in concert with others seeking to end their own pregnancies and then later with medical professionals and feminist activists, as has been seen with other feminist health practices (Murphy, 2012). As an interviewee in Peru explained:

> this is a topic that young women spoke about first with their peers. And it's among peers that they exchange the techniques that they use with each other. So it was at that level that they were able to strengthen the evidence-based information, to be able to bring them safe information in order to achieve these levels of effectiveness of the product.

As medical anthropologists have shown, efficacy is more than simple effect, it is processual, relational, and situated (Hardon and Sanabria, 2017). Latin American women were, therefore, not just uncovering an efficient regime – they were *creating* it.

It is clear that across Latin America, activists take a sense of pride in being the ones to have created the misoprostol abortion regime, rather than receiving it from the medical community. The struggles bound up in this were noted by one interviewee, who explained that 'it has taken years, and unfortunately many difficult situations for many women, to find the ideal route, and the right dose'. In her influential book on abortion accompaniment in Argentina, *Código rosa* (code pink), Belfiori (2021, 18) writes: 'we have been changing the story from being "passers of data" to being active subjects of these practices. We create the code, we interpret it, we share it. And we make it visible.' The mythology of 'the poor Black women in the favelas' was also frequently mentioned by *acompañantes* I interviewed as a symbol of innovation, resourcefulness, and rebellion.

The experimentation that led to this effective regimen then fed into the medical communities' clinical trials with misoprostol and informed the regimen that came to be officially recommended by the WHO. The WHO (2022) guidelines recommend 'the use of 800 µg [micrograms] misoprostol administered vaginally, sublingually or buccally. ... Repeat doses of misoprostol can be considered when needed to achieve success of the abortion process. In this guideline we do not provide a maximum number of doses of misoprostol.' Since 2005, the WHO has recognized misoprostol as an essential medicine and acknowledged it as a safe method to end a pregnancy, even if they classify the sourcing and use of it outside the medical system as 'less safe' (Assis, 2021). The WHO's 2019 list of essential medicines includes misoprostol in the 200-microgram form for the 'Management of incomplete abortion and miscarriage' and the 'Prevention and treatment of postpartum haemorrhage where oxytocin is not available or cannot be safely used' (WHO, 2021a). It is also included with mifepristone but with the unprecedented warning 'Where permitted under national law and where culturally acceptable', and no guidance on what this combination is used for is given within the document (WHO, 2021a; see also Assis and Erdman, 2022).

Elsewhere, the WHO do issue guidelines on how misoprostol can be used to terminate pregnancies, and the existence of it at all on the list is used by healthcare providers and activists to argue that it must be accessible in all contexts because it is an essential medicine. The WHO's policy on abortion medications, particularly their guidance document *Safe Abortion: Technical and Policy Guidance for Health Systems*, first published in 2003 with a second edition in 2012 (WHO, 2012), has helped to usher in abortion reform across the world (Erdman et al, 2013). Their guidance offers evidence-based recommendations on how to use misoprostol in combination with other medications or by itself, and acts as a globally recognized, trusted source. Beyond the WHO, other organizations have legitimized misoprostol through formal recognition, including by FLASOG, the Latin American Federation of Obstetrics and Gynecology Societies (Chia, 2018). This means that feminist activists who perhaps did not know how to recommend an effective regimen of misoprostol can access guidelines much more easily (Larrea et al, 2024).

But experimentation has not stopped with the global recognition of the WHO-recommended dosage. While many *acompañante* groups who support people to self-manage their abortions outside medical settings spoke about following the WHO-recommended regimen of 12 pills, typically across three doses, plenty have continued to tailor the regimen, based on their own findings, for their own communities. The WHO protocol on safe use provides a legitimized source that facilitates clear and accurate guidance on how to use misoprostol for abortion seekers, activists, and providers, but for many this is a starting point, not the end goal. In terms of the number of pills used, one *acompañante* in Peru explained that in most cases they use 12 pills but if the abortion is not complete after 24 hours, they recommend taking 2 more and, in most cases, this will result in a complete abortion. This extra dose is possible with misoprostol because no dangerous overdose amount has been found. Other groups find that they do not usually need to recommend the full dose of 12 pills – for example, one group in Mexico uses two doses of 4 pills while another uses just one dose of 4 pills. One *acompañante* in Mexico explained that she saw the number of pills needed as not just a physiological issue, but an emotional one:

> it depends, very possibly, on how the woman is feeling, on the support she has, if she feels well, calm, if she knows that she is, that she has people who will accompany her if the matter, let's say, becomes more difficult, if she has to go to a hospital, right? Or if she has networks that can give her assistance if things get a little more complicated.

The regimen needs to be flexible, taking these factors into account. As the *acompañante* explained, women who experience a level of calm are more likely to have a successful abortion with just four pills. Groups also tailor the route of administration according to the person's preference, as some people see sublingual or buccal use as more linked to 'menstrual regulation' and vaginal use as more linked to abortion (Zamberlin et al, 2012). Also, in contexts where abortion is criminalized, the sublingual or buccal routes tend to be recommended so as to keep the use of misoprostol hidden since, should the person end up seeking medical treatment, any partially dissolved pills may be found in the vagina.

Acompañante groups have also drawn on their experience of accompanying abortions to make recommendations on additional strategies that can be incorporated. For example, some have found that the integration of plants such as rue or Andean mint, an approach adapted from ancestral knowledges on provoking an abortion, can help to aid the process (this is discussed in Chapter 5). One group explained that they advise people to avoid eating chocolate when taking the pills, since they noticed a potential causal link between chocolate and low efficacy of misoprostol; however, this wasn't noted by any of the other groups. Another noticed that people who were taking prescribed anxiety medications seemed to have a lower efficacy rate, so this informed their protocol. An *acompañante* in Colombia explained that they recommended a diet for people to follow to minimize the amount of blood they lose during the abortion. She explained, 'we were not going to tell anyone, get an iron supplement and eat a lot of red meat and a lot of liver, because it is very expensive' and some people may be vegetarian; instead, they recommended cheap and easily accessible food sources such as herbs, grains, chickpeas, lentils, and beans, as these were more affordable for the local community compared to expensive red meat. Another *acompañante*, in Peru, also stressed the importance of nutrition, noting that diarrhoea is a common symptom during the medical abortion process so it is better to choose lighter meals over heavier ones. She also explained that they recommend that people stay hydrated as that will help them to generate saliva to dissolve the pills.

One specific finding that came out of this creation of an effective regime is that misoprostol is not effective in the first six weeks of gestation. This has fed into the protocols of many groups, with the recommendation being that people wait until the sixth week of gestation before attempting the abortion. One *acompañante* explained that she had noticed this issue when she was supporting people with abortions and had spoken to others in her country as well as people in other countries who had also noticed it. She said: 'Although it has not been investigated by the WHO, we, with all the accompaniment groups in the world, have been able to agree that the same thing happens to them and we have been able to integrate this information into our protocol.' An interviewee in Peru explained that for pregnancies of six to eight weeks, they use 800 micrograms of misoprostol every four hours, but only two doses. She supported misoprostol abortions up to 18 weeks, and for those, she used 400 micrograms every four hours for up to five doses. Some interviewees spoke about how they would develop specific protocols for pregnancies over 12 weeks of gestation. One *acompañante* in Peru explained that passing the foetus and placenta is more challenging with more developed pregnancies, so their strategy, which was 'developed based on experience, as well as accompanying these women', involved women blowing into a bottle, which they found helps people to expel all the material successfully.

Another finding is that ultrasounds are not necessarily an essential part of the abortion process. Until fairly recently, some accompaniment groups have required evidence of an ultrasound before offering the pills, and medical professionals have deemed this essential. However, as many interviewees explained, obtaining an ultrasound requires money and interacting with medical staff, and it provides proof of a pregnancy, which can then be used to prosecute someone who later has an abortion or miscarriage. In many Latin American contexts, urban areas have small clinics that offer ultrasounds for a relatively low price, and here the results are not attached to people's broader medical records. However, some accompaniment groups found that ultrasounds were not necessary, as they rarely saw a significant difference between the gestational age indicated by the ultrasound and the estimate given by the pregnant person based on the date of their last period. This was recently corroborated by a research study showing that the self-reported date of last missed period 'can reliably estimate the stage of pregnancy in individuals seeking first-trimester MAB [medical abortion] services', which 'expands access to comprehensive and safe abortion care, especially for low-income individuals or those living in areas with limited access to technology' (Cely-Andrade, 2024, 6).

As all these strategies show, *acompañantes*, rather than strictly following one protocol use their own experiences to tailor the medical abortion process to their own communities and the people they're supporting (Bercu et al, 2022). My findings here are validated by other researchers. Larrea et al (2024) conducted interviews with abortion activists in Latin America and the Caribbean and found that many were critical of the WHO approach. While many agreed that the guidelines gave them a framework to work from, they disagreed with the WHO approach to quality of care, which did not centre women's autonomy, justice, ancestral knowledge, or emotional support. They believed that while the WHO guidelines may work for formal health systems, they were at odds with the feminist approach to abortion care that was key to their activism and accompaniment. Similarly, one *acompañante* I interviewed noted that although the new WHO approach gave a freedom to those seeking an abortion as they no longer set a limit of 12 pills, the WHO still views 'safe' abortions as being supported by trained medical professionals, 'so it is not so autonomous, in that sense, because you have to be checked by health personnel, right?'

The experiences that informed these adapted strategies and protocols can be understood as a form of tacit knowledge development. This knowledge did not need to be developed through clinical trials carried out by medical researchers, as *acompañantes* drew on their own abortions as well as their experience of supporting others through abortions to note patterns and outcomes that then fed into their accompaniment practices. As Burton (2017b) found in her work on the Argentine group Socorristas en Red, through accompanying thousands of abortions, the group have constructed knowledge that allows them to be valid voices in knowledges and practices of medical abortions. They have systematized data on abortion accompaniment from their 'daily insistence' on abortion (Burton, 2017c). An *acompañante* in Peru explained: 'We began to share valuable information, didn't we – knowledge that we had acquired throughout this process of providing information and being close to the women.' Here, efficacy is constructed through what Zurbriggen (2019) terms '*actos corpo-aborteros*' (bodily-abortive acts), as *acompañantes* provide embodied support and knowledge making, as opposed to clinical and distant service provision. Such embodied knowledge building shows the interweaving of manual and intellectual tasks, whereby *acompañantes* are thinking with their hands, heart, and brain (Cusicanqui, 2018). This tacit knowledge was described by one interviewee in Peru as '*casuística*' (casuistic), which describes a type of knowledge learned from one case and applied to others (Freeman and Rodríguez, 2024a). This recognition of casuistic knowledge development takes seriously the 'lay expertise' generated and shared by activists who don't usually have formal medical training (McReynolds-Pérez, 2017) and challenges what Harding (2009, 418) calls the 'familiar philosophic assumptions' of 'Dominant science'. This casuistic knowledge does not stay statically with individuals, but is shared across groups, locally and globally, as a form of 'peer-to-peer education about the medical technology and its impact on the body' (Bercu et al, 2022, 134). This development of a feminist protocol through embodied experience reclaims power held by the medical community and locates it within communities of people 'getting together to share experiences and learn about their own bodies through direct observation' (Murphy, 2012, 25).

An *acompañante* in Argentina told me about her abortion group's strategy to construct the data they felt was lacking on misoprostol use. When they began supporting people with their abortions, they created a data file for information such as sociodemographic data and the person's gynaecological and wider health history to better understand the communities they were aiding. They then gathered data about how people were experiencing the abortion process, 'then that allowed us to know [at what dosage of] misoprostol the bleeding generally starts, from the second dose, sometimes after the third dose'. They asked people to rate the pain they were experiencing on a scale of 1 to 10, and they 'were also interested in knowing whether they were alone or accompanied, because perhaps the pain also had to do with emotional issues, of feeling alone at that moment'. The *acompañante* also explained that across the early years of their accompaniment, they saw a dramatic fall in the number of people needing to access medical care. She said that at the beginning they had a fear about the risks of abortion and would recommend that anyone with a fever or heavy bleeding should seek treatment at a medical facility. Over time, based on 'the lessons ... learned from the medication', they became less reactive and instead would monitor fevers and recommend medications to ease them, and they got a better sense of how much blood should be expected. As the *acompañante* explained: 'we learned a lot as we were assisting abortions and learning from the women's experiences'.

Another interviewee proudly explained how through their lay expertise, she and her fellow *acompañantes* had a better understanding of misoprostol than some doctors, as they have been the ones 'listening to the experiences of the women who tell ... what their whole process has been like, delving into their history, knowing what they take, what they don't take'. Similarly, an interviewee in Peru who had been accompanying abortions since 2001 said: '[I] was incorporating what I had learned, because for me every woman was a learning experience' as 'each situation is different and, as you attend more and more, you incorporate more things and you become an expert'.

These learning processes, the generation of knowledge, and the development of expertise has then been collated by various *acompañante* groups. As part of their political approach of making abortion knowledges as democratic as possible, abortion knowledges are shared widely through more formal training, via informal mentoring, in local, national, and international workshops and events, and through the plethora of guides and information sources that groups create, which might be manuals, videos, podcasts, information hotlines, zines, and more. To prevent individuals having to (re)develop this already-produced knowledge, networks have been effective at retaining their knowledge while continuously reworking their practices and adapting their protocols to best support their own communities.

Casuistic, tacit, embodied knowledge has become a key tenet of the de-medicalization of abortion: the political conviction that abortion can be self-managed by individuals, between friends, or with the support of feminist groups, not just in medical settings. This de-medicalized approach acts as an extension of the early days of experimentation with misoprostol. As I, together with a colleague, have argued elsewhere, this knowledge building that has transformed the use of misoprostol shows how the idea of 'toxicity' is contextual and shifting (Freeman and Rodríguez, 2024a). Misoprostol is labelled with the warning of 'reproductive toxicity', but for someone seeking an abortion, 'toxicity' can mean freedom and a solution to an unwanted pregnancy. As Liboiron et al (2018, 333) argue, '[t]oxicity is not wayward particles behaving badly', and a chemical that is a 'bad actor' (Liboiron, 2016) for some is a liberatory one for others. Through domesticating the 'toxicity' of misoprostol, on people's own bodies and through accompaniment knowledge-building, women and pregnant people have harnessed toxic side effects to become intended effects. 'Side effects' are always culturally specific and circumstantial (Etkin, 1992), and the creation of not just one, but many shifting regimes transformed the 'side effect' of abortion to the desired effect of misoprostol.

Spreading the word of misoprostol

The creation of a safe and effective dosage of misoprostol was an important step, but the next challenge was to make sure this regimen reached the people who needed it. While information on the safe and effective use of misoprostol exists, all too often those seeking this information have instead encountered inaccurate and potentially harmful information (Erdman, 2012;

Hyman et al, 2013). Smaller activist and *acompañante* groups have filled a key space here, given that larger non-governmental organizations (NGOs) have often been prevented from sharing information about abortion access. US President Ronald Reagan's 'global gag rule' in 1978 meant extra-legal abortion services were challenging to provide, as organizations were banned from receiving US aid money if they even provided information about abortion (Nolan, 2022). To illustrate the impact of a lack of information, I include at length the following story that was told to me by an interviewee in Argentina, who I call Cristina, who self-managed her own abortion using misoprostol in 2007. This experience was formative in her becoming an activist and going on to help people access the information on misoprostol that had not been available to her.

> I used misoprostol in 2007. I was going to have an abortion with a doctor and then my partner at the time talked to a friend and the friend told him, stop, there are some pills. I spoke to that guy's partner at the time, who had used the pills, and she showed me a blister pack. She had two left, I think. She shows them to me. And she explains to me a regime that she [had] from when she had used them. I started to look for information. The first information I found was on the internet. There I see that it had appeared in a newspaper, *Página 12* – there was an article by Mariana Carabajal, a journalist who is dedicated to these issues. [The article was about] a public hospital here in the autonomous city of Buenos Aires that has always worked in the line of reducing harm, that said that abortion mortality was decreasing and that they were beginning to see that misoprostol was starting to be used. And not much else. I tried to contact the gynaecologist who had given this girl the instructions on how to use the pill. She never wanted to see me. It was very … she didn't want to … I called her, called her, called her.
>
> And at the same time, I was looking for the pills. I went out to get the pills. I bought them, I used them. From a pharmacy. I went to several pharmacies. My boyfriend at that time went to several pharmacies until they sold it to him. He found someone to sell it to him. In one day we had the pills, but I didn't have the instructions, or rather I had this information that this girl had given me. The gynaecologist didn't want to see me, I didn't know what to do. So, what I decided to do was move forward. And with the information that I had from the girl, I did the process. It was not following the recommended dosage – I took much less. I remember I took one pill every four hours. And it worked the first time I took it.
>
> I didn't want anything to do with that situation. I was convinced that I didn't want to continue with the pregnancy and in fact I was very happy when I saw the bleeding. I mean, for me, when I … it

was like a big shock, you see when they talk about this narrative of abortion only as something painful, when in my perspective, in my personal experience and also in the experience of other women who I have spoken to, the painful and distressing thing was to be pregnant. I remember the anguish I felt from the moment I found out I was pregnant until I was able to resolve it. The moment I saw, I remember I got out of bed and saw the bleeding, I was happy. I was happy. That was it. What I needed to happen was happening. And ... well, yes. Then that gynaecologist did do the after-abortion care. She did agree to see me afterwards. Everything went well, there was no problem. I had expelled everything. But I remember I spent about seven days taking one misoprostol pill every four hours.

Cristina's experience in 2007 provides one example of the challenges that people face when they cannot access accurate information about misoprostol. She had to find her own information through word of mouth and the internet, and this information was not wholly accurate. Luckily for her, the abortion she so desperately wanted was successful, but that certainly was not guaranteed given the dosage she followed.

Similarly, another interviewee in Argentina, who I will call Sara, remembered misoprostol being used for abortions in the mid-1990s when she was in high school. But as she explained, 'we used it wrong, with one tablet or two', which sometimes worked and sometimes didn't. Sara and her friends learned about misoprostol from a friend who used Oxaprost (the brand name for a pill that included misoprostol and diclofenac, a medicine that reduces inflammation) for joint pain in her knees. As Sara recalled: 'and she is the one who started to know that Oxaprost could not be used when she was pregnant. We were 17 years old, and she was the one in charge of saying "Are you pregnant or what? Take this."' Sara went on to explain that her friend 'wasn't an activist or a militant or anything, but she read the package insert'. She said: 'I knew from her because she read the package insert, she said, "Well, use this." And we used it and, uh, the cases that I know of were successful. I can't explain why.' The sharing of information about misoprostol was initially informal across Latin America, such as in these examples, but this became more formalized over time.

One of the first major developments in formalized feminist strategies of sharing knowledge about misoprostol beyond immediate networks was the establishment of abortion hotlines. The region's first independent hotline was set up in Ecuador in 2008, with more countries following in the 2010s (Braine and Velarde, 2022). Abortion hotlines are prevalent across Latin America and provide accurate, empathetic information to callers who require support in procuring or using abortion pills. These hotlines intervene in the silence created by governments who fail to provide access to or information about safe abortions (Jelinska and Yanow, 2018). A particular advantage of hotlines is that they are a relatively low-tech technology, and if a number is shut down, a new one can be reopened. The most important prerequisite is not any real technological expertise, but rather knowledge on how to adequately support someone with a medical abortion (Drovetta, 2015). The introduction of hotlines democratized knowledge, and rather than needing to know someone personally who could provide information, people could call the hotline and receive anonymous, safe advice. This gave autonomy to a wider group of people to take control of their own reproduction outside medicalized settings (Calkin et al, 2022). One challenge with abortion hotlines is ensuring that people have access to the number to call. It is, therefore, common to find numbers plastered, scrawled, and graffitied on walls and in public restrooms, restaurants, and trains, as well as being shared on websites and social media (Erdman, 2011; Bloomer et al, 2020).

The importance of these hotlines frequently came up in interviews. Some were set up by activists and some by healthcare workers. For example, an interviewee in Argentina recalled the importance of a hotline set up by the Fundación para la Salud del Adolescente (FUSA, Adolescent Health Foundation), which ran under a 'harm reduction' principle, informed by highly successful harm reduction strategies for abortion in Uruguay. The people running the hotline could not prescribe misoprostol or provide information on where to procure it, but they could give information on the safest way to use it, what side effects people might experience, and what to do in the rare care of complications. A different interviewee in Argentina explained the importance of transregional connections in the setting up of activist abortion hotlines. She explained how the Dutch abortion organization Women on Waves trained up a group of activists in Ecuador as the founder, Rebecca Gomperts, was keen to advance the growth of feminist hotlines. The Ecuadorian group then trained up others, primarily in Chile and Argentina, and shared their experience of developing a hotline so that the practical know-how and abortion knowledge spread across the region.

Other groups in Latin America then followed. For example, in Peru, the group Colectiva por la Libre Información para las Mujeres (CLIM) have run their Línea Aborto Información Segura (Safe Information Abortion Hotline) since 2010, sharing information on how to safely use misoprostol. The CLIM hotline was noted in interviews as a key turning point that gave people in Peru a clear point of contact to access for themselves or direct others to. The fact that this is a telephone hotline means that people do not need an internet connection or advanced technology equipment to access it, although CLIM have diversified their information dissemination methods. Nowadays, when you go on their website, a small box appears with the following text:

> Hi, I'm MisoChat, the chatbot of the safe information abortion hotline and my task will be to provide you with information about abortion and misoprostol. This information is based on the Safe Abortion Medication Abortion Guidelines of the World Health Organization (WHO) and International Federation of Gynecology and Obstetrics (FIGO) among others.

MisoChat is a new extension of the methods to democratize knowledge and ensure that all people have access to information on how to use misoprostol safely.

Alongside hotlines, another crucial way of sharing information about misoprostol in Latin America has been 'manuals'. Manuals, handbooks, or guides are documents prepared by groups that typically comprise text and images explaining how to use misoprostol alongside information about side effects, symptoms, contraindications, and risks. Some are short and briefly explain the protocol, whereas others are lengthy and may include features such as testimonies from people who have self-managed their abortions, feminist prose, and a history of misoprostol use. These manuals may exist in book form, available to buy at feminist bookstores and markets and then shared between friends, or they may primarily exist as PDF files to be downloaded and shared by email or WhatsApp.

The manual that the interviewees in this study most commonly referred to as being 'the first' in Latin America was by the Argentine group Lesbianas y Feministas por la Descriminalización del Aborto, founded in 2009. They were set up from a politically lesbian position to support access to abortion with misoprostol and to take the 'drama' out of abortion (Mines, 2011). In 2010, they published *Todo lo que querés saber sobre cómo hacerse un aborto con pastillas* (Everything you need to know about how to have an abortion with pills), which went on to be downloaded 500,000 times, with an additional 20,000 copies printed out and distributed free of charge (Szwarc, 2024). An interviewee remembered being at an Encuentro (a national women's meeting) in 2009, when an early version of the manual was being distributed, a year before it was officially published; she said: 'that's when everything changed. It changed everything.' Encuentros have taken place in Argentina every year since 1986 (in addition to regional Encuentros), and these were central to abortion becoming a primary feminist issue at the national scale, so the launching of this manual at the 2009 Encuentro was certainly fitting (Sutton and Borland, 2013). One *acompañante* in Argentina felt that 'this manual kind of made it possible to know that abortion pills existed and that we could make them ourselves ... the manual was like the first milestone'. She noted that they and other activists 'had already heard that abortion pills could be used' and at the time they 'also thought that it was possible, but in general they [the pills] were linked to health professionals', whereas the publication of the manual 'broke a frontier' for them and they then developed an accompaniment group. The group created leaflets that could be easily printed and shared and focused on including images to make the process as clear as possible. She felt that this served as a way to share information but also 'to know and demystify issues that socially circulated' about abortion in Argentina.

Another manual that appeared commonly in interviews was the Peruvian group CLIM's *Hablemos de aborto y misoprostol* (Let's talk about abortion and misoprostol), which, like the Argentine book, was widely available in printed form as well as in a PDF file. One interviewee remembered going to the meeting of a sexual and reproductive rights NGO where everyone attending was given a copy of the manual as a gift; that, for her, illustrated the political importance of such meetings as a space to share knowledge on abortion. Another recalled being at the launch of the book and being impressed at the way it included the WHO protocol but 'added much more information about pre- and post- care, as well as during', which she thought was 'fundamental for the understanding of the process'. The tangibility of this manual was a common theme, with interviewees calling it 'the little purple booklet with fuchsia' or 'the pink one! I have it right here.' Another interviewee told me about how she had called the CLIM abortion hotline when she needed information about self-managing her own abortion and then went on to become an abortion *acompañante* herself:

> I have the CLIM book as part of my activism to help girls. That also seems crazy to me. I have been lucky enough to meet the CLIM members, who at that time were already working. We have shared workshops together. I have learned from them. I have even worked with them a little bit.

These manuals have, therefore, been important in providing information on how to use misoprostol, but they have also played a bigger role in network building and solidarity formation.

Before the existence of the manuals and hotlines, interviewees spoke about how they would share information 'in a somewhat disorganized way', in the words of one interviewee from Peru; she said: 'We were a little bit afraid – that is, we felt a little bit responsible for providing information in a disorganized way.' The dissatisfaction with this approach led to groups creating their own protocols. One interviewee explained the process of creating the protocol for her group's manual:

> Our protocol took us a year, first, to learn about misoprostol, to learn about our processes, about the pregnancy process, about our

reproductive system ... obviously that and all the information that had already been given to us and provided by our colleagues in Ecuador and Argentina. And, after a year, we had a protocol of care, so we would know if they ask me this, I am going to answer this? What questions do I have to ask?

They then printed this protocol out, decided on the schedule when they would offer their services, and developed a set of ground rules, particularly to protect the privacy of those they were supporting. Once the protocols, whether in a manual or for a hotline, were developed they soon spread across national and international contexts. One interviewee who had set up an early hotline told me of the pride she had in sharing the protocol her group had developed and seeing other Latin American hotlines use their exact same approach: 'We have realized that our protocol has travelled all over Latin America and it is good, isn't it? We feel really proud to have a very comprehensive protocol.' Often this knowledge sharing about misoprostol was through informal friendships and contacts, and at other times it was more formalized. One interviewee in Argentina remembered how her group was contacted by groups in other parts of Argentina and together they went through a training process run by people from Uruguay, a country often seen as one of the frontrunners of abortion access in Latin America.

The impacts of this shared knowledge through hotlines, manuals, and other strategies are significant. The sharing of a regime on how to use misoprostol 'opened up a different panorama', according to one interviewee in Peru. She recalled how in the mid-2000s, abortions with misoprostol were seen as second class compared to vacuum aspirations, but the dissemination of knowledge changed this completely. Another interviewee, an obstetrician, explained how she had known of misoprostol since the 1980s, but the networks who shared information about it created new understandings of how it could be used and accessed. Before routes of dissemination such as manuals, the use of misoprostol 'just wasn't talked about' and each person using it was forced to self-teach and search for opportunities to learn more about it. In the early days, as an interviewee in Peru explained, information would circulate around neighbourhoods and some of this information would be 'wrong and erroneous, but at least there was some information'. She went on to say: 'I read the manuals and that's where I more or less understood what the procedure was ... the protocol helped to make everything more condensed.' In the words of an interviewee in Argentina, 'the introduction of misoprostol together with a much stronger, much more articulated, and much more informed feminist articulation' of how to use it is what transformed the landscape of abortion access in Latin America.

Misoprostol and the politics of scientific knowledge

The story that unfolded in this chapter, from the stomach ulcer drug misoprostol being experimented with for abortions in Brazil to this knowledge spreading among across Latin America and into the medical community, often amid great controversy, and then the creation of a feminist regime that has been widely disseminated, is a story of the politics of scientific knowledge. Misoprostol was not developed as a pharmaceutical in Latin America, but that is where it went through the 'reinscription process' that led to its new life as an abortifacient (Hardon and Sanabria, 2017, 122). Misoprostol was designed to be a cheap and fairly effective medication for preventing and treating gastrointestinal issues that result from taking NSAIDs. But chemicals are 'unruly' (Calkin, 2021), and this medication leaked and traversed beyond its intended use.

The knowledge about misoprostol and its use for abortions was developed in the global 'southern periphery', and as this knowledge reached wider audiences, it was 'remade' in northern scientific spaces in order to become legitimized in a global North-centric culture that only accepts Western (or 'Dominant') science as 'real' (Harding, 2014; Liboiron, 2021). The southern periphery could be a space for experimentation, but misoprostol was only recognized as a safe and effective abortion medication when it was made 'legitimate' by the scientific community (De Zordo, 2016). 'Traditional' scientific research confirmed misoprostol's efficacy for abortions so that administration guidelines could be created (Hardon and Sanabria, 2017), but as this chapter has shown, feminist groups have been central in creating their own regime, tailoring this regime for their context and communities, and sharing the protocol with those who needed it. Latin American women were the ones who 'rewrote the script' of misoprostol (MacDonald, 2021, 393), and their bodies were, and continue to be, their own laboratories for working out how to best administer the medication for a safe abortion as well as a site of ongoing rearticulation of the politics of knowledge around abortifacients. Often this rearticulation has taken place in clandestine ways, but it is the 'friction' (Tsing, 2005) created at these margins and the interaction of the local and the global that has also created the possibilities for clandestine experimentation and the use of misoprostol for abortions. This exemplifies the importance of scientific knowledge that develops in marginalized communities at the 'periphery' and the effects this knowledge development can have on global science and millions of people's reproductive lives (Soto Laveaga, 2009).

The experimentation of Latin American women with misoprostol has led to a global change in abortion access. For example, as medical abortion has boomed across the world, the WHO has had to shift its way of classifying abortion safety. While previous classifications created a neat division between safe, legal abortions and unsafe, illegal abortions, there is now a spectrum of classification from safe to less safe to least safe (Suh, 2021). The WHO was forced to accept that medical abortions that take place outside medical settings and with no medical professionals involved can still be safe and that they are not in the same category as clandestine practices such as the insertion of foreign objects into the uterus (Larrea et al, 2024). The impact of the development of misoprostol as an abortifacient by individuals and activists in Latin America is, therefore, significant. Drugs alter the chemistry of our bodies, but they also have the potential to alter our experiences and our networks of social relations (Greene and Sismondo, 2015). The example of misoprostol exemplifies how technoscience influences feminism while feminism also transforms technoscience (Murphy, 2012).

Yet I am wary of telling this as a universal success story. If I, in the United Kingdom, access a first trimester abortion through our National Health Service, I will be given the abortion pills mifepristone and misoprostol. But women in Brazil, the 'cradle' of the development of misoprostol as an abortifacient (De Zordo, 2016) and the home of the people who experimented on their own bodies with misoprostol, 'are denied access to a technological innovation that they introduced to the world' (Assis, 2020, 120–121). As knowledge of the abortifacient properties of misoprostol spread, restrictions on its use have increased. Across the world, in countries such as Brazil, Egypt, and Thailand, misoprostol has been removed from pharmacies and can only be accessed by doctors in hospital settings, precisely so that its use for abortions can be limited (Jelinska and Yanow, 2018). Access to misoprostol is most heavily restricted in Latin America and the Caribbean, despite it being registered for obstetric use worldwide (Assis, 2021). These drug restrictions are, ostensibly, in the name of combatting the informal supply of misoprostol to protect public health (Assis and Erdman, 2021), depsite the huge amounts of evidence on its safety and efficacy. Assis and Erdman (2021) argue that misoprostol's 'double life' emerges from a public health rhetoric of unsafe abortion and that, therefore, abortion criminalization is not the *cause* but, rather, the *consequence* of misoprostol's double life.

If this chapter has traced the story of how misoprostol 'became' an abortion pill, the rest of the book explores the afterlife of this becoming, from the *acompañantes* who have facilitated its use to the strategies to access it, the role of the law, and the drug's relations with other reproductive technologies. While this chapter has covered some of the strategies developed by *acompañante* groups to develop and disseminate information about using misoprostol, the next chapter unpacks who *acompañantes* are and how they have radically transformed the landscape of safe abortion access in Latin America.

2

Supporting Misoprostol Abortions: The 'Accompaniers' Facilitating Access

Abortion is criminalized across much of Latin America, which makes getting information on how to access a safe abortion incredibly difficult. *Acompañante* groups have been established to address this need. They provide emotional and practical support for those seeking to end a pregnancy (Burton, 2017a; Zurbriggen, 2019). *Acompañar*, meaning to accompany, is understood slightly differently between groups, but most use it to mean the process of explaining how to have an abortion using misoprostol (alone or in combination with mifepristone), where to locate the pills, what to expect, and what to do in the case of an emergency. Volunteers will often go through the process with the person having the abortion, either in person or virtually, while many also run sessions on the law and group therapy-style support groups. But it is key to note that *acompañamiento* is more than just the facilitation of access to care – it is a political project that works towards abortion liberation.

Acompañante groups work from the political position that everyone has the right to manage their own reproductive lives and that with the right information and support, practically anyone can self-manage their abortion. Broadly speaking, accompaniment can be understood as a feminist model of care whereby activists provide information and support, and often the pills, to people wishing to have an abortion. Importantly, accompaniment groups have proven to be an enormous success in Latin America. The Argentine group La Revuelta reported that 99.4 per cent of women accompanied by them had a successful abortion on their first attempt (Burton and Peralta, 2016). The successes of the feminist model is exceeding progress made through clinical trials. *Acompañamiento* is the praxis that has made misoprostol 'magic'.

This chapter introduces a variety of accompaniment groups and describes their politics, how they support people to have abortions with misoprostol, and why they have been described as the 'engineers' of abortion access (Burton, 2017b). In particular, this develops reproductive justice scholarship by exploring how *acompañantes* fight for the right not to have children and take an intersectional approach to provide support for poor, Indigenous, and rural women who face the greatest barriers to safe healthcare. It also illustrates how accompaniment work has challenged preconceptions of who can provide an abortion, what knowledge is needed, and where an abortion can take place.

What are accompaniment groups?

Generally speaking, *acompañantes* are groups or individuals who mobilize to provide accurate information and support for self-managing an abortion using misoprostol (sometimes in combination with mifepristone) while providing emotional support, legal guidance, practical resources, and post-abortion care where needed (Veldhuis et al, 2022a). The emergence of *acompañante* groups is often identified as having taken place in the early 2000s, when 'several feminist groups around the world started organizing to support women who were self-managing medication abortions outside the formal healthcare system and the legal indications' (Larrea et al, 2024, 49). They began in key nodes in Latin America – Mexico, Argentina, and Ecuador, in particular – and then spread across the region. *Acompañante* groups may, therefore, seem like a relatively new phenomenon, but the practice of *acompañamiento* has a longer history of community support, feminist solidarity, and ancestral knowledges (Rojas et al, 2022). Feminist activism supporting people to access abortions can be traced back to global examples such as the Jane Collective in the United States in the 1970s, clandestine networks in France and Italy, and activist support on both sides of the US–Mexico border (Keefe-Oates, 2021; Braine and Velarde, 2022). And even before that, women have long shared advice and techniques on how to end pregnancies. Therefore, while the particular assemblage of people supporting the use of abortion medications emerged in the early 21st century, 'abortion itself has long been an area of autonomous health action and self-determination among women' (Braine, 2020, 89).

Nevertheless, accompaniment groups have seen a rapid increase in recent years, largely due to the *marea verde* (green wave/tide) that has swept across the region (Belfrage, 2023). One interviewee I spoke to in Mexico explained that there had been very few groups who were publicly visible in their accompaniment practices 'and it wasn't until the green tide in Argentina that more women began to become visible, right? And just last year [2020] it was like a boom.' In Mexico alone, 'it is estimated that, in addition to four national NGO-led accompaniment networks, there are currently over 350 independent grassroots accompaniment collectives operating across the country' (Belfrage, 2023, 7). While there is no singular model of abortion accompaniment (Atienzo et al, 2023), there are several key elements that can be used to encapsulate what accompaniment groups are: a commitment to providing abortions outside medical contexts; autonomy; holistic care; and collective care.

First, and perhaps the defining feature of accompaniment practices, *acompañantes support* access to self-managed abortions using misoprostol (alone or with mifepristone) outside the formal healthcare system. The recommendation of how to use the medications may be based on the WHO guidance and may mirror the regimen a person would receive from a medical professional, but the process itself takes place outside clinical settings (Moseson et al, 2020). *Acompañantes* do not see themselves as healthcare providers, but as activists and volunteers 'with training in safe medication abortion who provide evidence-based information, guidance, and support throughout the self-managed abortion process' (Veldhuis et al, 2022a, 40). *Acompañante* groups, therefore, reject the clinic-based, medicalized model as the only safe way of accessing abortions. For Singer (2018), *acompañante* activism is a form of direct action that acts as a challenge to reproductive governance by taking abortion outside medical spaces. However, it is important to note that *acompañante* groups are not rejecting medical professionals outright, and many groups have them as part of their cohort, as is discussed later in this chapter, but they are rejecting the assumption that only abortions that take place in medical settings can be safe or that they are preferred. Feminist accompaniment is, therefore, a non-clinical form of care that goes much deeper than merely indicating how to use a drug (Mateo, 2024).

A second, related, element is the principle of autonomy. This word was used frequently by interviewees to describe their work and activism as they support people to make their own decisions about their lives when options are constrained by the state. Abortion accompaniment was born out of the need to provide abortion care where it was denied by the state, but it can also act as an alternative to clinical abortion services in contexts where legal abortion is available (Veldhuis et al, 2022b). *Acompañante* groups seek to give people the power to decide which option is best for them and aim to support people to make autonomous decisions about their reproductive lives in a non-isolating way (Burton and Peralta, 2016). By involving people in their own decision making and expanding the options available to them, *acompañantes* are promoting the autonomy of all people in the community (Wollum et al, 2022). Moreover, the term autonomy is also used to describe how the groups themselves function. Braine (2020), for instance, uses the term 'autonomous health movements' to describe how activists work in community contexts and social justice movements, as they are not constrained by frameworks in the same way medical professionals are. Autonomy is, therefore, a key tenet that *acompañantes* strive for in their activism.

Third, providing clear and accurate information is an essential part of *acompañante* activism, but what differentiates it from medicalized approaches is the focus on holistic care. Different interviewees used different terminologies to describe this principle, but a common thread was a commitment to seeing the person needing the abortion as a full person and incorporating all elements of their life to help provide them with the best support. For one interviewee, it was about accompanying people at the *nivel holístico* (holistic level), which for her involved both practical and emotional elements of care. Another used the term *acompañamiento integral* (comprehensive accompaniment) because, rather than simply asking for a medical history and explaining the process, they would talk with the person needing the abortion and ask: 'What do you feel? What do you want?' This approach informs how *acompañantes* conceptualize a 'safe abortion' – it needs to include safety 'not only in the medical sense, of the body, but safe in the aspect of mental health and emotions'. This comprehensive approach recognizes that '[c]ompassionate care and emotional support can be just as important in this process as providing information and medication' (Walsh, 2020, 178). As Veldhuis et al (2022a, 39) write, 'holistic accompaniment is a horizontal model that involves trusting women, not asking for the reasons for their abortion, preventing criminalization, economic support, respecting autonomy, emotional accompaniment, and being flexible'. An understanding of the physiological effects of misoprostol is important, but *acompañamiento* prioritizes emotional support and a respect for the mental and physical health of the person having the abortion, which results in a more expansive understanding of abortion care.

Fourth, the collective is a common thread that runs through *acompañante* groups. Collective in this sense refers the person needing the abortion being part of a wider group of people seeking and supporting bodily autonomy. This is sometimes referred to as a 'horizontal' approach, as information and experiences are shared across *acompañantes* and people seeking abortions, rather than a top-down transferal of information, as in the medicalized model (Veldhuis et al, 2022b). This horizontal approach means that accompaniment groups are co-constructing knowledge with those who are using abortion and sharing their symptoms, experiences of pain, and emotions during the process (Mines et al, 2013). Self-managed abortion, 'by involving a number of actors who enable access to care and are present at different points in an individual's abortion trajectory ... challenges the idea of abortion as a solely individual act' (Nandagiri and Berro Pizzarossa, 2023, 6). In creating 'new assemblages for feminist practice' (Belfrage, 2023, 25), a whole 'constellation of actors' can be part of creating access to safe abortions (Berro Pizzarossa and Nandagiri, 2021, 24). This constellation encompasses people who support people having abortions in practical ways, such as through providing pills and information, but also those who provide the emotional and affective aspects of abortion care (Nandagiri and Berro Pizzarossa, 2023). The collective is, therefore, an important value that ensures people needing abortions are part of a wider feminist network of caring individuals who are committed to making sure that all people can access safe and supported abortions.

These values – a commitment to providing abortions outside medical contexts, autonomy, holistic care, and collective care – all underpin *acompañantes'* approaches to providing access to safe, effective abortion, but *acompañante* groups are often involved in broader feminist activism too. They seek to make abortion a visible issue and disrupt the silence around it to challenge abortion stigma and highlight the role that abortion plays in fighting for bodily autonomy (Atienzo et al, 2023). Some groups see their purpose as one of education as well as providing access to abortions. One interviewee in Colombia said that her group would talk about 'how the use of misoprostol was found through the Black women in the favelas in Brazil, well, because part of the … , like the mission was also, like, education in general, like, the history of abortion and all this'. Others do this education work through creating resources, and one interviewee in Peru noted that her group made a video on medical abortion that has reached over 100,000 views on YouTube as well as other testimonial videos with people talking about their abortions in order to destigmatize abortion.

Other groups make interventions in public space to bring abortion into people's consciousness, and it is often the younger generation of activists who have been the most public regarding abortion. As Sutton (2020, 1) explains, in Argentina, 'the influx of a young generation of activists and supporters has gained increasing visibility'; they were '[m]arching, chanting, dancing, and using their painted bodies as a canvas for protest messages' in the run-up to the national debates on abortion legislation. Similarly, Martin (2023) details the embodied activism so central to feminist and pro-abortion organizing in Peru. In a context where bodily oppression is high, 'those same bodies regulated by the state are the only tools available with which to protest, given the limited possibility of legal change or working with institutions' (Martin, 2023, 22–23). One interviewee in Peru spoke about the protests that her group organizes, while another in Mexico said that she put on a play about abortion that was explicitly aimed at the general population, not just people who were already pro-abortion. The group used a Theatre of the Oppressed format, with the audience participating in role-play around genuine situations so that they could act out what they would do in a given scenario. The interviewee discussed the deep impact this can have on audiences and said that at one event, a woman told the group that she had an abortion 40 years ago. Until that event, she hadn't told a single soul. *Acompañante* groups are, therefore, creating pathways to abortion access, 'but also truly fighting to dismantle patriarchal systems and incorporate feminist values into all levels of society' (Keefe-Oates, 2021, 191).

Reproductive justice underpins *acompañantes'* viewpoints on who and what type of abortions they accompany, whether or not this term is used explicitly by the collectives. *Acompañantes* fight for the right of anyone who wishes not to be pregnant, ensuring they are not forced to continue with a pregnancy. Some groups I spoke to were very clear on their intersectional approach, particularly in terms of trans and Indigenous communities. One interviewee in Peru had been part of a different *acompañante* collective that did not fully align with her values: 'when I discovered queer theory, the issue of trans inclusion, and it was something we didn't agree on with my other companions'. This led her to establish a different collective with likeminded *acompañantes*; as she explained: 'so far it is something that we are clear about, the issue of being trans-inclusive feminists. And now we are entering more into the theme of anti-racism, decoloniality, intersectionality.' Another explained the importance of being visibly committed to supporting trans and non-binary people who need abortions: 'With our transfeminist collective, we not only talk about and are active in LGBT rights in general, but there is no feminism or LGBT activism without considering reproductive and sexual rights as well.' Similarly, an interviewee in Peru said her group decided to offer accompaniment to trans men after noticing that other groups did not. These *acompañantes* are, therefore, putting their political values of inclusivity into practice in relation to trans rights.

Other interviewees spoke of the importance of delivering care that meets the needs of Indigenous communities and other marginalized groups. One *acompañante* in Peru explained that there are 'sectors of the population that do not have access to abortion or information about it, such as Indigenous, Quechua, impoverished, and Afro-descendant women' and so her group has 'to start from this intersectional analysis of how we function as a network, who we are excluding when we do a supportive practice'. Another interviewee in Mexico spoke of how her group tries to sensitively meet the needs of Indigenous communities, but emphasized that 'there are collectives in Indigenous communities ... And I think that's very good. I mean, we can't be everywhere'; she said this is important, to avoid 'saviourism', because 'you can't go to a community, for example, and say, I'm going to accompany you in your process ..., no, never. What could be better than someone from your own community?' These interviewees are responding to a context whereby the majority of *acompañantes* are based in metropolitan areas and are more likely to be university educated and less likely to be from Indigenous communities than the average population.

In terms of the types of abortion that *acompañantes* accompany, all *acompañante* groups will support the termination of pregnancies in the first 12 weeks where there are no additional factors to consider. Some will also support people outside these criteria, and some interviewees spoke passionately about the need to support people to end pregnancies over

12 weeks of gestational age. Three interviewees in Peru described how the COVID-19 pandemic led to them assisting people with more advanced pregnancies. One explained that during the lockdowns, 'because they could not even go out', people struggled to keep the pregnancy hidden from their families and women were often 'in the presence of their husbands who didn't know about their pregnancy'. The second said that her group saw more advanced pregnancies during the pandemic when 'most cases were over 15 weeks. Now it's gone down. But out of 10 cases, 8 were over 15 weeks.' As the third supposed: 'It is because it is more difficult to go out and look for an alternative outside and obviously you stay at home, and time goes by and time goes by, more and more time goes by.' These groups, therefore, became more accustomed to supporting abortions over 12 weeks during the pandemic.

Acompañante groups are, therefore, people who enable access to abortions outside the formal medical system in a way that offers support, empathy, care, and dignity. They are forming new infrastructures of abortion care by providing a collective and holistic model of care beyond the state (Duffy et al, 2023). These are the central tenets that encompass the hundreds or even thousands of collectives that have emerged across Latin America.

What does *acompañamiento* consist of?

Acompañamiento covers a broad range of practices, and each group or collective develops an approach that best suits their socio-politico-legal context, the communities they work with, and their own personal approaches. This section details where *acompañantes* locate themselves on the spectrum of provision (from providing information only to providing in-depth, in-person accompaniment), what support looks like, what practical assistance they provide, and the emotional labour that comes with accompanying. While the previous section set out the key principles of accompaniment, this section sets out the detail of different practices.

A key split between abortion activists concerns whether people seeking abortions should be accompanied through the process or not. One interviewee in Peru, Daniela, believed that giving people the information they need to have a safe and effective abortion is sufficient; she asked: 'What is the point of accompanying? They welcome you, what do they do?' Another explained: 'The only thing we try to do is to provide information and that this information allows you to destigmatize, allows you not to criminalize, but to provide. Because providing information is not a crime in our country'. Daniela did think that things are changing and that the divisions are not strong as they had been previously; as she put it, 'meeting points have been opened' and activists realize they are fighting for the same goals – 'to establish coordinated actions, safety, to get access to the pills and access to health professionals who welcoming'. A different interviewee felt that, due to concerns for her own safety and the legal situation, she could only provide information. Each person's decision about the level of support they want to provide is personal.

Some groups feel very strongly that the emotional support and solidarity engendered through the collective is what differentiates *acompañamiento* from service provision. The Socorristas en Red in Argentina, for example, request that people who ask for their support attend a group workshop. I spoke to a Socorrista about this process and asked her what happens if someone says 'I don't want to go to a meeting, I just want the pills'. Her response was: 'OK, but we are not pill sellers. We are a collective that gives information and accompanies them to make it safe.' She explained that a lot of people contact her sure that they know exactly how to take the pills but when they describe how they would take them, it is in a way that would be unlikely to lead to a complete abortion. So she makes sure that people are aware of the misoprostol protocol and that they can ask for other information, as the group is open to providing information about alternative routes to an abortion: 'We try to be very clear in what we do and we tell them, "if you want to move forward, we move forward, if you want other information, tell me."' As she explained: 'In other words, we offer accompaniment. If you want to go to the workshop and choose another option, that's fine.' For the Socorristas, the group workshop is an integral part of the process, whatever route the person decides to take afterwards. Another interviewee, in Peru, described a similar sentiment: 'For us, it is not only to inform but also to accompany. [The collective] was born that way, as accompaniment more than anything else.'

One interviewee had been part of a group of people interested in supporting abortion access, but they were divided on whether that should involve providing information or giving in-depth support through the process. This interviewee decided she felt most comfortable just providing information, but the others wanted to accompany abortions in-person, so they went on to join the local chapter of a larger *acompañante* collective. Similarly, an interviewee in Mexico described being part of a group that split over the question of whether to provide information or accompany. She went with the group who

> set up the [abortion] hotline mainly with the intention of protecting our privacy and that of the people we were accompanying, because at that time there was a lot of insistence among ... many collectives on face-to-face accompaniment, in person, and what we saw was that not everyone wanted a stranger to [be] in their home. There was a lot of resistance in this aspect, and we also ran several security risks, didn't we? Going to a stranger's house, often at night, to do illegal

things. So, we thought that the hotline was a good way to solve those security problems and we also raised it as another option to access a safe abortion.

Another interviewee in Mexico reported similar experiences:

One woman had two children, so she said she preferred to be alone so that her children would not wonder what was going on with an external person there. So it's like asking them what would you feel more comfortable with, right? Whether I'm there or whether I'm on a call or a text, you let me know. Some live at home with their parents and do it in the small hours of the morning, so you can only use the phone and nothing else.

An interviewee who was a medical professional in Peru but had also accompanied abortions outside her formal work for many years didn't see in-person accompaniment as necessary:

It's training the patient, orienting her, and doing the telephone counselling, very rarely face-to-face. In-person there have been very few times actually, cases like the daughter of a friend, or some patients ... I would say that all this time I have physically accompanied a maximum of ten patients. For example, I accompanied a young woman who was terrified of doing it alone. She came from [a rural area] so that I could accompany her here, so we stayed in a hotel.

In some groups, *acompañantes* tailor their support on the spectrum of just information to in-depth support depending on what the individual requires. One interviewee explained this is 'because there are some women who just want information. There are others who want, like, you to be present on the phone. There are others who would like to see you.' Another explained that in most cases they just provide information, 'but there have been occasions where [the person has] been accompanied face-to-face' or via phone when needed. One *acompañante* in Peru said their approach depended on whether there would by anyone with the person having the abortion; she said, 'I have had cases of girls whose mother knows, their family knows and accompanies and supports them, or they live with their partner and they support each other', but also noted that they can offer in-person support if the person doesn't have someone already. An interviewee in Mexico explained: 'If they ask for virtual accompaniment, we do give it, but mainly we give the information over the phone and that's usually enough.' Her group created a protocol or manual of the kind detailed in the previous chapter, which they send to those they support so that they have all the information they need.

She recalled that before the manual existed, they would have to explain everything over the phone, but it is 'a lot of information and sometimes ... well, it's also a stressful moment', which can mean the person doesn't take in all the information accurately and in full. The manual means that the person having the abortion can access all the information that they would have been able to ask the *acompañante* about.

There have been shifts in the ways groups feel they can best provide support. One interviewee explained that her group changed their position on the information–practical support spectrum over time. She said: '[In the beginning] I was very focused on accompanying in a physical way. And I feel that as time went by, we knew what time to give to each [part of the process]' to ensure that no one felt alone during the parts where they needed most support. She also explained: 'We give it [in-person support] to those who need it. But, for example, in the first weeks it is not necessary, because the procedure is very simple', but for more advanced pregnancies of 15 to 20 weeks, 'some accompaniment is necessary, especially because of fear or lack of information or because the person is alone. In that case, we give them a whole day.' Similarly, another noted that in-person accompaniment was reserved for 'the more complex cases'.

The type of accompaniment provided can also vary with the stage of the process. One interviewee explained: 'We were there for all the previous moments in-person, like getting to know each other, explaining everything to them, helping them with the pills, maybe even getting them a prescription', but 'at the moment of the bleeding, the [passing of the] gestational sac and the abortion itself, many girls told us they did not want [us there] because they did not feel comfortable having an abortion in front of someone'. Another interviewee believed that the character of the *acompañante* plays a role in whether they are willing to offer in-person accompaniment. She told me, 'obviously we have to feel safe to do it', and recounted situations where anti-abortion Catholic groups had tried to incriminate them 'so there is a kind of mistrust'; but she also said: 'I think it also depends a lot on the character of the *acompañantes*.' She saw herself as 'a little more suspicious', whereas she had an older *acompañante* friend who was more open to unknown situations and she would say to her 'hey, but we don't know her', to which her friend would reply 'no problem! I'm going!'

With the development of communication technologies, and then the need to provide support at a distance during the COVID-19 pandemic, there has been a significant growth in virtual accompaniment. This virtual accompaniment shares some similarities with 'telehealth', whereby abortion medications are delivered by mail and information and support is then provided virtually (Larrea et al, 2024). Often, the service is based in a country with liberal abortion laws but supports abortion access in restrictive settings. While the people I interviewed did not see themselves as practising telehealth, *acompañante* groups work in similar ways, though not always in such a formal manner. They frequently use social media and instant messaging services, which allow for anonymous communication through a variety of formats such as text messaging, video calls, voice notes, and photographs (Duffy et al, 2023). *Acompañantes* often use secure encrypted platforms, such as Signal and Telegram, in contexts where confidentiality is essential. One interviewee, who lived in Peru but was visiting family in Canada when I spoke to her, said: 'Can you believe that being here I'm doing telephone counselling with miso?' She told me, 'last week I did a 21-week accompaniment' and explained that an abortion at this stage would often be accompanied in-person, but she was able to support the person (who was struggling to pass the placenta) virtually, using her phone. Even though she was supporting the person virtually, she felt confident in understanding the stage the person was at in the process and was able to guide her until the placenta passed with no issues.

Technology has expanded the horizons of what abortion accompaniment can look like, but that does not mean that technology suits everyone. As one interviewee in Mexico detailed:

> The accompanied women, they may not have continuous internet access, right? Well, then, we have also carried out accompaniment via telephone, calling them, well, many times we call them because they don't always have credit on their mobile phones to talk to us, so we are communicating, sending text messages like old people, right? Or even through Messenger on Facebook, there are also girls who suddenly don't …, they have a lot of control over [the use of] their mobile phones or they don't have another way.

Virtual support can still be time-intensive. One *acompañante* described having to be in contact with one person at an early hour: 'I had the cell phone at about 4 o'clock in the morning, "have you taken the pill yet?"' She recalled: 'Once I set an alarm, I remember, because the girl would fall asleep and I was afraid she wouldn't take the pill.' Virtual support, then, is not necessarily less 'accompanied' than in-person support.

Different groups have different levels of checks that they require before providing support. Most *acompañantes* are strict about only speaking directly with the person who is going to have the abortion. As an interviewee in Mexico explained: 'We always, always, always, always, always try to be with the women who are … going through the pregnancy'. Another in Mexico said: 'We always make contact directly with the woman we are accompanying, don't we? Because sometimes boyfriends contact us.' Once they are in contact with the person directly, the *acompañante* will ask for additional information and begin to explain the process. One interviewee in Mexico described their procedure:

> First, we make sure that she has already taken a pregnancy test, that she is sure she is pregnant ... then see how many weeks she is, from there check how she is physically healthy, in case she has anaemia ... if she is allergic to any medication ... eh ... if she has already had an ultrasound where she can check the number of weeks and whether it is an ectopic pregnancy or not. In other words, that she is a suitable person for the procedure and that her health is not at risk.

They then explain what the person will need to do to be ready for the abortion in terms of the protocol, and they check that the person is aware of the location of their nearest medical facility in case of complications and find out whether someone will be with them during the process. They also let them know how to stay in contact with the *acompañante*. Another described a similar protocol, which 'indicates that she must have the pills, an ultrasound that indicates that there is no ectopic or placenta previa and the exact weeks ... to have a place and someone to be with her. Preferably someone she loves, a friend, a companion.' Another interviewee in Mexico explained:

> Once the context is established and it is known that they are in a safe place, we explain the procedure, we go through a questionnaire, we do a questionnaire to check the physical conditions of the accompanied person and to be able to accompany them, well, better, right? To see if there are any issues that could be risky, to see if they are taking any other medications, issues like that. We agree on a date for the abortion. We see if there are any difficulties in obtaining the medication. We help with the logistics of all that.

The *acompañante* may then, if it is desired, provide support, virtually or in-person, through the process until the abortion is complete. An interviewee in Colombia explained that the accompaniment didn't just end when the bleeding stopped; rather, they get in touch with the person 15 days and then one month after the abortion to check that they are doing well.

The provision of solidarity and support is a crucial part of what it means to accompany. Supporting people to self-manage their abortions does not mean that it is 'solo care' (Bercu et al, 2022). People are empowered to be active participants in the abortion process, enabled through the support of accompaniers. A common theme from the interviews was the importance of making sure that people do not feel abandoned in a context of stigma around abortion, and perhaps criminalization. As an interviewee in Peru reflected on her own abortion experience:

> The most important thing is that you know that if you start to bleed more than usual, you will have someone who will be able to help you and who will not let you die. Because the feeling of abandonment, that no one is going to help you, is the ugliest feeling in the world. I, with all my resources and everything, without being able to tell anyone, what I was afraid of was dying, infected, bleeding to death, dying of whatever. But dying because I couldn't go to anyone.

In a similar vein, an interviewee in Mexico told me:

> Because another thing that prevents the girls from being safe in the accompaniment is that they are completely alone, they don't have a friend, a mother, they don't even have another woman with them who they can rely on if they faint, get dizzy, have ugly, unpleasant symptoms. Who is going to help them? There's no one. In the best of cases, they have friends who are the same age as them, very young, who don't know what accompaniment entails. The girls think that they just take a pill and that's it, right? So, that's where we are ..., without exercising power [over them], explaining to them in the most loving way possible that they have to take responsibility. Sometimes they don't realize what is going to happen until little by little we guide them, and the days that we have before they can do the procedure, [we use to] to guide them on how exactly, what is going to happen and what risks they face.

This refusal to let people feel alone through their abortion ran through the interviews. People described abortion accompaniment as a loving act, an act of providing care. One interviewee in Mexico used the Nahuatl word *apapachar*, which refers to tenderness, comfort, or, as she described, cradling.

Support can also extend beyond the person who is having the abortion. One interviewee in Peru explained how she has often had to provide emotional support for others, such as a partner who may be feeling intense fear that they may lose their loved one. Another, in Mexico, recalled an experience where a girl had procured abortion pills herself but they were accidentally sent to her neighbour's house 'and the gossipy neighbour goes and tells her parents'. So the girl got in touch with the interviewee:

> [She] tells me 'I'm sure I want to have an abortion and I know how to do it, I don't need accompaniment, but my parents do need accompaniment. Can you give it to them?' And I well ... 'Yes. bring them.' Then the parents came, we were round the table with coffee,

talking, yes, explaining to them how it works, how it is ... and why her daughter wants it – she talked about it – being with her, accompanying her decision and she was ... it was a very nice experience because the father told her 'I am willing to register him as our son if you keep the pregnancy' and things like that, and she said, 'I don't want to be pregnant, that is ... I don't want a pregnancy, I don't want to experience it.'

For those who go beyond abortion provision, *acompañamiento* means practical support such as dealing with logistical and security issues, helping to arrange transport or financial resources, helping with legal and bureaucratic issues, and helping to navigate state and medical surveillance (Sutton and Vacarezza, 2023). An interviewee in Mexico described the variety of ways they give support, often for those who required or desired a procedural abortion and, at the time of the research, needed to travel to Mexico City for one. This entailed 'resources to cover transport from the states to Mexico City, but also, for example, local transport, right? Because, no, not all women live in their state capitals, right? And so they have to go from [where they live] to the state capital and then come to Mexico City.'

She also said that networks may need to pay to 'cover accommodation – no, not because the treatment requires them to stay in hospital, but more for logistical reasons' because 'most of the services operate in the morning, and there isn't always transport that arrives early or sometimes they live in dangerous communities. It's not safe to go back at night.' The group had a network of guest houses and hotels near bus terminals that they booked so that they knew they would be sending the person needing the abortion somewhere safe. As the interviewee said, this practical support is based 'on the needs, isn't it? In other words, it's not like we have ready-made packages of "abortion package one" or "package two". It's more like, it's more like seeing with them directly on the call what resources they have, what they need from us.' Support can, therefore, involve practical elements, but it is also an emotional process.

Literature on accompaniment practice has begun to recognize the emotions bound up with the work and activism. It has been described as loving, tender, empathetic, joyful, pleasurable, and intimate (Kimport et al, 2023; Belfrage, 2024). it is important to acknowledge these aspects alongside the risk and sacrifice that come with *acompañamiento*. One interviewee in Peru spoke of the complex emotions she experienced when she began to accompany abortions: 'I was scared shitless. I mean, I was scared to death. What's more, I saw it as dangerous, clandestine, and all that it has on top of it.' She felt that she was committing a crime and moreover felt the weight of the emotions of those she was accompanying: 'If they are burdened, you are burdened. With guilt, with shame.' So she worked with those she supported 'to take away the guilt so that they don't feel bad'. It was the context of criminalization that made accompaniment challenging for this interviewee, as these emotions 'are not and cannot be distinguished from the marginalization of abortion accompaniment itself' (Kimport et al, 2023, 12).

I spoke to one *acompañante* in Argentina who struggled with the 'on call' nature of abortion support. She explained how she would often want to avoid picking up the phone she had that was linked to the abortion hotline 'because it gave me a lot of stress, because people had to call me during the abortion and I felt uneasy about having to be available for the emergency'. She recalled: 'It could be in the middle of the night ... you could be having a coffee, in the middle of a class, on a bus. I mean, all those situations have happened to me. Like, having a beer with friends.' She said these tended not to be urgent situations where somebody was experiencing complications, but they were calls from women who were nervous and needed reassurance and to talk through the process with someone who understood it. This was draining emotional labour for her. One interviewee in Peru, who I will call Ana, explained how difficult the emotional work can be when accompanying people you do not like. She explained that not all people treat *acompañantes* well; instead she found that some people spoke to her 'like they're a customer' because they were often paying for the pills. She said: 'They tell us "are you going to help me or not, I only wrote to you because I wanted the pills, if you don't have them, then bye-bye", things like that.' Ana described how in these moments she has wanted 'to send them to hell' but instead she explained the misoprostol protocol and supported them. She even recalled one situation – 'the case of a girl who was super rude to me' – where she explained to a friend: 'But I don't feel comfortable, I don't even feel safe because I know that her boyfriend is a neo-Nazi who has harassed other women. So what do I do? So in the end it was like, "I'm going to do it."' Ana felt conflicted in these sorts of situations because she wanted to enact her political values around *sororidad* (sorority) but did not feel that these values were being respected. She further explained that by accompanying in a context of clandestinity, she already felt 'super insecure' about her activism, and these sorts of situations exacerbated that: 'It's not cool to feel insecure doing something that is already insecure.'

Acompañamiento, therefore, consists of a range of practices. This range means that those seeking support can find what best suits their needs, if they are able to access the information. One interviewee in Peru explained that feminist organizations are able to refer people on to certain groups

> because sometimes *compañeras* have certain protocols that are very cumbersome for some *compañeras*. For example, some women don't want to send an email with all their data. They want to just write to another *compañera* on WhatsApp to also send audio and tell her about their experience, and some feel more comfortable that way.

Rather than measuring 'effectiveness' by the number of complete abortions, *acompañantes* seek to 'enable autonomous decisions' by providing the information and pathways that allow people to make the best decision for them (Larrea et al, 2024, 56).

Working with and against medical professionals

Common questions I get asked when I talk to people about my research are: Is misoprostol safe? What happens if something goes wrong? However, when accurate information is followed, complications from medical abortions are rare, and as misoprostol is not a medication that shows up in urine or blood tests, in the event that someone does access medical care, the abortion will be indistinguishable from a spontaneous miscarriage. The development of medical abortions has transformed what an abortion consists of and who is needed to provide it. This can be viewed as professional 'deskilling', as abortion has moved from being a physical, invasive procedure to one that can simply involve the dispensing of a medication (Joffe et al, 2004). This 'puts more power in the hands of the patient herself ... since the woman ingests the pills herself, it is arguably the woman who "performs" the abortion' (Joffe et al, 2004, 791). These developments have led to both opportunities and tensions between *acompañantes* and medical professionals. Here, I explore three of these points in more detail: clashes with health professionals, medical professionals working with *acompañante* groups, and the shift to activists training doctors.

First, throughout Latin America there are countless events of medical professionals blocking access to abortions even where those routes should exist, providing misinformation about abortion access, calling the police in cases of suspected abortions, enacting obstetric violence on people who present with a suspected abortion, and providing abortions in emotionally and physically harmful ways. *Acompañantes* have often had to navigate this themselves, and they act to prevent these harms from being experienced by those seeking an abortion. As McReynolds-Pérez (2017, 359) argues, '[m]isoprostol activists have managed to overcome what had been a serious stumbling block, which is that medical professionals often obstruct access to abortion'. *Acompañante* groups are able to provide a different pathway to abortion care – one that allows people to circumvent the violence and stigma that is all too often faced in the formal health system (Larrea et al, 2024). For Fernández Vázquez and Szwarc (2018, 167), 'the abortifacient use of misoprostol has provided feminists with a possibility that combines direct action, agency, redistribution of knowledge and allows them to break the monopoly of medical knowledge regarding safe abortion'. Therefore, medical professionals and medical spaces can be harmful for those seeking an abortion, and *acompañamiento* provides an alternative, feminist, empathetic, feminist model of care to circumvent this harm.

Second, some *acompañante* groups have medical professionals as part of their contingency while others set up friendly relationships with them. It is common for *acompañante* groups to include a number of people with a variety of skills. As Sandra in Mexico explained, of the 22 people in her collective, 'there are doctors, there are nurses, there are lawyers, there are graphic designers, there are social workers', which means that whatever circumstances arise, 'well, we already have the connections'. Others in Peru explained that one group has an obstetrician-gynaecologist as a member and they are able to write prescriptions for misoprostol, and another has managed to find a doctor but it was a complicated process for them because in Peru 'the obstetricians still take their oath to take care of the unborn'. Another interviewee, who works in rural Peru, was told by the obstetrician who is part of her group that 'you know more about abortion than, possibly, my obstetrician colleagues' because medical training in Peru deals with miscarriage care and post-abortion care but not with the medical abortion process. This interviewee noted that she and her companions felt highly trained in dealing with first trimester abortions but 'in matters related to more advanced topics', particularly with gestational age or suspected ectopic pregnancies, they consulted their obstetrician.

One interviewee, a trained medical professional who also worked within an *acompañante* group, explained that the others in the group would contact her with questions or to get clarification: 'For example, one of the girls did an accompaniment about three days ago … they send me a picture and they say, "… the patient is bleeding too much, what can we do?"' The interviewee then asked what pain management the woman had been taking and, as she described: 'then they send me the pictures and I said, "well, yes, she definitely has to go to the hospital"' – 'tell her that there is no way they are going to realize that she has induced' the abortion; 'let them test her because there is no way for them to know that she has taken the pills'. The woman in question went to the hospital, where she received a manual vacuum aspiration and recovered well. The interviewee concluded the story with: 'And that's it. I think that the more knowledge and empowerment that women have, and the security that they are not going to be discovered, the better.'

Acompañante groups have also created strategic relationships with 'friendly' medical professionals who are not part of the group itself. While complications are rare, there are some cases where people need or desire medical attention, but they also need to be protected from obstetric violence and legal consequences (Larrea et al, 2024). By developing networks of trusted healthcare professionals and training those who have had an abortion on what to say when people seek care, the risks of harm in medical spaces can be reduced. One interviewee in Peru explained that her group had contacts in hospitals so that in the event that an abortion is incomplete, the situation can be resolved quickly. Another interviewee, in Argentina, said that her group had always been aware of the WHO guidelines and kept up to date with developments, but she explained: 'In parallel we were always talking to fellow doctors, right? We didn't do anything or give any advice without consulting or being in a network. So there was something very interesting in terms of how we built bridges [and] networks.' She likened this to earlier on when they were developing knowledge of how misoprostol could be effective to terminate pregnancies, when, as she put it, 'we had to talk to the pharmacists, uh, and, and, and organize ourselves and also, uh, be in close contact with lawyers'. *Acompañante* groups create alliances with the formal healthcare system because so many people seeking an abortion engage with this system (Burton and Peralta, 2016). Whether getting tests or ultrasounds, seeking medical advice on termination, or going for check-ups after the procedure, the link between abortion seekers and health services exists (Burton and Peralta, 2016). Furthermore, healthcare professionals have not been removed from the development of misoprostol as an abortifacient; they are deeply entwined with its development thanks to their off-label use of it (Fernández Vázquez and Szwarc, 2018). By being proactive in forming positive alliances with healthcare professionals, *acompañante* groups are able to manage risks.

This 'friendliness' goes both ways. Medical professionals have been key in redirecting people who desire an abortion to accompaniment groups. Most of the people who contact the Socorristas en Red in Argentina report that this option was 'suggested' to them by health system staff (Burton and Peralta, 2016). This shows the trust that the group has gained from many years of providing abortion support. There are, therefore, clear points of solidarity between *acompañantes* and medical professionals, but activists have been typically wary of over-reliance on them or sycophantism; activists have been steadfast in ensuring that medical professionals fulfil their obligations (Keefe-Oates, 2021).

Third, in an important development, *acompañantes* are now being asked to feed their knowledge and expertise on abortion back into medical practice. Notably, this has happened in Argentina since the country's progressive abortion law was passed in 2020 and became law in 2021. Feminists have been asked to train medical professionals and work on joint projects, and as Szwarc (2024) details, the Argentine group Lesbianas y Feministas, who developed the first abortion manual in the country, have trained different medical associations. One interviewee in Argentina recalled Lesbianas y Feministas being invited to give a workshop at the national conference of the Argentine Federation of General Medicine: 'Just imagine! They, not doctors, explaining the functioning of misoprostol and how to perform an abortion with medicines, to doctors who were in health centres. If I had been there, for me it would have been pure glory.'

Moreover, the Argentine group Socorristas en Red have developed a post-abortion care and accompaniment protocol in collaboration with the gynaecology department of a public hospital (Szwarc, 2024). This recent initiative involves support and counselling on the abortion process with Socorristas en Red and then referral to the hospital for post-abortion care. A clinic is open for anyone who wants to consult a medical practitioner after their abortion, to provide additional support for those who desire it, and this serves to grow the network of professionals open to working with the Socorristas (Keefe-Oates, 2021). One Socorrista I interviewed explained that she had been involved in training doctors in one Argentine city and was shocked at how poor their knowledge of medical abortion was. She described how she would

> leave our instructions because I can tell you that there were ob-gyns with 20 years' experience who recommended swallowing misoprostol, keeping it in the stomach. And then you say let's see, yes, if you are training, specializing all the time, you can't just stick to what you learned at the university in 1984. You have to keep training. If something is happening, then you have to know what's happening.

Beyond Argentina, Ipas, an NGO that works to expand access to abortion and contraception, developed an intervention in Bolivia in 2018 that uses abortion accompaniment as a 'blueprint' to support people to have abortions with volunteer community agents trained by Ipas (Acre et al, 2023, 2). Similarly, an interviewee in Colombia worked for a health organization providing abortions that used a counselling model that draws on accompaniment approaches; as he described, this 'accompanies the woman's decision, validates her rights, validates the woman's autonomy, validates the woman's intimacy, validates confidentiality. This counselling consultation is framed in that way – it is framed in that the woman is the owner of her decisions.' He argued, therefore, that accompaniment doesn't only happen in more radical spaces. These examples 'show the importance of communication and collaboration between systems, giving pregnant people the array of options of access to care and methods that they need and deserve' (Yanow et al, 2021, 220). The medical profession and NGOs are beginning to take *acompañante* models seriously.

The question of 'safety' is, therefore, in part managed carefully by *acompañantes* who have developed safe models of abortion care and who work with medical professionals as part of their groups or in collaboration, with such success that the medical professionals not only recommend the *acompañantes* to people seeking an abortion but also ask the *acompañantes* for training themselves. While abortion accompaniment has been seen as 'less safe' or as a provisional interim solution (Larrea et al, 2024), these developments illustrate how *acompañamiento* has transformed the landscape of abortion access in Latin America and shifted understandings of what 'safety' means (Berro Pizzarossa and Nandagiri, 2021). However, there is a geography to this across Latin America, with the 'friendly' medical professionals much easier to find in places such as Argentina and Mexico compared with Honduras or El Salvador (Walsh, 2020).

Motivations for becoming *acompañantes*

The *acompañantes* I interviewed often described their abortion activism through their political motivations, and this is often reinforced by *acompañante* groups. The Argentine group Socorristas en Red, for example, are explicit about the feminist politics underpinning their activism. 'Socorrismo' – which translates as first aid, first response, or life-saving – is an accompaniment practice that 'goes beyond providing medical aid or helping individual women; it is also a political act that destigmatizes and dedramatizes abortion. It is a feminist practice against a patriarchal system' (Zurbriggen et al, 2018, 113). Socorristas en Red are also clear that their work seeks to undermine traditional stereotypes of women as domestic and 'natural' caregivers (Burton and Trinidad Peralta, 2021). By creating their national network and structuring their work around the solidarity of women taking care of one another, collectively and publicly, they are overturning traditional notions of care (Burton and Trinidad Peralta, 2021). The form of care enacted by the Socorristas is one of caring *with*, not caring *for*. Thus, for many *acompañantes*, their work is a feminist political project or form of direct action, not service provision (Larrea et al, 2024).

One clear theme that ran through many of the interviews with *acompañantes* was how formative their own experiences with sexual and gender-based violence and with their own abortions had been and how these experiences had motivated them to become *acompañantes*. These were typically isolated, scary, and risky experiences that made them want to support others to have radically different abortion trajectories. Natali, in Peru, for example, said: 'I think one of the things [that led me to accompany] was that I had an abortion when I was 24 or so, right out of college. And I didn't have anybody. I mean I didn't know where to look for information.' Similarly, a Peruvian *acompañante*, who I will call Lucía, explained: 'The worst thing was not that I wanted to have an abortion. The worst thing was how abandoned I felt when I did it. And the lack of reliable information. So, I believe that my mission on Earth is that, to prevent anyone from going through this situation.' Another interviewee told me about her two abortions 'in emotionally unstable and economically unstable conditions', which, she said, 'made me want to learn more about the issue, to investigate more and to accompany. Because somehow, I did not do it in the right conditions, nor with the right accompaniment. I felt the need, that commitment of wanting to do it for others.' These interviewees all narrated a causal link from their negative abortion experience to the motivation to ensure that the same thing did not happen to other people.

While those interviewees completed their abortions entirely alone, another recounted her experience of seeking support and experiencing obstetric violence. Catarina, in Peru, found sourcing misoprostol to be a highly traumatic experience and she was unable to locate enough of the medication in order to have a complete abortion. So she went to the hospital, presenting with a miscarriage so that she could receive the treatment to complete the abortion. Catarina explained that she personally experienced obstetric violence and saw others facing it too. She recalled that there was a 15-year-old girl admitted to the ward with a perforated uterus from an abortion, and as Catarina was being put under anaesthetic, she could hear the hospital staff discuss this girl in a derogatory way, saying it was her own fault for getting in this situation because she had 'opened her legs'. When Catarina awoke from the anaesthetic, the girl was dead.

Others narrated their own abortions in relation to feminist organizing. One, in Peru, had gone through her abortion alone and was surprised to realize she did not have adequate knowledge: 'I was extremely ignorant about abortion even though I was in favour of *libre* [free] and *gratuito* [monetarily free] abortion. So this showed me that it was an issue I was really unaware of even though I was part of other feminist organizations.' This led her to reposition her feminist organizing towards abortion. Another explained that the 'costly and complicated' abortion she had experienced at 19 led her to get more involved in feminist understandings of abortion and she began to accompany her own friends in an informal way: 'I realized that there was a lot of false, wrong information, that it was necessary to socialize our own experiences.' She then founded an accompaniment collective to share knowledge, information, and experiences to avoid piecemeal, individual attempts at supporting people.

For one interviewee in Argentina, who I will call María Luisa, it was attending a meeting about accompaniment that was a transformative experience that helped her to reflect on her own abortion. She witnessed a woman tell another that she was pregnant and needed an abortion. That woman was able to help her, provide information, and answer her questions about medical abortion. María Luisa was impressed with this woman's calmness and expertise on self-managing abortion. She recalled that, after the first woman had left:

> I bombarded her with questions, lots of questions, why do you bleed, why don't you bleed, why, why, everything. And that was the first time I was able to tell a person other than a family member that I had an unsafe abortion a few years ago. And I knew I could do that because I knew I wasn't going to be judged, and that gave me a lot of relief ...

It was due to the sense of guilt, responsibility, for refusing motherhood when it's supposed to be such a beautiful thing. And, well, that was a way in which I was repairing a history of an unsafe abortion many years ago.

This experience made María Luisa want to become the person she needed when she experienced her own unsafe abortion. She described this encounter as her 'moment of awakening' and dealing with what had happened to her but also 'politicising it in choosing to be an *acompañante* for those who need it and to be able to provide information, to accompany, to make people feel that they are not alone when they choose to have an abortion'. Siskindovich (2018, 122) theorizes the abortion experience as 'an imaginative political opening', whereby it is connection with others, through *sororidad* and solidarity, that creates pathways to a safe abortion. For these interviewees, their abortion had been such as 'opening', galvanizing them to want to create safe pathways for others.

For other interviewees, it wasn't their own personal experience of abortion that led them to become *acompañantes*, but the abortions they were seeing in their communities. One, a medical practitioner, was working in rural communities in Peru in the 1990s and 'saw that many women had abortions with herbs, with knitting needles, with Mejoral [an analgesic], with a series of things that really compromised their lives'. She felt powerless to support these women. She was not given enough petrol to drive patients to the nearest city, which could take 12 hours in the rainy season, and this meant that any patient presenting with haemorrhaging from an unsafe abortion could die. This led her to conclude that in that area 'at that time, life was not worth anything'. She resolved to devote her career to facilitating access to safe abortions so that that sort of situation would not occur again. Another interviewee, who had worked in the health system in Argentina, 'got involved in abortion because of dramatic situations that many women in the neighbourhood have gone through'. In the early 2000s, she saw the results of both unsafe abortions and the effects on people's lives when they could not access a desired abortion while, as she put it, 'we in the health team did nothing'. She decided to rectify the situation by becoming an abortion activist.

For other interviewees, it was the situation of gender as well as sexual and reproductive issues that they were encountering more broadly that motivated them to become an *acompañante*. One interviewee described the low-income area where she grew up in Peru, where she learned about the 'many problems surrounding women and how they assume their rights; that is, how women manage to live with dignity here in this territory'. She explained: 'Because as I have grown up, from my personal experience I have lived through a lot of sexual violence in my home, with my family. So that shaped me.' Another spoke about how she became interested in sexual and reproductive health after learning about the history of sexual and reproductive violence in her own family. She found out that her grandmother and mother had both been raped as teenagers and forced to have children alone at 13 and 14, respectively. She then began studying obstetrics and saw cases that 'marked' her. In one example, she saw to a 12-year-old girl admitted with herbs coming out of her vagina; she said:

> I didn't know what was going on. When they admitted her, I saw how they first reproached her, they screamed at her horribly, they told her that God was going to punish her for what she had done and that she should pray to God that her baby would be well, because if it was bad she was going to go straight to hell.

She felt unable to intervene or speak to the medical staff about this violence because, as she explained, 'they had all the power and I was a student who just knew how to take vital functions. I had no power.' The interviewee recalled how the girl came to the medical practice three more times for check-ups and was being beaten by her parents. In the fifth month of the pregnancy, the girl took her own life.

Others were motivated to become *acompañantes* after hearing about the practice from others. Sandra, in Mexico, for example, set up her own group after watching the 2014 documentary *Accompaniment* about the group Las Libres in Guanajuato, Mexico (Centro Las Libres and Ipas, 2014). She then put a call out to see if anyone would be interested in setting up a network with her, and nearly forty women came along. Then, with three of those women, she set up her own network. Sandra described this as a significant political awakening for her, as when she was a teenager she had been active in her local community in collecting signatures for anti-abortion petitions. Another interviewee, in Colombia, explained that she went to a workshop run by activists from a Chilean accompaniment group. The workshop ended with a call out to anyone who would be interested in accompanying abortions, so she got in touch, motivated by the workshop itself as well as the political situation in Colombia, as Iván Duque had recently been elected president and she was fearful of the repercussions for abortion access and women's rights.

Acompañantes, therefore, experience many different routes to the practice. What is consistent through their experiences is a political component, whether due to feeling so abandoned in their own abortions that they wish to support others or feeling radicalized by the situations they have seen in their communities or work. Accompaniment was a way for the interviewees to 'live their feminist values' (Kimport et al, 2023) with the understanding that abortion accompaniment 'is a transformative process with the power to reconfigure women's subjective sense of themselves as political subjects entitled to abortion rights' (Singer, 2019, 175). It is through collective action that these rights can be made possible in the present, even where they have been denied by the state.

Accompaniers' knowledge building

The previous chapter detailed the process of knowledge building that 'discovered' the abortifacient properties of misoprostol and developed a dosage and protocol leading to a safe and effective abortion in the majority of cases. But across Latin America, knowledge building has also taken place within and between *acompañante* groups in order to develop this feminist model of care and provide autonomous abortions. While there is no formalized or hierarchical global movement for self-managed abortion activism, *acompañante* groups and the networks between them, which often span the globe, are fundamental to building and sharing knowledge about autonomous abortions in horizontal and dispersed ways (Braine, 2023). They are 'generating' a different kind of feminism that begins from situated experiences but interweaves theoretical aspects (Burton, 2017c). Knowledge building about abortion is not just to help individuals in the moment that they need it, but moves through feminist networks to benefit a much wider collective.

This knowledge first moves between people, which may be in ad hoc ways or through attending workshops, as detailed in the previous section. Some of these individuals decide to join already-existing collectives, whereas others find that none exist in their location or that existing groups don't offer the exact type of support they are interested in. An interviewee in Peru described the process of establishing a group with other people who were interested in abortion accompaniment:

> During the first phase, we had been learning, beyond our own abortion processes, not all of us had had abortion processes, but I had …, three out of four [of us had]. That's a lot. So we talked a lot about our own processes. How it had been, how much we had paid, what had worked for us, what had not worked for us.

Starting from their own experiences, they were able to identify the particular barriers, needs, and emotions surrounding abortion access in their context, and from there they began to build the structure for their collective. The interviewee's partner was an obstetrician and could provide some advice. They also researched the approaches of other *acompañante* groups. Another interviewee described the early days of their group: 'We started meeting about once a month, I think, to tell each other, like what has happened and what complicated cases maybe someone has had', such as a pregnancy with twins or a particular medical condition. As Burton (2017c, 103) argues, a feature of *acompañante* groups is their 'incessant reflection on their own practice', and when groups are being established, this forms a key part of their knowledge building.

With smaller or newly created groups, training on what accompaniment consists of is often conducted by other collectives. One interviewee in Mexico explained that when her group was forming, one member went to visit another part of Mexico to be trained by a group with more experience. They explained that this was 'hands-on' training which was useful precisely 'because they can tell you a thousand things in theory, right? But when you put it into practice it is very different.' Within established groups, new members then need to be trained on how that collective accompanies abortions. An interviewee in Mexico described their 'extensive' process of 'intensive training for a week. It's like that, hours from ten [in the morning] until six in the afternoon, from Monday to Friday', to cover legal issues, stigma, the medical procedure itself, the framework of human rights, and the concept of reproductive justice. After the week of training comes a period of supervision where the new recruit shadows a more experienced *acompañante*, listening to them support someone. Then they begin to take over the *acompañante* role, while being supervised. She explained that it can take between three and six months before the person is able to accompany someone through an abortion without supervision. The Socorristas en Red in Argentina also have extensive training, with self-study, shadowing, and support from other Socorristas, as well as the opportunity for training by regional and international organizations (Zurbriggen et al, 2018). Not all groups have such an extensive process; as one interviewee in Colombia recalled, 'the training they gave me was like a shadowing of about three accompaniments'. This training, from people who already have the knowledge, whatever the training may consist of, is essential, because, as one interviewee in Mexico remarked: 'Well, there isn't a school of abortionists, isn't there?'

This knowledge building isn't just about practical expertise. Maffeo et al (2015, 225) describe the importance of 'accompaniment between feminists'. They describe how *acompañamiento* can bring up a multitude of thoughts and feelings so 'being able to lean on a colleague, to talk about our own difficulties and fears, is also an important part of our feminist action' (Maffeo et al, 2015, 225). They particularly stress the sharing of experience and knowledge by those who have been accompanying for longer, those from other geographical contexts, and people with different backgrounds of activism and militantism in order to deal with complex situations or to resolve concerns. This is, in the Argentine context of Socorristas en Red, 'in the first instance, a process of healing and loving catharsis, which then turns into political and conceptual reflections on Socorrista activism, which becomes flesh again in subsequent Socorrista accompaniments' (Maffeo et al, 2015, 225). An interviewee in Peru explained how accompanying as part of a collective is important for generating a sense of solidarity. She noted that during the COVID-19 pandemic, some *acompañantes* were struggling with anxiety and so they were able to support each other as well as speak to one of the psychologists who were part of their collective. The emotional support between activists and the solidarity they offer one another is crucial.

Outside the groups themselves, national networks have mobilized informally and formally to share information and expertise. For example, an interviewee in Mexico described how she has relationships all across the country, and she can talk to those people about particular legal issues, how to access misoprostol, and how to access funds for travel when needed. Another interviewee in Mexico explained how her group 'mobilizes alliances' depending on the issue. For example, they collaborate with a pro-abortion Catholic group when there is a conflict over a religious issue, and they support groups in particular states of Mexico when there has been an abortion-related issue in the courts there. One interviewee in Peru actively trains people who want to accompany abortions across the country. She described this skill sharing as 'the more technical knowledge, but also the human accompaniment, accompanying the decision making, what this implies, making sure that the woman is not alone. Basically accompaniment in all its dimensions'. Another interviewee, who co-ordinates national training in Peru, spoke of their approach of training 'young people' across all regions so that when young people seek abortion support, they can get this from their peers, who are typically older teenagers or in their twenties. She believes this helps to create a sense of trust, especially in a context of typically poor access to sex education and high levels of gender-based violence. National networks have, therefore, played a role in sharing knowledge, pills, and solidarity.

Acompañante groups are also often part of wider national or regional networks. While networks work at the local level first and foremost, recent years have seen the growth in the exchange of information, strategies, and pills across Latin American borders (Walsh, 2020). This is through informal networks but also via national and international meetings that share information and experiences (Veldhuis et al, 2022a). Red Compañera, for instance, is a network that connects 25 collectives across 19 countries in Latin America and the Caribbean to improve accompaniment practice while also strategically influencing legal debates on the decriminalization of abortion. This involves in-person meetings as well as the generation of resources, such as evidence on abortion and joint publications. The network was formally established in 2021, having emerged through meetings of like-minded individuals and collectives that took place in Ecuador, Uruguay, Indonesia, Chile, and Peru. These events came up in interviews. For example, one *acompañante* in Peru spoke of how she had been inspired by abortion organizations in Mexico and then travelled to Quito in Ecuador, where the first meeting on abortion hotlines and *acompañante* networks in the region was held in March 2017. Another recalled the meeting in Indonesia in July 2018: 'we met women from Ecuador, women from Chile, women from Argentina, Venezuela, Uruguay, women from El Salvador, Guatemala'. This was the beginning of the idea to form a network of networks.

The informal connections that were being made before Red Compañera was established allowed groups to gain knowledge on how to form their own collective. An interviewee in Peru, who established a collective with like-minded friends, spoke of groups who had come before in Argentina and Ecuador who were then able to travel to Peru to share their knowledge. She remembered hearing about a particular group in Ecuador, which she thought was 'very cool, very risky, very powerful, very audacious', and they decided to follow the Ecuadorians because, as she put it, 'we were so fed up with the criminalization, we were so fed up with hearing about women dying in clinics'. Two members of this nascent Peruvian group, therefore, travelled to Ecuador to find out more, and the Ecuadorians then travelled to Peru to support them to set up their group. The interviewee recalled how financial opportunities then emerged from international groups to facilitate this knowledge exchange, and they were able to travel to Argentina and Venezuelans were able to visit Peru.

Once the groups are established, connections between them are vital to secure access to abortions for anyone who gets in touch. One group in Mexico found that they get contacted by people across all of Latin America, so, as one member told me, they have had to 'make these networks, although we may not know each other physically, we know each other through messages', and that has allowed the group to 'have our directory in case we receive any girl from other countries, to channel them to these girls from their country'. They feel that it is important to redirect these people because national groups 'know much more about the reality of abortion in those places'. In some cases, however, if the group they redirect the person to doesn't reply to them, they will accompany abortions transnationally.

This transnationalization of knowledge and experience has contributed to the current reality, whereby people are able to access a safe abortion even where it is criminalized (Fernández Vázquez and Szwarc, 2018). One interviewee in Mexico described this sharing of knowledge as incredibly 'generous', as everyone involved is committed to improving abortion access for all. All of these examples demonstrate 'the need for transnational political coordination and solidarity' (Sutton and Vacarezza, 2023, 383).

Who is an abortion provider?

Abortion accompaniment groups have transformed who can be an abortion provider and who gets to hold abortion knowledge. *Acompañamiento* is a form of care that rejects the paternalistic and authoritarian practices that are present in the doctor–patient relationship, and it has led to multiple forms of violence experienced by people attempting to access an abortion (Gudiño Bessone, 2023). In response to these harms, *acompañantes* have developed a model of care that is not trying to replicate the medicalized model of providing technical information on how to use misoprostol; they have instead subverted this power dynamic and created a way to 'use medical knowledge to empower women to control their own reproductive lives in face of political and institutional opposition' (McReynolds-Pérez, 2017, 357). Self-managed abortion has, therefore, reconceptualized who the 'provider' is and what it means to 'perform' an abortion, as the person having the abortion is in control of the process, assisted by a 'support team' in the way that they, personally, need (Jelinska and Yanow, 2018, 88). *Acompañantes* have shown that safe, supported abortions beyond the state are possible.

In so doing, *acompañantes* have taken abortion knowledge outside medical spaces and have shown how knowledge can be developed and shared in alternative ways. Through learning from one another and creating networks within countries, across Latin America, and across the world, *acompañante* knowledge has grown and blossomed. As one interviewee in Mexico explained, their aim is to share this knowledge to challenge the 'monopolization or centralization of knowledge'. While these knowledges have often been developed in order to avoid the harm inflicted in medical spaces, that does not mean that medical professionals are absent from this knowledge building. *Acompañantes* often collaborate with medical professionals or have them as part of their groups, and this has led to a hybrid form of scientific knowledge that draws on medical understandings of how misoprostol works but combines that with core values of a commitment to providing abortions outside medical contexts and ensuring autonomy, holistic care, and collective care – a model of care for providing safe abortion access outside state frameworks. By normalizing the facilitation of abortion as accessible and safe, accompaniment practice has transformed the kind of knowledge that is needed to support an abortion (Karlin and Joffe, 2023). *Acompañante* expertise may be different from that offered in medical settings, but it is far from second best.

Reproductive justice is at the heart of the *acompañante* approach – whether or not it is articulated using this term – because a simple 'pro-choice' framing is wholly inadequate in contexts where abortion is outright criminalized, heavily restricted, or stigmatized. In locations where choice is not a possibility, *acompañantes* have stepped in to support people with their right not to have children. While Assis (2020, 128) argues that '[m]isoprostol has changed the landscape of reproductive justice as a technological discovery', what I hope has become clear throughout this chapter is that it is not the chemical properties of misoprostol alone that has changed the landscape of reproductive justice, but the committed activism of abortion *acompañantes* who have shifted abortion knowledge and care outside the medical sphere and into the hands of those who need an abortion.

3

The Mobilities of Misoprostol: Pharmaceuticals on the Move

Knowledges around misoprostol and *acompañante* groups that support its use have flourished across Latin America, but these alone are not sufficient if the pill itself cannot be accessed. As information about how to use misoprostol effectively has surged across Latin America, the most significant obstacle has been practical access to the medication (Fernández Anderson, 2020). Misoprostol is available with varying ease across Latin America. In some countries, such as Peru, nicknamed the 'paradise of miso', it can be found in pharmacies that agree to sell it without a prescription. But other contexts experience multiple obstacles to access, including legal prohibition, cost, requirement to have a prescription from a doctor, and scammers. For instance, in Chile, misoprostol is heavily restricted by the state, and that leads to supply issues with insufficient 'stock' (Chia, 2018). The consequence is that 'black market' sellers have a greater incentive to provide access to misoprostol and can inflate prices.

Misoprostol has democratized access to a safe abortion to some extent, but the access to information and the medication still leads to inequities along class and geographical lines, with people in urban centres with internet access, who are part feminist networks, and who know healthcare professionals most likely to receive accurate information about misoprostol (Fernández Anderson, 2020). In response, a range of actors, from international non-governmental organizations (NGOs) to small volunteer-run collectives, mobilize misoprostol to transport it to those seeking abortions. Numerous strategies are employed, tailored to the specific context and geography of the location. These include relatively low-tech strategies such as buses and postal systems as well as more resourceful tactics such as 'abortion robots' and systems of smuggling pills.

This chapter utilizes scholarship on the politics of mobility, particularly Mimi Sheller's (2018a; 2018b) concept of mobility justice, to interrogate the power tied up in what gets to move and how. Access to mobility is uneven and stratified along lines of gender, race, ethnicity, class, age, sexuality, disability, and other factors, and these inform people's access to misoprostol and how they are able to facilitate the movement of the pills. As Sheller and Urry (2006) argue, the 'mobility turn' in the social sciences needs to account for how materials move, not just how people do so. Mobility is central to understanding abortion because 'across scales, from the clinic to the nation-state, bodies, pills and knowledge are on the move in ways that reflect, reinforce and contest power relations' (Calkin et al, 2022, 1416).

Misoprostol has the qualities that make it easily mobile; the pills are small, they are thermo-stable, and they have a long shelf life if stored appropriately (Elati and Weeks, 2009; Calkin, 2021). There can be some issues with misoprostol because it is unstable in the presence of moisture (Bower et al, 2024), and this issue was raised by an *acompañante* in Peru. She remembered being at an international meeting of *acompañantes* where they noted that when they had moved pills from locations such as Peru to warmer and more humid places, such as Mexico and Venezuela, they had not been effective in completing an abortion. It was interesting that this *acompañante*, based in Lima, characterized the Peruvian climate more according to its coastal region than its tropical regions. This of course is less surprising given that the majority of *acompañante* networks who move pills are based in metropolitan areas on the coast or in the mountains, rather than the tropical rainforest. As she explained, the reason that these pills were ineffective was 'not because they are *bambas* [knock-offs], not because they were poorly made ... [but] because they are kept in a place, stored in a place that is not the best, right? Very humid, very warm.' When stored properly and kept away from moisture, misoprostol travels well.

The mobility of misoprostol has also been made possible by the deregulation of economies and the liberalization of trade barriers as well as the development of technologies (Calkin, 2019). The movement of pills across borders is highly challenging to govern, and authorities have found themselves unable to completely shut off flows (Calkin, 2023). Moreover, the growth of abortion hotlines and websites that facilitate pill mobilities have made abortion pills 'readily accessible via a few clicks of a mouse' (Sheldon, 2016, 90). This has all led to the general belief that 'pills have legs' (Assis and Erdman, 2022, 2243), but this can give undue agency to misoprostol and erase the work and strategies of the activists who give these pills legs. This chapter, therefore, pays attention to the people, places, and strategies that enable misoprostol to move to those who need it. It first focuses on four sites where misoprostol is procured: pharmacies, the black market, laboratories, and networks; then it details some of the mobility strategies enacted by activists, how misoprostol is paid for and how the movement of pills has shifted the spaces where abortions take place.

Pharmacies

Due to misoprostol's 'legitimate' life as a stomach ulcer medication, it exists legally in pharmacies across many parts of Latin America. National regulations on the sale of misoprostol vary across countries, and price hikes and the restriction of its use to hospitals or for gastric ulcers mean that access is unequal (Dzuba et al, 2013; Erdman et al, 2018). For example, Brazil restricted sales of misoprostol when its use for abortions became known and Chile restricted the sale of misoprostol in pharmacies in 2001, when it became widely recognized as an abortifacient (Vivaldi and Stutzin, 2021). However, while in many contexts a prescription is required to buy misoprostol from a pharmacy, in practice, staff may sell the pills without one, especially if they can raise the price (Lara et al, 2006). In one study of misoprostol sales in Mexico, only 44 per cent of pharmacy staff reported requiring a prescription for sale of misoprostol (Weaver et al, 2020). This is in a context where, as is the case across Latin America, pharmacy staff do not need to be trained pharmacists and '[m]any drugs are sold for indications not medically approved' (Coêlho et al, 1991, 247). Misoprostol has not always been so accessible in pharmacies, and one interviewee in Peru described purchasing the pills from pharmacies in Colombia and bringing them back to Peru – now Peru is lauded as the *paraíso del miso* (paradise of miso).

Similar to Peru, in many parts of Mexico, 'there are usually not many obstacles, even if it happens that the pharmacy doesn't want to sell you the medicine. But, in general, you can get it at the pharmacy.' Moreover, an interviewee in Colombia explained that 'a woman can go to a pharmacy without a prescription and the pharmacist can sell [misoprostol] to her'. From my interviewees' perspectives, then, misoprostol is easily available at pharmacies in Peru, Colombia, and Mexico. An interviewee in Costa Rica, however, reported a markedly different situation. There, misoprostol has not been approved by the national administration for obstetric purposes, 'so that means there is no access'; she went on to say that 'in order to have access to misoprostol I need a prescription from a doctor who certifies that I have gastric problems'. Similarly, an interviewee in Venezuela explained that while some large pharmacy chains will stock misoprostol, and it is possible to buy a prescription, some pharmacies, 'even if you have the prescription, will not sell the pills to you'. The pharmacies sell them to 'medical personnel only, doctors, nurses, and even in that situation, they will prefer selling to male doctors and male nurses'. As she explained, that means 'it's very unlikely that, I don't know, a 20ish-year-old woman with a prescription will get the pills easily'. While, as she described, there may be a pharmacist who is 'some cool chick that went to pharmacy school, and she's a feminist, and she's like, I got you', they are 'very few. Very, very few.' Interviewees in Argentina reported varying levels of accessibility and being able to buy misoprostol from a pharmacy without a prescription was seen as more challenging than in Peru, Colombia, and Mexico. They said that it was often easier to buy a forged prescription but that there were some 'militant pharmacies' who would sell misoprostol for abortions. However, even in contexts where, as interviewees reported, misoprostol was easy to buy without a prescription, that doesn't mean that people needing to buy the pills for an abortion always experience the situation in the same way. People may be unaware the pills are available, they may not be able to afford them, or they may experience hostility at a pharmacy. As discussed later in the chapter, this is where activists and *acompañantes* have an important role to play.

Before knowledge on misoprostol was being widely disseminated by abortion activists, pharmacies were not just the places where people could buy the pills; they were also the places where people were receiving information on how to use them (Vázquez et al, 2006). Poor information and even deliberate misinformation from pharmacy staff has led to people experiencing variable results when following the regimen suggested to them; the result could be a complete abortion, but it could also be a continuation of the pregnancy or an incomplete abortion that requires further treatment (Mateo, 2024). Interviewees in Peru spoke of situations where the pharmacist would tell the person they only needed to use six pills and would refuse to give them more, would sell them an additional (and unnecessary) medication or would tell them to use the pills vaginally, which could leave undissolved material that could be used as evidence of an abortion. This creates confusion for the person having the abortion because, as one *acompañante* explained, 'they prefer to trust the pharmacist … that is there … round the corner from their house' as opposed to 'person X who doesn't say his or her name and is providing the information or [giving information from] a book'. The perceived medical knowledge of pharmacy staff often takes precedence even where, in the case of using misoprostol for an abortion, they may not know the safe and effective regimen.

Pharmacies can also be hostile spaces. One interviewee told of a time when she bought pills from a pharmacy and was charged a heavily inflated price and was mistreated; as she described, the pharmacist said '"hurry up or we're going to call the police" – they threw the pills at me, so [they were] very hostile'. Another interviewee explained that she frequently bought pills from one pharmacy for her collective's stock and they always looked at her 'weird', while a third said, 'there's one place where we always buy that the pharmacist looks at us with a "so many abortions, girlfriend!"' look. Pharmacies will also typically charge more to people who don't have a prescription. Interviewees reported prices two to five times higher than the cost for the pills when a prescription is provided. As one interviewee in Peru explained, pharmacies have to keep records on how much misoprostol they sell 'and that's where the negotiation lies, and that's why they manage the price – that is, the market has been setting the price based on demand'. If pharmacies need to manipulate their sales figures, then they want a financial incentive. There can also be question marks over the effectiveness of the pills, since, as the interviewee continued, 'sometimes you don't know the expiration date because they only give you the pills loose or in a bag so you don't know if they are real or not. That is why we take a gamble every time.'

One important role of activists and *acompañantes* has been to facilitate access to misoprostol in pharmacies. A collective in Peru described how they devised a 'heat map' of local pharmacies, tagging each one with information about how much they sell misoprostol for and whether they require a prescription. Another collective generated this knowledge on pharmacy access together with the people they have accompanied, though they didn't create a visual representation; one member of this group said that 'in a way, [we] have mapped almost all the districts' because 'we have mapped the places where, well, women, other women, tell us where they get the medicines and how they have gotten them'. Similarly, another interviewee said that if someone contacts them after an abortion,

> we take the opportunity to ask, 'And where did you buy the pills?' 'I bought them at such-and-such a place. No, no, they didn't ask me for a prescription.' 'And how much did it cost?' 'So much.' So, with this information, let's say, as we systematize it, we can update it and provide it to other women who call.

Acompañantes also do groundwork to test the experience of buying pills from pharmacies. As an interviewee in Peru described, 'we actually look for places. Basically, we knock on doors. We verify that it is a safe place. We make sure it's open all the time to sell us the medication; that yes, they will sell them to us.' This generates shared knowledge that reduces friction when someone needs to quickly purchase the pills from a reputable seller. The journey to finding misoprostol from a pharmacy can also be 'labyrinthine' as not all pharmacies will stock the pills and the ones that do may not sell them if they suspect the person wants them for an abortion (Mateo, 2024). Activists help people to find a route through the labyrinth.

Acompañantes also help to facilitate access to prescriptions in order to increase the likelihood that a pharmacy will sell misoprostol and do so at a lower price. One interviewee explained that 'there are many colleagues who give you the prescription' because they 'obviously know the need'. An *acompañante* in Peru told me how her collective managed to get a prescription for misoprostol that they have used to buy pills for two years; it's 'some crappy prescription that looks like parchment because it's so old', but it opens up the possibility of lower prices. A male doctor friend was aware of her activism around abortion and said to her: 'If you ever meet someone who needs a prescription, let me know and if I can help, I'll do it.'

Another strategy is to only send certain types of people to buy misoprostol. One *acompañante* in Mexico explained that as a woman in her fifties, she 'is able to buy misoprostol much more easily than a *compañera* in the network who is 21'. Other groups send men. Two interviewees in Peru described this approach. One explained that 'getting misoprostol as women is more difficult than as men', so her collective has asked 'a male colleague … to buy … the pills, or [male] friends'; another said, 'we found the key through the "ulcerous old men"'. Their older male friends would pay much lower prices than 'girls' who went to buy misoprostol. The interviewee explained that even if the pharmacy staff 'might suspect it, at the place where we bought it they can't confront it, because there's nothing to confront.'

Therefore, the situation is one whereby misoprostol is widely accessible in pharmacies across Latin America, but not without issues of restrictions, inflated prices, hostility, and misinformation. As one interviewee in Peru put it:

> I think that's the relationship that you have with misoprostol. It is almost never used for what it is intended for, which is ulcers. Every person who goes to the pharmacy and asks for misoprostol are people who want to have an abortion, especially when they ask for 12 pills.

The practice of buying misoprostol from pharmacies for reasons other than abortion is a known cover, but one that continues, especially when it provides an additional income stream for pharmacies. It is seen as a 'safer' way to procure the pills; as one interviewee said, 'it was safer from a pharmacy – I didn't buy it from a stranger'. These 'strangers' form the next section of the chapter, as when, for a variety of reasons, people cannot access misoprostol from a pharmacy, they turn to the black market.

The black market

The term *mercado negro* (black market) was frequently used by interviewees to describe the informal markets through which misoprostol is bought and sold. This often has negative connotations of scams and criminal enterprise, and pharmaceuticals purchased on the black market are typically considerably overpriced and have the potential to be diluted or adulterated (Hulme et al, 2020). Black market misoprostol, however, is widely reported as being high quality and safe; it is the context of criminalization and stigmatization that forces the creation of a clandestine market. The pills may not have the right paperwork or be sold by an approved vendor, but that does not necessarily have any bearing on the quality of the product (Thakur, 2023). Therefore, while much of the literature on black market pharmaceuticals focuses on the prevalence of 'fake' drugs, this is less common in the case of misoprostol in Latin America. As one interviewee in Peru explained, 'I have some beautiful *yerberas* [herbalists] who provide you with misoprostol and who give you counselling focused on human rights and who do not judge you and who see it in a different way.' That said, scammers and opportunists do seek to capitalize on the desperation and urgency of those trying to buy misoprostol, so the black market is at once an important site of pill mobility and a site with the potential for deception. An *acompañante* in Peru described the situation as follows: 'besides being the paradise of …, of misoprostol, it is also the paradise of informality, isn't it? … And that has a good side, because it allows you, well, to do things in a creative way but it has a bad side too.'

In their search to find a way to end their unwanted pregnancy, many people will turn to the internet as their first port of call. There, they may find clear, accurate information and empathetic, feminist support, but they may also encounter scammers and anti-abortion activists. Informal vendors tout their wares across various platforms such as the e-commerce site Mercado Libre or social media sites like Facebook Marketplace, Instagram, and X/Twitter. As the World Health Organization (WHO) reports (WHO, 2024), the growth of e-commerce and the complexity of global supply chains has made it easier for vendors to sell substandard or falsified pharmaceuticals, particularly in low- and middle-income countries. Websites and social media make it easy for those with fake, overpriced, or non-existent pills to feed off people's desperation, and this makes it more challenging to find the accurate information and appropriately priced pills that are also available through the internet. This is, at times, their strategy, and online misoprostol sellers are often shrewd with their marketing and design. One interviewee in Peru explained that some online sellers copy the style and language of feminist pro-abortion sites in order to siphon off potential customers: 'They copy messages from any feminist network. And obviously they scam them and sell them at any price and [sell] anything.' In their study of misoprostol use in Brazil, Facioli et al (2024) found a clear circuit used by scammers: they market themselves on Instagram and then move potential buyers into the more private space of WhatsApp chats to facilitate an anonymous negotiation on the purchase of the pills. These vendors frequently engage in 'fake-talk' to provoke fear of fake pills and reassure buyers that their own abortion pills are legitimate and trustworthy (Calkin, 2024).

These websites are highly visible across much of Latin America, and as an interviewee in Costa Rica described: 'You Google, "Cytotec Costa Rica" and you will get the sites, but they are insecure sites because you don't know if there is a doctor, if there is a consultation, you don't know anything.' However, another interviewee in Venezuela reported that in her country, 'it's not even as open as a Facebook group. It's people on WhatsApp and

WhatsApp is super important here in Venezuela to find misoprostol and to find abortion medication.' So people are given a contact and 'it's someone on WhatsApp – you don't know exactly who these people are. And then you ask them [for misoprostol], so it puts you in a level of risk that is absurd' because these are not feminist activists but people who sell misoprostol as one source of income alongside recreational drugs and weapons. As she elaborated, 'the scarcity of it makes it a very valuable thing and something that, you know, like people can take advantage of you'. Beyond the internet, advertisements for misoprostol can be found in public space through flyers, stickers, and graffiti, targeted in locations where younger populations are present, such as university campuses (Gynuity Health Projects, 2007). Misinformation, as well as legitimate information, about misoprostol is rampant, whether on or offline.

While in the global North it is rare to find fake misoprostol pills (Murtagh et al, 2018), they have occasionally been reported in Latin America, where people have been sold pills made from flour or sugar or other medications that will not lead to an effective abortion (Gynuity Health Projects, 2007). One interviewee even saw pills that had been made out of plaster. This may be because selling 12 fake misoprostol pills for US$20 provides much more purchasing power for a scammer in a low-income country such as Honduras or Bolivia than in the global North. Moreover, those seeking to purchase misoprostol may also find themselves receiving 'packages' (often marketed as 'combi-packs') that don't include misoprostol, include misoprostol but also other unnecessary medicines, or include medications that are ineffective (Drovetta, 2015). One interviewee in Peru explained that there were many misoprostol scams and these only seemed to worsen with the COVID-19 pandemic. She said that some sellers on the internet will ask for the money in advance but never send the pills or they will send ineffective ones and ask for more money when those inevitably don't lead to an abortion. Other interviewees reported stories of supplying misoprostol being used as a front to rob or sexually assault people when they arrive to purchase the pills.

Given the risks of buying misoprostol through the black market, feminist networks have deployed strategies to help people recognize scams and re-route them to safer options. Just the possibility of falling prey to fake drugs or scams affects how people access abortion pills (Calkin, 2024). One interviewee in Argentina spoke of a strategy to try to deal with potential scams, which was to make sure people were aware that the misoprostol (being sold there under the Cytotec brand) came in a hexagon-shaped tablet. It may still have been of dubious quality – 'whether that was Cytotec or not, how did we know, it was a very complicated black market' – but this was one rung of knowledge that pointed towards a medication being misoprostol. Others attempt to tackle scams by publishing lists of scammers so that people trying to buy the pills can check that their seller is not on the list (Larrea et al, 2024), some have developed digital self-care tools to facilitate information provision (Luigi-Bravo and Gill, 2022), and some run websites with information about safe abortion. A common issue here has been censorship with pro-abortion websites taken down or blocked by governments and tech companies such as Meta moderating content that includes 'abortion' and associated words (Shenkin and Abee, 2024). International networks such as Women on Web are forced to create 'copycat' websites with new links to force censors to play 'whack-a-mole', use images rather than words, and use languages beyond English (Shenkin and Abee, 2024). This is a far from ideal situation as it makes it challenging to build trust and useful websites are inaccessible or deprioritized in search engine rankings.

The black market is, therefore, a space of both risk and opportunity. It has opened up access to misoprostol when people are not able to buy the pills through a pharmacy or a feminist network, but it has also exposed people to scams, misinformation, and violence. Feminist activists have played an important role in intervening in this black market space by warning people of the risks and providing information on safer ways of procuring misoprostol.

Laboratories

Misoprostol's 'other life' as a stomach ulcer drug means that it can be legitimately manufactured in contexts even where it cannot be legally used to terminate pregnancies. Since Pfizer's patent of misoprostol expired in 2000, pharmaceutical companies have been permitted to make generic misoprostol, and many laboratories across Latin America, including in Brazil, Colombia, and Peru, have chosen to do so (Gynuity Health Projects, 2007). This is an important development that allows activist networks to develop relationships with laboratories and purchase misoprostol directly from them, cutting out other 'middlemen' such as pharmacies or black market actors. These relationships allow activists to buy in bulk and sell or donate misoprostol to those who need it more cost effectively. I spoke to members of one large *acompañante* collective in Peru who explained that it is their relationship with a Peruvian laboratory that produces generic misoprostol that allows them to sell misoprostol cheaply to those needing abortions. A member of another group explained that they established a 'contract with a pharmaceutical company to provide medicines. So, we have a stock every month.' This is not to say that these pharmaceutical companies are themselves working as feminist activists; instead, they are selling misoprostol for their own financial benefit (Belfrage, 2023).

Peru is often singled out as the location with a strong presence of laboratories producing misoprostol and developing relationships with feminist networks. One interviewee explained that seven brands of misoprostol are available in the country, with three being imported and four being manufactured within Peru. There is some geographical dimension to their movement, with two of the Peruvian brands being more prevalent in the south of the country. She explained that her group had 'tracked down all these companies that sell [misoprostol], the *laboratoritos* [little laboratories]' and found that they are frequently small companies with a handful of employees who manufacture very few pharmaceutical products. 'So it's obvious,' she asserted, 'they are companies that are formed to earn money with miso and that must be linked to all this clandestine business.' Interviewees saw national production of misoprostol as a benefit because it could be used soon after its manufacture date. As one interviewee described: 'The misoprostol that I buy [from abroad] expires after a year, year and a half' so 'even if you keep them or bring more, it's always at risk of expiration'. More local misoprostol reduces the time, and lessens the barriers, to get it to those who need it. One interviewee recalled the shift that came with the national production of generic misoprostol in Peru: '10 years ago, it was only Pfizer. It was Pfizer and other laboratories, but there were no Peruvian laboratories or you could not find them', 'and Cytotec is expensive because it is from Pfizer'. This meant that 'when you go and ask for the pill, without a prescription, they are probably not going to sell it to you at that price, they are going to sell it to you a little more expensive' so 'if Cytotec should be sold to you for 7 soles, they will probably sell it to you for 10, 11, 12 soles. But, then, it costs you more than 150 soles, more or less, a dose.' However, with generic misoprostol, 'in theory, they should sell it for 2.60 soles, for example, per pill. So, it costs less than 30 soles to have a dose', so even if it is sold at a heavily inflated price of 5 soles per pill, that is still far cheaper than the branded equivalent.

However, the national production of misoprostol has not been a universal panacea. When ANMAT (the Argentine National Administration of Drugs, Food and Medical Devices) approved misoprostol, it began to be produced by the public laboratory in Santa Fe as well as by private companies. As an interviewee explained, the province of Santa Fe has been generally more progressive, but she surmised that 'there was only one company producing misoprostol and it could be that there was an increase in demand and they ... took advantage of the opportunity and said we are going to charge more'. She said that this monopolization of misoprostol, and the subsequent rise in price, led to an increase in obstetric mortality rates – as she put it, 'that's how direct it is'. Another interviewee explained that this resulted in a lawsuit against the monopolization of misoprostol and that now 'everything is different, everything is better now because there is competition'. Another issue, reported by an interviewee in Peru, is that reproductive health advocates have had issues trying to get these laboratories to commit to registering misoprostol for obstetric purposes. By producing it as a 'stomach ulcer drug', they are able to circumvent the regulatory approvals system and stigma associated with being a pharmaceutical company that produces drugs that are even abortion-adjacent. The result is that it is harder for health professionals to procure misoprostol for its other obstetric purposes, such as managing miscarriages, preventing postpartum haemorrhage, and inducing labour, and accurate indications for other uses cannot be included in the medical insert.

The national production of misoprostol in laboratories has created opportunities for activists to procure high-quality pills at low cost. This means that they can sidestep scams, misinformation, and pills that have been stored in suboptimal conditions. While there have been issues with monopolies and being able to register misoprostol for obstetric indications, laboratories have played in important role in facilitating the mobility of misoprostol and, in turn, its use for abortions.

Accessing pills through networks

Beyond pharmacies, the black market, and direct access from laboratories, a fourth way of getting misoprostol is through pro-abortion (or at least pro-'family planning') networks at both international and national scales. International NGOs and other private and public sector organizations have created flows of pills from the laboratories in which they are produced, which are largely in India, to the contexts where people need them. One international NGO came up time and again in interviews as one that donates pills to *acompañante* groups as part of their mission to expand safe abortion access around the world. This NGO had a particularly strong presence in Mexico and sent abortion pills to smaller organizations and activist groups. This relationship was highly valued by interviewees because the NGO will usually send mifepristone as well as misoprostol. The so-called 'combi-pack' is favoured for its higher efficacy and fewer side effects, and because mifepristone is harder to buy and much more expensive than misoprostol. One interviewee in Mexico reported directly receiving 30–40 *combos* (misoprostol with mifepristone) every 15 days, whereas another explained that they referred the people who contacted them to this NGO, which would then send the pills directly to the person needing them. Another interviewee said she only received mifepristone from this NGO because misoprostol was relatively easy and cheap to buy in pharmacies in her Mexican state; in this way, she only had to charge for the cost of the misoprostol.

Another way that abortion pill access is facilitated is through social marketing organizations. These groups, which can be non-profit or for-profit, 'use market mechanisms to promote and distribute reproductive health products and services, often at subsidized rates, through global SRHR [sexual and reproductive health and rights] programs' (Belfrage, 2023, 15). To instigate behavioural change, they use campaigns and other 'social marketing' strategies, such as the adoption of long-acting reversible contraceptives (Belfrage, 2023). Social marketing organizations, therefore, donate misoprostol (often in combination with mifepristone) to local NGOs or activist groups in order to disseminate pills within national contexts.

Another type of network involves international abortion activist organizations, and the two most commonly mentioned by interviewees were Women on Web and Women Help Women. Women on Web is a Canadian organization founded by Dutch doctor Rebecca Gomperts in 2005. Women on Web uses a telemedicine-style model whereby someone needing an abortion can input their information as part of an online medical consultation and be prescribed abortion pills by the medical team at the organization. The doctor then writes a prescription, which is sent to NN Agencies, a pharmaceutical company in India, who then send out either individual or bulk orders (Calkin, 2023). While Women on Web are not handling the pills themselves, they are facilitating self-managed abortions more directly than the organizations described earlier. Women Help Women, meanwhile, was founded as a splinter group after disagreements among some members of Women on Web about the more medicalized model the organization had taken. Those members set up Women Help Women in 2014 to expand access to abortion pills and develop partnerships with local activists on the ground (Shochet et al, 2023). People who need an abortion fill out a form that is reviewed by staff, who then arrange for the abortion pills to be sent. The key difference between the two groups is that Women Help Women does not require a prescription to be filled out by a medical professional.

Interviewees reported that their groups received donations of abortion pills from both Women on Web and Women Help Women, while individuals accessing the websites and requesting the pills themselves was less common. This is because, at the time of writing, accessing the pills from Women on Web costs €70–€90, depending on the buyer's location in relation to Women on Web, and accessing pills from Women Help Women costs €75. While Women on Web have stated they set a sliding scale price because 'abortion pills should not be expensive', the average monthly net salary in 2024 was US$186 in Venezuela, US$370 in Colombia, and US$402 in Bolivia (Statista, 2024). Uruguay had the highest net salary at US$1,088, but even there, abortion pills costing US$77 will be out of reach for many given that women typically receive 60 per cent of the income received by men and abortion seekers are disproportionately young and have low incomes. So, for local groups, partnerships with these organizations and receiving donations through them offers a crucial way to circumvent out-of-reach prices.

There are, then, regional and national networks of organizations and activists that mobilize abortion pills. There are some groups who find themselves more likely to receive donations from the organizations mentioned here or can more easily buy misoprostol in their context and then share the pills with *acompañantes* in other parts of Latin America. For example, an interviewee in Peru explained: 'There is a *compañera* here who has a network in Mexico, so there are *compañeras* in Mexico who also have stored pills, and they can send them to another network here if they make contacts, right? That's how it works.' Others move them within countries, particularly from urban centres to more rural areas or from larger groups to smaller ones. One group in a rural area of Peru described how they would regularly request misoprostol from a national collective based in the capital, Lima. Another interviewee in Peru mentioned knowing someone who ran a medical clinic and was able to access misoprostol for its other obstetric uses and share this access with others. These relationships are often based in having 'a friend in feminism', but the growth of networks such as Red Compañera, discussed in the previous chapter, is generating additional linkages that can lead to shared knowledge as well as strategies for making misoprostol mobile.

These networks are able to move pills between themselves due to their slippery mobility. Misoprostol is a 'legitimate' stomach ulcer medication, and it is approved for abortions across many parts of the world and is recognized by the WHO as an essential medicine. The networks take advantage of this global acceptance of misoprostol and then use legal loopholes such as staff who prescribe or arrange the delivery of the pills being located in countries where abortion pills are legal. Once pills enter a country, they are indistinguishable from pills that arrive 'legitimately', so networks use the 'regulatory ambiguity' of misoprostol to move pills internationally (Calkin, 2023). These strategies are very hard for governments to shut down and so they are typically only able to halt the movement of pills when they are intercepted at the border (Calkin, 2023). The pill-moving networks outlined here challenge the arbitrary laws that dictate for what purpose misoprostol can be taken, what side of a border it can be taken on, and whether a medical professional needs to be present.

Feminist groups at a range of scales are, therefore, providing information on how to use misoprostol, but 'some feminist groups also bring medicines into local communities, establishing make-shift pharmacies that not only create community-level access but compete with and drive down prices among other private sellers' (Erdman et al, 2018, 15). These international, regional, and local networks mobilize verified misoprostol pills and move them effectively to those who need them.

Mobility strategies

The four sites discussed in this chapter – pharmacies, the black market, laboratories, and networks – all represent ways that activists and *acompañantes* can access pills. They then need to keep these in motion to prevent what Sodero (2019) terms 'coagulation'. When misoprostol coagulates, its movement is disrupted and it cannot circulate to those who need it. *Acompañantes*, therefore, discussed the strategies they use to keep misoprostol moving, from creating networks of 'girls who share with girls', hiding pills in groceries and teddies, and even repurposing robots. While I will not share all the strategies told to me for reasons of security, activists are creative, pragmatic, and resourceful when it comes to providing physical access to misoprostol.

One key strategy has been to keep the pills already in circulation moving. An interviewee in Mexico described how the misoprostol that is bought in pharmacies often comes in a package of 28 pills and so can be used for two or more complete abortions. So when someone contacts her group and

> tells us that she can't ... that she doesn't have the money to buy it, we look in our records to see if there is someone else in her state, near her ... in her own municipality or nearby who has used it, and then we contact her and tell her that there is another woman who needs it. If she has the pills, she can donate them to them, and, yes, then it's more like they can find each other to give them to her.

A different group in Mexico uses a similar strategy and, as a member explained, because they have no funding, 'it is complicated for us to support them financially', but they do ask people who have bought the pills and had some left over: 'We invite them to donate those pills to other girls, not that they give them to us, but that they give them to another girl, right? Also so that, well, we advocate for creating a network not only among collectives but also a network among girls who have abortions.'

While these groups in Mexico did not handle the pills themselves, other groups would receive them back as a donation. An interviewee in Peru said: 'We are always thinking about the dynamics of how to, let's say, recover the pills that are bought by those who are accompanied, to be able to redistribute them', so 'we organize ourselves' so that if someone buys a full package of misoprostol pills and only uses half, they ask her to donate them. However, she continued: 'This has also been a logistical issue to see who can go and pick up the misoprostol, and then, when they know of another accompaniment in the same place, they can hand it over.' Another interviewee in Argentina spoke of how 'it took a lot of solidarity, it was talking to other women – "if you were able to get it, please give us the pills you had left over"'. She said that some people were sceptical and thought that they wanted the pills back to sell them on, but they would reassure them, explaining that it was to pass them on free of charge to maximize the number of people who can access misoprostol. Across all of these contexts, the sharing of unused pills keeps them circulating and reduces the economic and political barriers to procuring pills.

Utilizing the postal system may seem like a mundane mobility strategy, but across parts of Latin America, it can be a relatively reliable and quick way of moving the pills. While some interviewees lamented the unreliability of postal services and noted that they are more efficient in metropolitan areas, the postal system was frequently used by *acompañantes*. When pathways to abortion access are limited, even a service with low trust or faith in its effectiveness becomes an important element in supporting abortion access. The more frequently discussed issue was the challenges of receiving pills if the recipient lives with family or a partner who they are trying to keep the abortion hidden from. An interviewee in Mexico described how they support people in this situation: 'We send it to the mailing office, and they can collect it there' or use an alternative address; 'Sometimes if they have, like, a good friend and the friend is helping them, we'll send it to the friend. I've sent it to hotels. They receive it at the lobby of the hotel.' Another *acompañante* in Mexico said that for people who, for reasons of 'privacy and security', can't receive them themselves, they deliver the pills to what they termed 'allied spaces' or they deliver the pills themselves to ensure they reach the right person discreetly.

In other situations, *acompañantes* 'camouflage' the pills so that when they do arrive at someone's house, it is not immediately apparent that they are abortion pills. One interviewee in Peru described tactics such as hiding the misoprostol in clothes, toys, and trinkets; then, if a 'girl has to explain to her family why the hell she's getting something from somewhere else and they want to see what it is and no, look, they don't think it's drugs, they think it's something else, right?' She even takes care in how she wraps these gifts: 'green paper, a pretty little bow, somehow, I don't know, [to] make her feel that we're embracing her, even though we're not, right?' Another interviewee in rural Peru explained that a larger group in Lima would post her misoprostol to share in her local community and the pills would be sent 'in little boxes of earrings'. The postal system is not cheap, however; an *acompañante* in Mexico told me that 'it costs almost three doses of misoprostol to send it from one city to another city in Mexico'. She said: '[It] makes me indignant because I feel that we are investing what we could be investing in donating the medicine to three other *compañeras*, three other girls, for what I call saving their lives, who surely don't have the means, nor the technology.' Nevertheless, sending people pills directly, despite the cost, is a key mobility strategy.

The COVID-19 pandemic heightened the challenges of moving misoprostol. One interviewee in Peru, who I will call Ivette, told me of a woman who was 10 weeks' pregnant 'but did not want to have it, not at all'. The woman was pregnant with her ex-partner, not the husband she lived with. This was at a time of lockdown and 'she was telling us she couldn't even go out the door of her house'. Ivette had to devise a solution to this: 'in the end, we were able to go to her house and give her a package in her grocery bags', and the woman was then able to use the misoprostol and simulate a miscarriage. 'She was super relieved that it was over', explained Ivette. *Acompañantes* are forced to be innovative and to tailor their strategies to complex situations.

Passing pills between networks and through the post are ways of moving pills to ensure access to those who need to use them for an abortion. But mobility strategies can have other political rationales too. Pro-abortion activists have used the transportation of abortion pills in innovative ways to publicize problems with abortion access (Freeman, 2020). The Dutch organization Women on Waves, for example, has a track record of using spectacles to raise abortion awareness. They used abortion drones in 2015 and 2016 to move abortion pills across borders, from Germany to Poland and from the Republic of Ireland to Northern Ireland, respectively. In 2018, the group then collaborated with Irish activists ROSA Socialist Feminist Movement to use a small robot, which was being controlled from the Netherlands, to transport abortion pills to a woman outside Belfast's High Court. A new abortion robot then appeared in Mexico in 2021, organized by Women on Waves' sister organization, Women on Web, in collaboration with local *acompañante* groups.

The robot, rAborta, first delivered pills on 28 September 2021, International Safe Abortion Day, in the Mexican state of Coahuila, which was at the time the nexus for the discussion on whether punishing people for an abortion was unconstitutional. Then 11 rAbortas were mobilized in 11 states to call for access to mifepristone and ridicule the situation where people have to rely on technology to access an abortion. As an interviewee from the group explained, the rAborta is actually 'a robot that is used for dogs', a dog treat feeder through which owners can interact with their pet via video and voice calling, and dispense treats by clicking a button on the app. rAborta was repurposed to dispense abortion pills following video consultations with the recipients. The interviewee explained that 'there were so many loopholes there that we can work with and make it legal and safe and everything', including controlling the robot from Mexico City, where abortion was already legal. An *acompañante* who was invited to be part of this campaign explained that 'as a media thing, it was great' because it brought together different abortion activists and was *algo mediático* (something that drew media attention) in a way that other activist strategies don't. The groups were then able to keep their rAborta to use in other ways and to serve as a discussion point about abortion access. These mobility stunts may not offer a way to deliver pills to the millions of people who use them, but they are effective in drawing media attention to barriers to abortion access and using humour to parody the absurdity of state laws. If a robot dog feeder can provide abortion access, why can't the state?

Paying for misoprostol

In the pharmaceutical industry, misoprostol is not expensive. One 200-microgram misoprostol tablet can usually be purchased for under US$1 in most low-income countries (Harvey, 2015). Its relatively low price is due to its 'other life' as a stomach ulcer medication, where the dose is high, with four 200-microgram tablets taken daily (Weeks et al, 2005). Nevertheless, its relatively low cost, for an obstetric medication, does not mean that the price is affordable for all those who are trying to purchase it, especially where contexts of clandestinity cause the price to rise.

Across Latin America, the price of misoprostol varies widely. One study found that the price of misoprostol through legal routes varied from US$0.48 per pill in Ecuador to US$15.80 per pill in Uruguay (Fernández et al, 2009). In Mexico and the Dominican Republic, it is available relatively cheaply and can be bought from pharmacies, frequently without a prescription, which makes it physically accessible; however, the economic situation of most women in these countries means it is still out of reach in financial terms (Larrea et al, 2024). In Guatemala, Honduras, and El Salvador, the cost of eight misoprostol pills costs between US$140 and US$160 from pharmacies, which, when the minimum wage is about US$150 per month, makes the pills completely unaffordable (Walsh, 2020). In Costa Rica, as one interviewee reported, a regimen of 12 pills can cost US$300, so while richer people are able to travel to Cuba or Mexico for an abortion, those who cannot leave the country are left struggling to pay for the pills. One interviewee in Peru gave the example of 14- or 15-year-olds getting in touch and having absolutely no recourse to funds as they cannot tell their family they are pregnant. She has had people get in touch who simply have not had the money to buy the pills. As she explained:

> We are in a poor area where women cannot have an abortion, and many times not because they do not know about it, but because they do not have the economic possibilities because the pills are expensive. And it's a privilege to get 150 soles [US$40] for someone who doesn't have a job.

In contrast, Chile has a higher average salary, but misoprostol is much more regulated by the state and, therefore, harder to purchase from a pharmacy. This means that many people access misoprostol through the black market, where the price is much higher (Larrea et al, 2024).

The fluctuating price of misoprostol on the black market can make it challenging for people to know how much to expect to spend on the medication or what would constitute an acceptable price. An interviewee in Peru recalled supporting a young woman who had been told the pills would cost 80 soles and so she passed over a wad of notes because 'she had thought it was 80 per pill, because that's how she had heard that her friend had bought it'. Another said that online sellers will often triple the pharmacy price. In the mid-2000s, the black market price of misoprostol in Brazil, Colombia, Mexico, and Peru varied from US$1 to $30 per pill (De Zordo, 2016). One interviewee in Venezuela explained that the cost of an abortion there, where 'it is highly illegal', means 'it is [like] the Wild, Wild West out there'. She said that the price could be between US$30 and $500, with black market providers raising the price depending on the week of pregnancy. This can mean that someone seeking to buy the pills can be given a certain price initially but when they return, say, two weeks later after getting the money together, they are told: 'Oh it's 50 bucks more now.' There are also problems when a person takes two doses (eight pills) but the abortion has still not begun and they need to quickly find four more pills to complete the third dose. The price also varies within countries. De Zordo (2016) reports that in Brazil the cost per pill can vary from US$10 in the north-eastern state of Pernambuco to $2,030 in São Paulo.

It is in the formal market, through pharmacies and organizations that sell the medication, where the prices are lower and the nature of the pills can be largely verified, but this does not mean that the pills can be purchased there. Whether it be national regulations, anti-abortion pharmacy staff, the inability to purchase misoprostol without a prescription, or the lack of privacy, pharmacies are not always an option. It is here that *acompañante* groups have intervened to facilitate more affordable or free access to misoprostol pills of reliable quality. Some *acompañante* groups work on a sliding scale or use a solidarity form of payment whereby people pay what they can, with those who can afford to pay more subsidising the cost for others. As one interviewee in Peru explained, her group has a set price for the

> standard amount of the full dosage, of the 12 pills. And we ask if they can pay that amount. If they can't pay, we tell them about the options and those who can pay, and there are some who can pay in full, we give them the whole dosage. There is an amount that we take from those who pay in full, the general amount, and that goes to the cash box of those who cannot pay.

The amount they charged was 120 soles (US$32), but she explained: 'this year and last year most of them could not pay the 120 soles. We had to lower the cost and we have given many donations and we had to stop because we could no longer donate.' An interviewee in Mexico described her group's model as having a fixed suggested price 'and if women can donate, it's a chain of solidarity. Like, women that can donate the full amount will subsidise the abortion of women that can donate nothing at all, or just a part of it.'

Similarly, another interviewee in Peru said that their standard price is 80 soles, but they reduce it for those who cannot pay this amount or even provide it for free in some circumstances. But they do ask those who can to pay the full 80 soles: 'It is not like an income, I mean, I don't know how to say it. It's like they pay the 80 and with those 80 we can buy another dose, and so on. So it is like that is the mechanism.' One interviewee in Colombia explained that her group has a fixed price of 50,000 pesos (US$12), but those who can afford to give more are encouraged to pay for the group's other costs or subsidise those who cannot pay the full amount. They then have a general bank account and 'what is also said is if you can't pay now, but you know in a few years or months you will be in a better place, please consider making these donations and in many ..., well, they are anonymous donations and a lot of them do come.'

One interviewee in Peru described her group's approach as one of 'differentiated accompaniment'; this recognizes the different needs and experiences of those who approach them for support. They have found that due to covering the costs for those who cannot pay, some within the group end up paying for things from their own pocket, as there are sometimes expenses beyond just buying the pills, such as airfares. She said that since not everyone in the group has their own resources to support this, they 'try to generate a fund to cover those kinds of things, expenses, but also to cover the complete procedure for those who can't, or half of it'. One *acompañante* in Peru explained that she would buy the pills herself in order to have a reliable supply of misoprostol for those needing it immediately. She said:

> I buy the pills in ..., in the *mercado* [market] ... It's a great place – it's full of people. You can't go to pharmacies in downtown ... especially without a prescription. So you go to the outskirts. Well, the market is downtown, right, but it is in a more remote place, right, farther away. So I always buy there. And since I buy them regularly, they are always 10 soles each, between 10 and 12, right, Cytotec and [generic] misoprostol. So I go there to buy them. I tell the people that I help with the accompaniment that they should buy them, and if they don't, I can buy them and they reimburse me.

She had heard of other *compas* (friends, other women who support abortions) who sell misoprostol at a profit and she said: 'to tell you the truth, it makes me uncomfortable because ... well, I don't have to explain to everyone. They think I am selling the pills, but no, not at all.' She was keen to make it clear that she only ever asks for the amount she paid herself, and never takes a profit. Another in Peru explained: 'We charge just to replenish, to have our stock. That is basically three or four soles per pill and we restock ... there is no profit involved.' She disagreed with other groups' practice of having a fixed price to cover the costs of buying the pills as well as any other costs involved in buying and moving them. 'I don't think it's transparent to have a fixed price without knowing how much the pills cost', she explained. 'I have colleagues who have been part of [a particular group], who still are, who don't know how much the pills really cost. There is no transparency.' Similarly, an interviewee in Mexico said: 'There are collectives that charge – for what reason? We don't know.'

Some *acompañante* groups receive donations of funding to purchase pills from NGOs that support broadening access to safe abortion (Belfrage, 2023). This allows groups to distribute misoprostol (sometimes in combination with mifepristone) for free or at a heavily discounted price. However, as Belfrage (2023) argues, this puts *acompañantes* in the difficult position of vetting who is deserving of free or discounted pills. Some *acompañantes* wanted those having an abortion to source the money to buy the pills themselves, to make them 'co-responsible' in the process and to move away from there being a charity-type relationship, whereas others saw this as feeding into a moralizing narrative where people are being economically disincentivized from seeking support with their abortion. These donations can result in fluctuating ability to support people. One interviewee in Peru described her group's 'case-by-case analysis': 'During periods when we have had doses, we have provided the medicine, right, at no cost', whereas 'now, we are waiting to have again … some small stock to be able to bring back the medicine.' Other groups don't receive donations of pills but do receive financial donations from other abortion or feminist organizations, from their own networks of individuals in the community, or even from friends abroad. One interviewee in Mexico explained that her relatively large group would donate pills to smaller groups, especially when they were able to get hold of combi packs that include both misoprostol and mifepristone.

What was consistent across the interviews was the refusal to deny anyone access to abortion pills due to lack of money. One interviewee in Peru explained that for those who cannot pay for misoprostol, 'the issue is very treatable, it can be discussed' and costs can be lowered as the priority is always that the person getting in touch is able to have the abortion, and another declared: 'We have had people who have not had a peso and I have not charged them.'

Spaces of abortion

The mobility of pills has meant that fewer people need to travel to a specific site where an abortion can take place. Before there was wide access to pills, people would often travel to a clinic, which may have been clandestine, for a procedural abortion. But now it is usually easier, cheaper, and preferable to have the pills do the traveling and then have a medical abortion in a place of the person's choosing. This was noted particularly by interviewees in Mexico, where abortion was legalized in Mexico City in 2007. People from other Mexican states would travel to the capital for an abortion in the years following the ruling. However, as self-managed abortions with pills became better known, people preferred to stay where they were; as one interviewee remarked: 'If it is very expensive to come from the north of the country to Mexico City, it would be much easier to do it with pills.' The mobility of misoprostol also opened up access for those who could not undertake travel to Mexico City; another interviewee explained: 'Many times, even though we cover transportation, all the resources, because of all these structural issues, it's impossible for women to come' … 'because of the issue of care, of work, because of their lack of autonomy.' A third interviewee reflected on the reduction in people traveling for abortions to Mexico City or even the United States, and recalled a friend telling her, 'if I had known that I could, right, go to the pharmacy and spend 500 pesos, I wouldn't have gone'. The mobility of misoprostol to people has reduced the need for travel and has, therefore, transformed the spaces where abortions take place.

Moving abortions outside the clinic puts them back in spaces where they occurred before the medicalization of abortion: homes and other private spaces. 'Home' can be a complex space, and as Vivaldi and Stutzin (2021, 235) argue, calling for the home as a political space for abortion 'involves a dismantling of the private/public dichotomy and an expansion of the conception of home itself'. Far from wanting to push abortion into the hidden, non-public space or equating 'women's issues' with the domestic space, abortion activists are fighting for home-based abortions as a way of creating care-filled spaces where people feel they belong. Being able to have an abortion in the privacy and comfort of home is frequently touted as a benefit of self-managed abortions (Veldhuis et al, 2022a; Engle, 2025). As Engle (2025) found in her research with people who experienced telemedicine abortions at home in the United States, being at home allows people to make the space as comfortable as possible and means they can have their choice of food, drink, and entertainment, and they can even have their pets with them.

However, many people are unable to have a medical abortion in their own home due to lack of privacy. An *acompañante* in Peru told me that the space where an abortion happens depends 'a lot on how the girl want[s] to do it' and if she could not have the abortion in her own home, she may go to a friend's home or to the *acompañante*'s home. She said described abortions mainly took place at night so that 'the girls could make the excuse that I'm going to a sleepover or, I don't know, I'm going to do some work. And she would come back the next day and that was it.' Another explained that she would never accompany an abortion in her own home unless it was someone she already knew, so they usually took place 'in friends' houses.

Borrowed houses. Things like that.' Sometimes no home would be available, so the person having the abortion would have to find a hotel room, and interviewees in Mexico and Colombia spoke of their groups being able to fund this, especially if there are 'pay by the hour' hotels. An *acompañante* in Mexico went one step further and had an *abortería* [abortion space] in her home for those who had no other private space. There, people could have a private bathroom, cable TV, Netflix, blankets, and meals so they could experience the abortion in comfort. Moving abortions beyond medical spaces is not about pushing abortion into the shadows, but providing the best physical space for someone during their self-managed abortion.

The spaces of abortion have also been transformed by the possibility of virtual accompaniment. Interviewees spoke of being able to support people through abortions across national borders, with one interviewee in Mexico supporting people from as far away as Angola and Spain. It is mainly people from smaller countries that do not have established accompaniment collectives who reach out to the groups that are visible online. The *acompañantes* they contact don't see physical distance as a barrier to empathetic, feminist care; if the person is able to access the pills, they can be supported virtually. The growth of the internet to raise awareness of supported, self-managed abortion in the first place, and then the advent of platforms such as Signal and Telegram where people can confidentially share information, photos, and voice messages, has made abortion accompaniment possible in new ways and new spaces.

Yet, rural spaces in Latin America have particular challenges that not even these technological leaps can address. The situation varies enormously across the region, but some rural areas have no access to telephone or internet networks and can be extremely cut off from urban areas or even small local towns (Larrea et al, 2024). In addition, these areas are most likely to be where people in economically precarious situations live and where people, particularly Indigenous communities, don't speak the national or dominant language. One interviewee in Peru spoke of how rural women face difficulties even if they are able to buy misoprostol from a pharmacy, as it will be expensive and they are unlikely to receive the correct dosage information. Moreover, in the rare case that they experience complications, they may not be able to access a healthcare facility. Another, in Peru, explained that in many rural areas of the country there are simply no pharmacies. In addition to issues with physically accessing misoprostol, the stigma around abortion can be fiercer in rural communities, and an interviewee in Peru declared: 'Being in the regions is not the same as being in Lima. It is not the same to say publicly that you accompany as to do it in the provinces. I know that if we said it here, we would get three complaints the next day.' All of this means that activist groups and *acompañantes* have to devise particular strategies to widen abortion access in rural areas.

Some urban-based *acompañante* groups try to share information and misoprostol with rural communities. One interviewee in Peru described the chapter-style structure of her group whereby more experienced members would train keen groups or individuals throughout the country, thereby disseminating knowledge beyond the metropolitan centres and into communities. Another in Mexico described how she would provide accompaniment in rural, Indigenous communities, but only alongside a member of that community. Other groups are developed within the rural communities themselves. I spoke with one *acompañante* whose group explicitly works 'in an organized and sustainable way to be able to support girls without resources ... outside the city, in Indigenous communities, rural communities, so that they can have an abortion'. She said: 'You can't find misoprostol in rural communities. There are no pharmacies. There are medical posts. And you can't ask for it there.' While there are clinics with doctors doing their training, the interviewee said that they tend not to speak Quechua, the local Indigenous language, or understand the lived realities of sexual and reproductive health in these communities. In the absence of ways to buy misoprostol locally, she described alternative strategies such as 'sending misoprostol by bus, where the driver gives the pills to the woman himself'. This driver 'does not know what he is carrying and is paid for this shipment' – 'he takes it to them and they can have the abortion and we do the accompaniment by telephone'. Even in areas with no pharmacies or postal service, *acompañantes* have worked to transform abortion possibilities in rural space.

Misoprostol for mobility justice

The 'magic' of misoprostol cannot be realized without practical access to the medication. As shown in this chapter, the ease of accessing misoprostol depends on a range of factors, including national regulation, availability in pharmacies and the willingness of staff to sell it, the possibilities of the black market, the status of national production and relationships with laboratories, the existence of international and regional networks, and the strategies implemented by activist groups. The situation, therefore, varies widely across Latin America, and in some locations, misoprostol is very hard to make mobile. As an interviewee in Costa Rica explained: 'There are some of us who know how to accompany, but because of the legal and criminalization issues in Costa Rica, we do not accompany because access to medication is minimal.' In contrast, 'in Peru it is not a big deal to find. ... It can be tedious, it can be a hassle, it can be expensive, sometimes, depending on your income. But it is possible, it is possible.'

The challenges of moving misoprostol in Latin America are considerable. Particularly in countries where abortion is criminalized or the use of medications outside medical supervision is prohibited, ingenious strategies are required to move misoprostol. As Calkin (2023, 44) writes: 'When a package of abortion pills appears at the door, shipped from abroad, direct to the abortion seeker, it seems miraculous.' This is an illusion, argues Calkin, and the apparently seamless flow of the pills belies the political, economic, and material contexts through which this movement has been made possible. In the Latin American context, it is frequently the strategies developed by activists that produce the seemingly miraculous arrival of pills. These strategies prevent the 'coagulation' (Sodero, 2019) of misoprostol and reduce the delays or obstacles to accessing the medication.

It is hard to overstate the justice implications of this facilitated mobility. The movement of abortion pills means: fewer people need to travel for a procedural abortion, if that is even an option; fewer people need to resort to other, less safe methods; and people are able to have an abortion earlier in their pregnancy, thereby reducing distress and the possibility of other complications. This is why elsewhere I have suggested that this movement of pills is, to an extent, 'emancipatory' for those seeking an abortion (Freeman, 2020). Mobility, in this case, can be part of creating a more just future (Sheller, 2018a). The mobility of misoprostol is deeply uneven but in fighting for reproductive justice, activists and *acompañantes* have democratized and enabled access to misoprostol across the region. All of this shows how key the global circulation of 'things' can be to mobility justice (Sheller, 2018a).

The mobility work of activists and *acompañantes* and the way this has transformed the spaces and possibilities of abortion access is extraordinary, but pockets of coagulation remain, and there are still significant challenges and risks in moving misoprostol. As one *acompañante* in Peru lamented after describing how her group accesses pills: 'It seems like I'm talking about drugs. I can't believe it's not legal if there's nothing wrong with passing [on] misoprostol.' Her exasperation encapsulates a common obstacle in *acompañante* pill activism in Latin America, and the next chapter turns to this issue of the law.

4

Misoprostol and the Law: Manipulating the Margins

Misoprostol occupies an unusual legal space: it is perfectly legal if used for the purpose of treating stomach ulcers, but illegal if used to terminate a pregnancy. This distinction creates a space of risk for those using and facilitating misoprostol for abortions, but it also creates opportunities. Misoprostol's 'double life' means it is available – it can be manufactured, sold, and ingested legitimately (De Zordo, 2016). Abortion activists have harnessed this marginality to support abortion access at the edges of the law. Through using specific language, employing code words, and writing 'scripts' for abortion seekers to use, the law becomes malleable, and a space can be opened up to provide abortion access without prosecution.

This chapter furthers thinking about knowledge by tracing the ways that *acompañantes*, activists, and abortion providers have developed specific knowledge about how to use and share information about misoprostol in a context of clandestinity. Through an analysis of their 'scripts' and protocols for how to accompany or have an abortion, this chapter provides a detailed case study of how knowledge is made and remade at the margins of law. Moreover, this chapter critiques understandings of knowledge by engaging with Linsey McGoey's (2019; 2020) work on 'strategic ignorance', particularly through the ways in which states choose 'wilful blindness' to avoid the thorny political and public health issues of abortion.

As set out in the Introduction, abortion laws in Latin America have typically been hyper-restrictive, but recent years have seen the introduction of progressive laws in countries such as Colombia, Argentina, and Mexico. Nevertheless, abortion continues to be a battleground between liberal and conservative actors and is a commonly used political pawn (Morgan and Roberts, 2012). As a result, other countries, such as Honduras, El Salvador, Nicaragua, and the Dominican Republic, have repudiated the move towards liberalization and instead have further restricted their abortion policies, tightening the legal exceptions for an abortion and even completely banning abortions without exceptions (Fernández Anderson, 2020). The linear progress narrative that often frames public discourse about abortion in Latin America can ignore the heterogeneity of the legal status of abortion across the region as well as the pendular nature of abortion politics as laws move back and forth following changes in government between the Left and the Right. The rationale for the regulation of abortion has historically been placed within a medico-legal paradigm, underscored by 'the belief that regulated systems of legal and medical control guarantee safe abortion' (Assis and Erdman, 2022, 2235). This belief stipulates that in order to enforce standards and manage safety and risk, abortion needs to be regulated through criminal law and medicalized control (Assis and Erdman, 2022; Nandagiri and Pizzarossa, 2023).

Criminalizing abortion of course does not prevent abortions from taking place (Faúndes and Shah, 2015). Before the 2020 ruling that allowed people to have a legal abortion in the first 14 weeks of pregnancy, abortion in Argentina was a crime punishable by time in prison except in cases of rape or danger to the life or health of the pregnant person. Even in this context, an estimated 372,000–522,000 abortions still took place every year (Sutton, 2020). When abortion is not legal, it is forced into clandestinity and even with the dogged determination of activists and *acompañantes* to facilitate access to safe and effective abortions, too many people are left 'to the mercy of the elements', forced to continue with unwanted pregnancies and to experience risks to themselves or the foetus, or to search for other strategies to terminate the pregnancy (Chaneton and Vacarezza, 2011, 131). These risks are not evenly experienced, and it is low-income, Indigenous, racialized, and rural communities that are most likely to experience the negative effects of criminalization (Wurtz, 2012; Singer, 2019).

Within this legal context, this chapter first sets out the challenges and opportunities of changing abortion laws in Latin America, then details the strategies used by *acompañantes* to ensure self-managed abortions remain hidden from legal authorities and medical professionals. It explains how the 'shield of healthcare' approach is employed by *acompañantes* to legitimize the care that they provide, and it explores the legal threats and harassment faced by activists and the anti-abortion actors stoking this. Then, it considers the role of the state in both maintaining and moving past ignorance of abortion.

The law and its limits

The law is undoubtedly used as a tool to actively pursue and punish those who have or facilitate abortions outside legal routes (if they even exist) and to socially criminalize abortion. This means that abortion is shrouded in stigma and becomes a political battleground, and people who have or are suspected of having had an abortion can suffer consequences, such as social isolation and loss of their jobs. Abortion restrictions result in a lack of information, the persistence of stigma, poor routes to care, and low quality of abortion services (Veldhuis et al, 2022c). Religious groups, whether Catholic or evangelical, play an outsized role in these legal debates, and since many Leftist political parties were supported by the Catholic Church during military dictatorships, the quid pro quo has often been to toe the Catholic line on abortion (Morgan and Roberts, 2012).

The purposeful use of the law to uphold abortion restrictions can be understood through the term 'lawfare'; a portmanteau of 'law' and 'warfare', which, 'with its dual connotations of war and the use of legal tactics, aptly describes the phenomenon where rights, legislation, and litigation are strategic tools in a broader sociopolitical battle between organized, antagonistic groups' (Gloppen, 2021, 3). Abortion lawfare, in particular, refers to the use of the courts and judicial strategies to prevent abortion liberalization, further roll back rights, and prosecute those who have had, or are suspected of having had, abortions. These strategies frequently pit women's rights to health against foetal rights to life from the moment of conception (Sieder and Espinosa, 2021). Rights discourses are, therefore, being weaponized by anti-abortion groups, and often to great effect – in El Salvador and Nicaragua, the recognition of the juridical rights of the foetus has resulted in abortion bans (Unnithan and Pigg, 2014).

The approach on abortion from national courts varies across Latin America. Mexico, for example, has in recent years ruled in favour of the pro-choice movement's arguments, which has led to the reaffirmation and expansion of sexual and reproductive rights (Sieder and Espinosa, 2021). Argentine and Colombian courts likewise have recently ruled in favour of expanding abortion rights. Peruvian courts, meanwhile, have taken a 'formalistic' approach by strictly following already-approved legal frameworks, which has reduced opportunities for more innovation or strategies to expand the legal grounds for abortion (Gianella and Álvarez, 2021). In Costa Rica, often held up as a bastion of human rights in Latin America, the government has actively sought to prevent the introduction of exceptions to an all-out ban on abortion even when ruled by the Inter-American Court of Human Rights (Morgan, 2021). And the Honduras government, which had a previous blanket ban on abortion, wrote that ban into their constitution as recently as 2021 (Roth, 2023). A similar approach is possible in Brazil, where a proposed constitutional amendment is currently being discussed in the National Congress that would criminalize abortion across the whole country and equate it with homicide, punishable by 6 to 20 years' imprisonment (Fernandez et al, 2025). It is, therefore, difficult to talk of a single legal approach to abortion law or lawfare in Latin America.

This is not to say anti-abortion actors are the only ones mobilizing legal tactics. Krauss (2021), in her work on abortion in Mexico, highlights that abortion lawfare is something that can be enacted from 'below' as well as 'above'. Across Latin America, feminist activists and those fighting for sexual and reproductive rights have made demands of the state to follow through on existing law and to use legal frameworks to expand abortion access. For these groups, abortion lawfare is a tool for change, not just a tool of oppression. The oft-lauded legal success of Argentina, Mexico, and Colombia, for example, can be traced to the gargantuan efforts of abortion rights activists organizing and campaigning, with one element of that being legal strategies (Encarnación, 2022). These legal strategies have often centred on rights frameworks, claiming that 'the right to have an abortion is a basic human right—and, therefore, an extension of democratic citizenship and social justice' (Encarnación, 2022, 98). This is frequently viewed as a less confrontational approach and is situated in a longer history of Latin American feminists fighting for democracy under dictatorships (Morgan, 2015; Encarnación, 2022). Activists have also successfully shown how abortion restrictions lead to structural discrimination – for example by highlighting that they disproportionately prevent poor women from being able to access safe abortions and that it is also poor women who are most likely to be prosecuted (Encarnación, 2022). The individualized, pro-choice framing so often used in the global North is seen as having less political currency in Latin America than rights and discrimination framings.

That does not mean that there is always a consensus on whether legal challenges should be attempted or what those challenges should look like. For example, one abortion activist in Peru explained that there are often divisions between what kind of legal change should be fought for in a context of extreme restriction. While some argue for a pragmatic approach of fighting for *causales* (exceptions, such as in the case of rape or threat to health), as they believed that was more likely to be successful, others refused anything less than *aborto libre* (free abortion). Feminists have also shared their distrust of the judiciary, which has historically not been favourable towards Leftist movements or challenges to patriarchal structures (Ruibal, 2021). Often, activists have decided to couch abortion in a broader movement for social justice in order to mobilize a larger support base, as was successful in Argentina (Daby and Moseley, 2022).

When legal challenges have been successful in leading to more progressive abortion laws, the results are significant. As well as providing legal routes to abortion services, this also protects those who have or perform abortions from legal recriminations (Taylor, 2023). As Burton (2021, 3) reflects on the legalization of abortion in Argentina, the decision 'recognizes that abortion is licit, that it is an act that underlies a decision that does not need to give reasons or justifications', thereby reducing the paternalism and discourses of compulsory motherhood that had previously dominated. Legal routes to abortion also go beyond just practical needs, but serve as an indicator of who 'counts' as an equal citizen with full democratic rights (Sutton and Vacarezza, 2023). Progressive legal change on abortion, then, is a crucial fight, but this does not mean that legal successes can solve all the problems with abortion access.

The legal triumphs regarding abortion in Latin America in recent years can belie the challenges of implementing these laws. When legal exceptions do exist – for example, in the case of rape, foetal abnormalities, or a threat to the health of the pregnant person – the pathway to actually accessing an abortion in those circumstances tends to be unclear. Regulations are not evenly implemented, cases are often put before the legal courts, medical professionals can exempt themselves under conscientious objection rules, and the law is often interpreted over-conservatively (Sutton, 2020).

Moreover, legalization does not necessarily lead to satisfactory abortion care through formal routes. In Argentina, for instance, despite the relaxing of the abortion law in 2020, abortion continues to be a public health issue, and it has become increasingly challenging to access misoprostol given that Javier Milei's Right-wing government has been reluctant to purchase and distribute abortion medications (Gudiño Bessone, 2023; Miller and Alcoba, 2024). Likewise, as one interviewee explained about Mexico: 'What we have seen in the country [is that] legalization does not guarantee you access or that the institutions will really facilitate the service and that they will do it in a dignified way, right, free of violence.' Another interviewee in Mexico reflected on abortion being legalized in her state but has found that they 'have had to deal with so many cases in which women receive inadequate, bad, or outright dangerous instructions from medical personnel, and this will not change once it is legal'. As she noted regarding abortion access in Mexico City, where abortion was legalized in 2007, 'in reality, it is not accessible – they are two very different things. Just because it is legal does not mean that there is access.' Another interviewee in Mexico spoke of how, even in contexts with progressive laws, 'there's always going to be barriers, always, and uncomfortable situations'. Laws can also entrench inequalities. One interviewee in Mexico reflected on what happened after the legalization of abortion in the first 12 weeks in Mexico City in 2007. The new law meant that those in the capital could access legal abortions but people in other states could only do so if they had the resources and ability to travel there. While abortion continues to be geographically uneven and permitted on certain 'grounds', barriers remain (Cammarota et al, 2022).

As well as practical obstacles to access, even when abortion is legalized in certain cases, the understanding of abortion laws tends to be low. For example, in their study of abortion in Mexico, Juarez et al (2019) found that most women in their sample thought abortion was prohibited in their state, and none knew the legal criteria that would permit them to have an abortion or what penalties existed for those who flouted the law. Likewise, a study in Colombia found that participants who self-managed their abortion after its legalization chose to do so 'because they thought that abortion would not be covered through their health insurance companies, that abortions were only available under circumstances that were not applicable to them, or did not think abortion services were available at all' (Ortiz et al, 2024). Changing the law does not automatically make people aware of their legal rights or give them the confidence to seek an abortion within state healthcare frameworks.

Progressive legal changes are also not permanent. For example, President Javier Milei's ruling party began discussing overturning the 2020 abortion ruling in Argentina soon after assuming power, and the decriminalization of abortion in Colombia in 2022 received intense backlash within hours of the ruling (Daigle et al, 2022). When more permissive abortion laws are passed, it does not mean that access necessarily follows. Colombia's Constitutional Court ruling in 2022 made abortion legal on request up to 24 weeks into a pregnancy, but in practice some healthcare providers have been unwilling to provide abortions and have claimed that they lack permits or the necessary training (Taylor, 2022). In addition, even after the federal decriminalization of abortion in Mexico, some states have been attempting to rewrite their own laws to reduce abortion access. The state of Aguascalientes, for example, passed a reform in 2024 to reduce the legal time limit for an abortion to six weeks, effectively criminalizing abortion for the majority of people who access one (Red Jurídica del Clacai, 2024).

Together, these issues mean that even with the legalization of abortion or the broadening of the 'exceptions' under which an abortion is permitted, many people still prefer to seek abortion care from *acompañante* groups. For instance, after the legalization of abortion in Argentina, people seeking to end their pregnancies continue to contact the Socorristas en Red accompaniment network because they trust them or they did not want to use the healthcare system to access an abortion (Keefe-Oates et al, 2024). Similarly, in Colombia, some people still prefer to use misoprostol to self-manage their abortion outside the formal healthcare system because fears of legal repercussion remain and abortion is still stigmatized (Ortiz et al, 2024), and online sellers are continuing to sell abortion medications without a prescription despite the new progressive legal framework for abortion access in Colombia (Arango et al, 2025). Where misoprostol has been normalized as a safe and effective way to have an abortion outside healthcare systems, and the legalization of abortion does not necessarily result in access, many people still choose that route even if they can access a legal abortion. There is, therefore, clear demand for accompaniment even when legal options through healthcare providers exist. Given these issues with legal approaches, many activists have focused their efforts on social decriminalization.

Social decriminalization

Social decriminalization refers to the argument that the societal acceptance of abortion is a key precursor to progressive legal developments. By shifting public opinion in favour of abortion, the law then seems antiquated and out of touch. A social decriminalization approach aims to combat the negative sentiments that pervade abortion, including shame, guilt, secrecy, and condemnation (Vivaldi and Stutzin, 2021). This strategy recognizes the limits of the law; activists 'want to transform the meanings and perceptions of abortion so as to destigmatize the practice and build the social consensus that helps create and maintain legal reform' (Sutton and Vacarezza, 2023, 381). As Assis (2020) and others point out, the social decriminalization approach was core to the legal success in Argentina, where recent years have seen a drastic shift in public opinion about abortion. Legal challenges to not exist in isolation, then, and activist strategies such as social decriminalization have been an important tool in laying the foundation for the possibility of legal changes.

In the face of tenacious anti-abortion actors engaging in abortion lawfare, the enormous amount of work that goes into raising pro-abortion legal challenges, and the limits to the law even when more progressive measures are implemented, social decriminalization has been an important additional tool to shift public discourse on abortion. While these debates rage on, activists and *acompañantes* have continued to work to provide access to abortion regardless of the law. Through rejecting gestational periods, exceptions such as in the case of rape and stipulations about the medicalization of the procedure, *acompañantes* create abortion access in the present.

There are two main reasons why abortion *acompañantes* create abortion possibilities in the present. The first is that the law does not move quickly enough, and the second is that legal, medicalized abortions are not the goal for all. Taking the first reason, legal change is rarely fast, and Pecheny et al (2022) argue that legal change on abortion in Latin America can be encapsulated through waiting: waiting for a more favourable government, waiting for political opportunities and bills to be debated, or waiting in the streets to hear the outcome of a verdict. Waiting is ever-present. It is due to an unwillingness to wait that activists instead provide action at the margins of the state. One interviewee in Peru rationalized her accompaniment praxis as follows: 'women continue to die ... I'm not going to wait ... for Congress [to legalize abortion]'. Another framed it with: 'I know it's not going to be legal here, I don't know in how many years, but I think that if we accompany one or two, we're helping a bit so that something terrible doesn't happen, right?' Waiting is a luxury that people needing abortions do not have.

As for the second reason, as detailed in earlier chapters, regardless of the legal situation of abortion in a country, accessing an abortion can entail obstetric violence, harassment, stigma, criminalization, and barriers to access. Most people in Latin America do not have access to a legal abortion in a medical facility, and even for those who do, it is not necessarily how they want their abortion experience to be. 'States of uncare' have failed to attend to this need, so activists step in to do 'the work of the state' (Vivaldi and Stutzin, 2021, 228; Duffy et al, 2023). *Acompañantes*, therefore, provide access to safe and effective abortions at the margins of the state, outside medicalized frameworks. The 'margins of the state' are those places where law and order are incessantly re-established by the state (Das and Poole, 2004). Accompaniment practices inhabit and manipulate these spaces and work to create 'different kinds of imaginaries from those available in the official sites and representations of justice and law' (Das and Poole, 2004, 23). This alternative imaginary, one of genuine reproductive justice, may technically be illegal and in opposition to the state, but it is an urgent response to the failings of the state. *Acompañantes* are bringing a new form of abortion care into being in what has been theorized as 'prefigurative politics'.

Prefigurative politics are practices 'rooted in survival' that seek to create 'alternatives to "what is" and prefigure "what could be"' (Lin et al, 2016, 302). This does not mean that *acompañantes* are scrambling to provide abortion care that copies state approaches; they have radically reshaped what abortion care can look like through their values of a commitment to providing abortions outside medical contexts, autonomy, holistic care, and collective care. While the conditions of being forced to create this alternative imaginary of abortion care are punitive and constraining, that has not acted as a limit to creating feminist, care-filled abortion realities.

Prefigurative politics and social decriminalization approaches are not universally dismissive of the law, and decriminalization is an important and worthy aim. Yet, activists working with these principles typically don't see changing the law as the key or final aim. Rather, decriminalization is a key tool to prevent people from being judicially punished for accessing or supporting abortions and a way to ensure provision through medicalized routes for those who desire them. But there is also a rejection of the assumption that anyone should necessarily care what the state thinks at all, with the attitude of 'we will provide abortions whether you *allow* us or not'. The problem with these approaches emerges in contexts of clandestinity when abortion *acompañantes* have to develop strategies to conceal their activism and abortion care, from both legal authorities and 'unfriendly' healthcare professionals. *Acompañante* practices 'constitute an escape valve that expands citizens' sexual and reproductive choices, but because they are makeshift, illegal, or unofficial, neither availability, safety (in the case of services), nor protections of basic rights are guaranteed' (Shepard, 2000, 115). The chapter now turns to these strategies.

Strategies of concealment

Even in countries where abortion is legal, the facilitation of self-managed abortions is usually not. This is due to the medicalization of abortion, whereby it is seen as a procedure that can only be practised under the supervision of a trained medical professional. Performing an abortion outside these limits can result in prison sentences, including life imprisonment. In the most restrictive contexts, accompaniment groups are forced to work underground and can only be contacted through mutual support networks (Walsh, 2020). This means that *acompañantes* tend to be highly considered about how they protect themselves and those they are supporting to access abortions. There are some exceptions to this, and I spoke to some *acompañantes*, primarily in Mexico and Argentina, who see their public presence and outspoken approach to abortion care as a strategy to keep themselves safe. But, on the whole, they prefer to evade the gaze of the authorities.

One problem that *acompañantes* face is that their abortion care is not going to be very well known about if they remain in the shadows. Because of this, they need to manage a delicate balancing act of making sure that people who need abortions are aware of their activism while remaining discreet enough that they will not attract the ire of the state. *Acompañantes*, therefore, manoeuvre the law carefully to provide sufficient information on abortion but also ensure that the state remains ignorant about their practices. This form of secrecy keeps a select group 'in the know' and leaves a larger group, in this case the state, 'out of the loop' (Burke, 2023, 16).

One strategy of concealment has been the use of code words. These code words and euphemisms allow those who support access to abortions to create space for denial (Thiel, 2015). Explicitly using terms such as 'abortion' and 'misoprostol' does not leave room to claim denial, so other terms need to be used instead. These expectations are often clearly enforced. One abortion Facebook group in Mexico, for instance, requires users wishing to join to confirm that they will never use the word 'misoprostol' in the group. Interviewees told me the terms they use instead, but this creates a possibility of risk if I include them here, as then the opportunity to claim denial disappears. Martin et al (2023, 6) quote a respondent in their work on activist strategies in the post-Roe United States who reflected on the use of 'camping' to refer to proving a place to stay for someone travelling out of state for an abortion: 'it's not a good code if everyone's using it … it loses its power when it can be identified by the police'. Keeping the code words usable as codes is, therefore, essential.

In general, the code words used in Latin America tend to revolve around food and Catholic imagery, and as described in a 2023 *CBS News* article about abortion access in Honduras, 'the challenge is obtaining the pills – never referred to as medication abortions, or with their pharmaceutical names, but as ordinary objects, code names that change from group to group' (Verza and Riquelme, 2023). The use of code words is not unique to Latin America – for example, since Russia's invasion of Ukraine in 2022, rape has been used as a tool of war, and group of activists decided to arrange for abortion pills to enter Ukraine so that they could be used by those who needed them. In a podcast about this, the interviewees explained how, to avoid detection, they relabelled the abortion pills as vitamin C – 'Vitamin C plus was mife, and vitamin C without the plus was miso' – and they also used this as a code word (Radiolab, 2023). This is of course all situated in a much longer history of abortion providers, legitimate or not, using euphemistic code words such as 'Relief for Ladies', 'Mystic Pills', 'female troubles', and 'diseases of women' (Roberts-Ganim, 2023, 18, 19). Code words, if kept within the 'in-group', are an effective way to share information without exposure to risks.

The development of secure technologies has helped to mitigate these risks. One interviewee in Argentina recalled how a few years previously: 'we activists deployed very, uh, clandestine strategies … we all used alternative networks to communicate, we had codes to talk about medication', which she lamented made her feel like a 'dealer'. However, she noted that the advent of secure messaging apps such as Signal and Telegram have offered new levels of security. An *acompañante* in Peru explained: 'the person who is being accompanied is asked to download the application [Signal]. If they can't, well, we look for other ways, don't we? But, in general, most people do have a smartphone, don't they, in our country', so typically they are willing to download the app. Another described how members of her group typically begin a conversation with someone on WhatsApp when they are contacted, but then move over to Signal or Telegram due to the tighter security these offer. A larger collective in Peru were able to add an additional layer of security by taking out phone numbers using the name of a company so that individual names could not be connected to specific phone numbers. Another collective makes sure all of their communications go through encrypted platforms, so they use Signal as their messaging app and RiseUp, a secure email provider, for their emails. As an interviewee reflected, code words are necessary on WhatsApp but 'on Signal we can say the other things' and even share photos.

For one interviewee, based in Peru, the level of security she feels she needs depends on the context of the person she is supporting. She explained how in Peru she uses the messaging app Telegram, particularly for more advanced interruptions, which could come with greater legal scrutiny. However, when her group is contacted by countries in Latin America where anti-abortion prosecution is fiercer, 'for example, in Guatemala, Honduras, and Nicaragua', Signal is used for the initial contact but 'only for contact and then everything is face-to-face because the political persecution is very strong'. This means they need to work with other collectives in these locations to facilitate the face-to-face accompaniments.

The question of digital security is widely discussed among *acompañante* groups, and some receive specific training on it. One interviewee in Peru explained that her organization ran a specific workshop for activists working on access to safe abortion after they were contacted by people wanting support on the subject. They gave them information to help them make the best decision for their circumstances. For example, they explained the different security features of messaging platforms such as WhatsApp, Telegram, Signal, and Facebook messenger so that the activists could evaluate which best suited their needs. She described how her organization works with a range of audiences and supports them to improve digital security for their specific requirements:

> So what we do is ask them what are your needs, your doubts, your fears? And with this we can know who the bad guys are, who your adversaries are – it's the State, your ex, your family, it's the place where you work, what do I know? And with that it's like. now we can propose a way of how we can improve our habits to feel more secure.

This approach was reflected in the pragmatism displayed by an interviewee in Peru, who said: 'the measures we take must also be based on the principle of reality, right? What we can and what we cannot do'. They could not afford for everyone in the collective to have a smartphone exclusively for use in abortion accompaniment, '[one], because of resources and, two, actually, because of convenience, too, right?' So, their strategy was to use their own smartphones but to use secure, encrypted platforms so that they felt secure in their activism. In another group, in Colombia, the *acompañantes* use their own phone but they insert a specific SIM card when they are accompanying someone; also when they are supporting someone, they use an alias. As she explained: 'the idea was to give the least amount of information, like about our personal life, you know, like, ah, I work here, no, it's like, ah, I work around here nearby, not specifically where.' Another said of the approach of her group in Peru:

> When we do the training course for abortionists, well, we do address these issues of safety, of self-care, but, also, let's say that we leave it up to the discretion of the *acompañantes* themselves, what makes them feel comfortable, right? Like it is a personal decision, how much you want to expose your real identity, isn't it? ... It's an issue of security for us, but also of security for those we accompany.

Groups will typically develop what they call a 'filter' to ensure those who contact them are legitimately in need of abortion support. As one interviewee in Peru explained, 'the first thing we do is ask how they got to us, or how they got our number or our contact details'. She sees this as a successful approach because, as she put it:

> It has happened that out of the blue they have written 'Hey, you have pills, right?' and then you say 'Who is it?' or 'How did you get my number?', and they don't answer ... It has happened to me twice that I have blocked numbers because it was strange – I don't know who they were.

Another interviewee in Peru had found keeping to a strict filtering approach challenging. She recalled a case where she was contacted by a young woman: '[She] couldn't tell me who had given her my phone number, she couldn't confirm who it was from and I didn't help her.' The interviewee would only support a person who had been referred by someone known to her, and while she said this case 'left [her] with a terrible feeling', she felt that she could not continue contact with someone who 'did not pass [her] filters'. These security filters are employed not only by those who support abortions but also by those who need them. One interviewee explained: '[People] write to us from fake profiles sometimes. They say it is for security [because] it is not a legal procedure. They want security from you and from their side.' Given the number of scammers that exist, people contacting her group want peace of mind. For example, as the interviewee noted, if pills are being sent to rural areas, 'how they can be sure that they will receive it. Or that the pills are not fake. Or that the information is true. There is insecurity on their part too, not only on ours.'

Once an abortion accompaniment begins, there are additional security strategies to consider. For example, if a group handles misoprostol themselves, then they need a plan for where it is stored and with whom. As an *acompañante* in Argentina explained:

> Those of us who were visible with the organization could not have the medication. The medication was in the house of an acquaintance or a friend or a person that only one of us knew where it was. We had a very complex system so that ... we could not give the medication to all the people we accompanied, so it was a kind of filter.

It is also essential that *acompañantes* know their own legal rights. One interviewee in Peru described the key information that they needed to have: 'nobody can enter your office without a judge's order ... the police cannot come, that is forbidden, it is illegal'. As she explained: 'everybody has already learned and a series of barriers have been put in place'. At every step of the accompaniment process, strategies of concealment need to be considered.

These security strategies are important to ensure there is no evidence of abortion accompaniment in contexts that criminalize it. However, it is when people access healthcare in the case of complications that they can become exposed to judicial punishment (Salazar Vega, 2019). Abortion is unique in being both a medical procedure and a criminal act, and this has led to medical staff often serving as the frontline of abortion criminalization (Roth, 2020). To avoid prosecution, it is essential that if people having an abortion seek medical care, they are able to hide that their situation was self-provoked. The properties of misoprostol are helpful here. The effects of using the medication are indistinguishable from that of a spontaneous miscarriage, and as long as no residue is found from using it vaginally, a doctor will not be able to tell whether misoprostol was used – that is, as long as the person having the abortion does not confess.

Acompañantes frequently 'train' those they support to make sure they know what to say in front of medical staff if they experience complications such as excessive bleeding and need medical care. Knowing how to 'perform' the role of someone who is experiencing a spontaneous miscarriage creates a 'theatre of ignorance'. Some people will choose to act distressed that they are experiencing a miscarriage of a desired pregnancy, while others will pretend they didn't even know they were pregnant. A convincing act will mean that medical staff won't have any reason to report it as a potential self-induced abortion, even if they suspect it may have been. For Necochea López (2014, 77) there is 'a form of power at work here, a subaltern kind of power that denies access to the "truth" or at least to a confession'. As an *acompañante* in Mexico found, doctors can suspect an abortion all they want 'but there is no way to corroborate it'.

Some *acompañantes* will use 'scripts' to practise with those having the abortion, to ensure they are prepared in the event of having to seek medical care. As an interviewee in Argentina put it, 'we teach women to lie'. They will typically report that they 'started bleeding out of nowhere' and can list the symptoms and timescale of the 'miscarriage'. As an interviewee in Peru explained, 'we always tell them that if they go to the clinic because it hurts a lot or something like that, they should always say that they started bleeding out of the blue'. At the hospital, another explained: 'they can surely question you about what happened. But they have no way of seeing that it was the misoprostol.' An interviewee in Colombia found people she supported with an abortion were often sceptical about a doctor not being able to detect their use of misoprostol, so she had to spend a long time reassuring them. But if they did need to seek medical care, they needed to understand how to behave there, because, as she explained:

> Some doctors in Colombia make a bad assumption when a woman arrives with an *aborto* [miscarriage/abortion], so, of course, we always told them that if you use misoprostol, nothing is going to happen. If

it does happen, you have to go to the clinic, they will … they may ask you, it is very violent, isn't it, to ask you if you had an abortion, what pills you took? I mean, they don't even … many times they don't even ask 'Did you have an abortion?' Instead they ask 'What pills did you take and who gave them to you?' So, we said that's a bluff. They don't know and there is no way to know – this is not detected in the blood, okay? So, sometimes, too, we would do like a little rehearsal of what things they could tell that happened.

Another interviewee, in Peru, said:

We always practise the discourse before, what to say, what not to say, what they cannot force you to say. They can't force you to confess, so to speak. They can't force you. You are going to indicate that you didn't know you were pregnant, that you have come and that you don't know anything. So they can get you taken care of as quickly as possible.

An *acompañante* in Mexico told me:

I tell them they are going to play the role of their life, right. If they have to go to the doctor, they are going to have to pretend that they really loved … we call what is expelled a product, but there, yes, we tell them they are going to have to call it a baby; it is a whole change, which is *fuerte* [strong], but it is the only strategy they have left. … But, they can't go to the hospital and say I have my product here, I mean, and they have to cry and say like, yes, they really wanted that baby, right?

She explained that they cover this information briefly when they begin accompanying someone but noted:

If the bleeding is no longer normal, we have to start a haemorrhage protocol. If we see that it doesn't stop, then, yes, and yes you have to say this. Remember they can't detect the misoprostol unless you say so. So, it's kind of a lot of reinforcement that they don't self-incriminate, right? You make sure you say this. It doesn't matter, they're going to tell you a thousand lies and it's not like that, is it? So it's like we have a period in which we reinforce everything that we said before, right, but that maybe they hadn't paid much attention to because it's a lot of information … So, well, we remember it, but … and at that moment, we reinforce like this. Don't incriminate yourself.

For another interviewee, in Peru, their approach is 'to empower women and tell them "you can go to a health service. You just have to be very careful about what you say and nobody can stop you, nobody can blame you for anything."' She continued:

> [We are] giving these tools to women who need to go to public services because, in reality, care for an incomplete abortion, for post-abortion care is denied in our country, isn't it, and we are not obliged, that is to say that we did or did not provoke an abortion. The health services, as we tell women, are obliged to provide healthcare, not to file complaints, right? So, we have to say it with the certainty, with the knowledge, with the laws, so that they can say 'okay, I am going to go and say such and such'.

One interviewee, a Peruvian obstetrician, recalled the fear and uncertainty that existed before these protocols were developed. She remembered that in 1990, she was contacted by the sister of someone who had used misoprostol and was in pain from an incomplete abortion. The woman was refusing to go to the hospital for fear she would be put in jail. The interviewee went to this woman's house and found that she had used misoprostol vaginally and orally and at too low a dose to be effective, resulting in the incomplete abortion. There was no more misoprostol available to complete the abortion, so they had to go to the hospital, but, she noted: 'before I went, I took care of cleaning the vagina well – that is to say, we had to do those things, to not leave evidence'. Then, at the hospital, medical staff were questioning the interviewee as a medical professional, but she was able to feign ignorance and say 'as far as I know, she hasn't taken anything'. The use of protocols discourages the use of misoprostol vaginally and gives people the confidence to seek medical care, knowing that their use of misoprostol cannot be detected.

In contexts of clandestinity and prosecution of self-managed abortions, strategies of concealment are vital to protect the identities of those who accompany abortions as well as those who experience them. Whether it be using code words so that those on the 'outside' cannot prove that misoprostol is being discussed, using secure technologies to ensure that conversations remain private, or using 'scripts' to practise feigning a spontaneous miscarriage, techniques of secrecy act to protect those involved. *Acompañantes* ensure that 'unfriendly' medical professionals and anti-abortion law authorities cannot prove that an induced abortion has occurred, even if they suspect one. Even when abortion is an 'open secret' (Kimball, 2020), actually proving one has taken place is challenging.

The shield of healthcare

In contrast to the levels of secrecy discussed in the previous section, many *acompañantes* are vocal and visible about their activism, and they argue that they are not flouting any laws since 'information is legal'. Even while abortion itself is not legal in most Latin American countries, providing information and pre- and post-abortion services usually are, and, furthermore, many countries do not criminalize the importation of prescription drugs for personal use (Rowlands, 2012; Assis and Erdman, 2022). Singer (2022) terms this an 'alegal' grey zone as groups carefully navigate the boundaries of what can be said and what needs to remain opaque. In this way, *acompañantes* navigate their activism where there are no laws that directly restrict support for abortions and use strategies to work outside the law but not necessarily in direct contravention of it (Duffy, 2024). Thus, *acompañantes* use the shield of healthcare by interpreting abortion laws broadly, drawing on the World Health Organization (WHO) guidelines, providing information through the use of the third person, and working alongside medical professionals.

Abortion 'on request' is prohibited across most Latin American countries but there are 'exceptions' such as in the case of rape, foetal unviability, and risk to the health of the pregnant person. These exceptions tend to be highly challenging to access in practice and involve petitions through healthcare and legal routes. *Acompañantes*, however, use the existence of these exceptions to make the case that abortions should be legally permissible in these cases, and they support people to access them where the state is failing in their duty. Through applying 'a broad understanding of the health exception', activists interpret the law in ways that make direct action such as abortion support or provision of information about abortion possible (Ruibal and Fernández Anderson, 2020, 705). While some states have claimed that this health exception should only be used when someone's health is in imminent danger, it can also be used where there is 'the possibility or likelihood of an adverse effect on or harm to the woman's health if the pregnancy continued' (González, 2012, 22).

A common strategy to interpret laws more broadly has been to argue that self-managed abortions respond to the need for abortions where the pregnant person's health is at risk. I spoke to one interviewee in Colombia before the 2022 ruling that made abortions available on request up to the 24th week of pregnancy. As she explained:

> We talk a little bit about the Colombian law specifically. So, that is when we explain to them that according to the law and according to the World Health Organization, they are not really doing anything illegal and that nowhere in the law does it say that people cannot give information about abortion, so we are not doing anything illegal either.

Similarly, in Argentina, before the 2020 ruling there, *acompañantes* argued, based on their interpretation of the law's health exception, that they were able to provide information about self-managed abortions (Ruibal and

Fernández Anderson, 2020). For them, an unwanted pregnancy is a clear threat to psychological health. As one interviewee in Argentina told me, 'everyone has the right to have an abortion because their overall health is at risk, so I give them the medication'. This strategy has been used not just by individual *acompañante* collectives, but also, in more formal ways, by sexual and reproductive health advocates. In 2008, a group of allies across Latin America created a network to systematize the application of the health exception within a human rights framework to better facilitate access to abortion services (González, 2012). These approaches have had some success – for instance, in 2015, 99.3 per cent of abortions reported by the Department of Health in Bogotá were performed under the health and/or life exception (Küng et al, 2018), and this has validated its use for *acompañantes* across Latin America as well. In this way, it is activists and advocates more broadly who are providing much-needed healthcare, using their states' own language.

Moreover, some *acompañantes* argued that because their own governments are buying misoprostol, they cannot then claim that it is dangerous and illegal. For one interviewee in Peru,

> misoprostol is not an illegal drug. Misoprostol is a legal drug, it is a drug that is used within the protocol of care for therapeutic abortions, which is legal in Peru ... misoprostol is used in gynecobstetrics, so it is an essential medicine for health according to the WHO, so they buy, the state buys their misoprostol.

Similarly, an interviewee in Colombia, speaking to me before the 2022 ruling on abortion, stated that they had no qualms about handling misoprostol because

> in Colombia, both misoprostol and mifepristone are medicines that are used for the practice of abortion, so there is no clandestine scenario or anything like that. There is simply an ... we have an agreement, a contract with whoever sells us the medicines and we bring them into the country because they are already accepted in the health plan.

Another approach taken by activists in relation to the provision of healthcare has been to draw on international and public health frameworks to validate their 'information provision'. Among the interviewees in this study, it was the WHO guidelines that were referred to most commonly. The WHO guidelines state that self-managed medical abortions are 'safe when individuals have a source of accurate information and access to a healthcare provider when needed or desired at any stage of the process' (Veldhuis et al, 2022b, 379). They also classify misoprostol as an essential medicine, and these two factors, safety and necessity, have provided *acompañantes* with an international, trusted set of resources to point to. In the words of an *acompañante* in Mexico:

> The point is that women should not be left without the right to have access to safe abortion. And I don't just say abortion, that's why I say safe abortion, with clear, reliable, scientific information. I mean, we, for example, when we accompany women, we always say, let's see, the protocol was not invented by us, it is endorsed by the World Health Organization, full stop, always.

This also came up in Peru when an interviewee told me: 'Now, for safety, we always refer to what is established within the protocol or the WHO, because that somehow gives us a degree of legal security. It is not just recommended by us, it is scientific information and it is a right.'

By using the shield that 'providing information is legal', *acompañantes* can be more public about their activism. As an interviewee in Peru explained:

> We use materials and information like pamphlets and brochures from different organizations. I go by the Colectiva por la Libre Información para las Mujeres, CLIM, which is a very good collective in terms of giving information that is legal in the country about misoprostol, about the effects, the side effects, etc. This can be provided legally.

Another, Sandra in Mexico, has always been highly visible about her abortion activism and has been profiled in the Mexican and international press. She remarked: 'we have done it without a problem and everyone knows it, and we post it on Facebook and we have done training in the women's institutes – the prosecutors here know it'. She does not sell misoprostol, and that is the key differentiation between committing a crime and providing legal information. While she is frequently told that she could get arrested, as she said: 'we haven't had any problems, everyone knows it, it's open'.

This provision of information is often deployed carefully in order to avoid incrimination. *Acompañantes* are very aware of the points at which the law can be played with, knowing precisely what can and cannot be said – for example, they often give information using the third person exclusively. This was explained by one interviewee in Peru:

> Now, all this information we provide is in the third person – that is, for example, I am not going to address you and say 'Cordelia, you can't take this', no. The way we provide the information is in the third person. The way we provide information, and this is one of our strategies to take care of ourselves as well, is how we try to be a little bit … like

having some distance and saying 'women who use misoprostol should not do such and such and such'.

In a similar manner, an interviewee in Venezuela who accompanied abortions in a clinic-setting explained:

> This very specific part, normally what you do as a clinic counsellor, is this trick with the language. You say something like if, you never use 'you', you never use 'I', you never use it. It's very weird, but it's 'the WHO recommends that if someone needs an abortion', 'if that person needs an abortion', 'the person' or 'the abortion seeker' or any of that, like you know you never make a direct reference to someone. Because what we fear in the clinics is that there's someone from an anti-rights group wired up and all of this. It sounds very ridiculous, but it's a lot of what you do, a lot of what I used to do when I was a clinic volunteer. So that's what you can say in a very, I don't know, in a very, very unpersonal way, because in that way you're following something that is … you're giving information, you're not giving a clinical advice or giving the pills.

This came up time and again in interviews, with Peruvian *acompañantes* telling me:

> In order not to have problems with the legal framework of our country, we have to give it [information] in the third person.

> At least in writing, we don't give them more information than we should, but like 'you can read this guide', or 'the WHO recommends such and such' – never say 'I recommend such and such', or 'I tell you this' or 'you should do this' if we don't know them yet. We make it a little bit more indirect.

And another in Mexico explained that they used this approach on their abortion hotline: 'we tried to do it in the third person mainly because we were advised that legally it could be a defence, right? It's, I didn't tell her to take misoprostol but … "a person who wants to have an abortion can go to the pharmacy and buy that."' This third person approach to abortion care has given *acompañantes* a layer of legal protection as they are able to legally share information about how to access a safe abortion in their country without incriminating themselves.

As discussed in Chapter 2, some *acompañante* groups have medical professionals as part of their contingency while others set up friendly relationships with them. This provides an additional shield of healthcare so that in the rare event of complications, the person experiencing the abortion will be able to seek care somewhere trusted and with someone trained in miscarriage management. These 'friendly' health system professionals work with *acompañantes* to guarantee rights and are committed to treating those seeking medical help with respect and care (Burton, 2017b). Not all medical professionals are inherently conservative or anti-abortion; rather, they exist on a continuum, encompassing 'those health professionals who act as insider activists from the public health system and reproduce a discourse of rights with regard to abortion and those activists who contribute to building networks from a multiplicity of approaches' (Fernández Vázquez and Szwarc, 2018, 175).

I spoke to one such 'friendly' obstetrician in Peru who straddled being a medical professional and an *acompañante*. She spoke of how the privileges of her position allowed her 'to deal a lot with the insecurity'. She felt less vulnerable due to her status, and that meant that she could perform roles that others couldn't, including purchasing misoprostol. Another interviewee, also a doctor in Peru, explained that those who work for a hospital have more freedom in prescribing misoprostol 'because there you're endorsed by the hospital label: hospital use'; 'the prescription is the indication that you can give to the patient, but under the hospital letterhead, so it's like you're using it formally within the hospital'. She explained that this was different from a doctor prescribing it from their own clinic, where 'there is a whole halo of persecution, of fear'; as she elaborated: 'I don't know anybody who wants to put their stamp under the word misoprostol. Among health professionals ... there's a lot of fear that they will link you, that they will link you to the topic' of abortion. Being a healthcare provider certainly does not eliminate the risk of being associated with abortion, but for *acompañante* groups, having alliances with healthcare providers does help them in their claim of providing essential healthcare when that is being denied by the state, and of having back-up in the rare event of complications.

In the event of complications, many *acompañantes* would prefer to have a 'friendly' contact at a private clinic rather than attend a public hospital. Hospitals were frequently viewed as more hostile spaces where the risk of being reported to the authorities for a suspected abortion was higher. This was detailed by one interviewee in Peru:

> If I saw any additional external complication, for example, bleeding or swelling, the protocol was to take her to a private obstetrician, no matter what. Because I also thought about what would happen if I went to the hospital, there would be much more exposure not only for them, but also for me. So the option has always been a private obstetrician.

Another interviewee in Peru had an alliance with a private gynaecologist who they referred people to not just in the event of complications, but for post-abortion care, because 'it gives them more security'. When supporting abortions outside legal frameworks, having these contacts was seen as a key way to provide legal and healthcare security. These health professionals use what Suh and McReynolds-Pérez (2023, 398) term 'subversive epidemiology' to 'routinely obscure the incidence of abortion and refuse to involve the criminal justice system' in cases of suspected induced abortions and are thereby 'obstructing the functioning of the state with regard to the regulation and discipline of women who seek out or complete induced abortions'.

Across Latin America, *acompañantes* use a shield of healthcare by interpreting abortion laws more broadly, drawing on international and national guidelines, providing information through the use of the third person, and working alongside medical professionals to ensure abortion access when it has been denied by the state while simultaneously staying on the right side of the law. One interviewee in Argentina saw this as a way of taking the moral high ground, saying: 'because we were very clear that it was to give information and [that] to accompany, that does not constitute any kind of crime. In fact, we were even reducing the number of unsafe abortions and their effects.' This, however, does not mean that *acompañantes* have been free from persecution and harassment.

Legal threats

The persecution of people who self-manage their abortions, or are suspected of doing so, is fairly well known across Latin America. This has a distinct geography and is particularly heightened in Central America. El Salvador, for example, has one of the world's most restrictive abortion laws and women and girls who experience miscarriages, stillbirths, or obstetric complications are actively prosecuted, with dozens of women imprisoned for up to 40 years if they are found guilty of aggravated homicide. Health professionals who suspect an abortion may have taken place are obliged to report it to the police, and if they fail to do so, they can face 12 years in prison and the removal of their licence to practise medicine (Women Resisting Violence Collective, 2022). This has given El Salvador the shameful title of first Latin American country to routinely incarcerate people who experience stillbirths and other obstetrical emergencies for the crime of homicide (Encarnación, 2022).

In Peru, 571 women have been taken to court accused of intentionally terminating their pregnancies and the number of complaints filed by the public prosecutor's office is far higher (Salazar, 2019), and in Mexico, 3568 people were reported to the police under suspicion of procuring or providing an abortion between 2007 and 2016 (Grupo De Información en Reproductión Elegida, 2018). Those targeted are disproportionately economically marginalized (Fernández Anderson, 2016). Therefore, while only a small fraction of those who self-manage their abortions in Latin America are prosecuted for this, it is still a possibility, and the stigma of being questioned for this 'crime' has a wider impact on that person and their families.

Persecution is also a real possibility for those who support people to have abortions. For example, one case I have written about with colleagues elsewhere shows the 'other side' of the *marea verde* in Argentina (Drovetta et al, 2023). Despite the ruling in 2020 legalizing elective abortion up to 14 weeks of pregnancy, abortion stigma and persecution still exist in Argentina. In December 2022, four members of the Socorristas en Red abortion network were arrested in Villa Maria, Córdoba. After an anonymous complaint and investigation for the 'illegal practice of medicine', the activists were arrested and detained for six days while their case continued. This case is a clear example of abortion activists being purposefully targeted, for three reasons. First, the 'illegal practice of medicine' is a crime that does not require detainment in prison. Second, two of the activists were abroad at the time and were arrested dramatically at the airport even though they had presented a written statement through their lawyer to say they would return to Argentina as requested. Third, the Public Prosecutor's Office used an adjacent offence, that of the illegal practice of medicine, even after abortion had been made legal in the country. The was, therefore, a case of 'abortion exceptionalism' that only served to whip up anti-abortion sentiment and insinuate that abortion is a risky, shadowy practice performed by criminals. Had these activists been 'illegally' practising another form of healthcare, such as alleviating joint pain or supporting hormone therapy, would they have received this level of legal scrutiny and drama? The arrest of the Socorristas shows that abortion activists are at risk of criminalization even in the region's more liberal abortion contexts.

This did not take place in a vacuum. One interviewee in Argentina noted that her group had to 'organize ... and also, uh, be in close contact with lawyers'; as she explained: 'we had situations of ... there were no lawsuits, but there were cases that were opened for possession of medication'. These strategies by the authorities can be understood as a form of abortion lawfare that takes up valuable activist hours and energy and prevents them from getting on with the 'real work' of supporting abortions. The same interviewee remembered a time when the home of a colleague was raided and 'they found the medication [misoprostol] which was, I don't know, like three pills, which is not even enough for one treatment'. She explained: 'the case was later dismissed, she was not convicted, nothing happened. But it was a very scary moment. At that moment, we all discarded all the medication we had, we stopped giving it, uh, we paused, like for months.' These legal threats have a 'chilling' effect and impact the capacity of people around the person targeted to continue their activism.

One interviewee in Peru spoke about the types of harassment that her group has received. She explained that at times it has been physical intimidation, such as when she went to a lecture at a university with the title 'It's called abortion, not menstrual delay' and aggressive anti-abortion activists shouted at people they deemed to be pro-abortion and surrounded them entirely. She said that it didn't escalate any further but 'it was a very violent experience'. Her group also received notarized letters from a member of a 'pro-life' group. She said: '[he was] sending his threats and saying that I don't know what and that he was going to denounce us in the Peruvian laws'. This didn't bother her at all; 'go on then, which one?' was her response. In addition, her group has been subject to 'the kind of thing that is not uncontrollable', such as members' email address being listed on gay porn sites so that they receive unwanted mail. Another interviewee in Peru had similar experiences, such as receiving attention for campaigning on a particular event, which resulted in rape threats by telephone and mail as well as insults and people spitting on her in public. She reflected that while she has been involved in abortion activism for 20 years, the harassment has been worsening as abortion has become more prominent in public and political discourse and the anonymity provided by social media has led to threats becoming more common.

I asked another interviewee in Peru if she had ever experienced harassment and her response was 'yes, of course!' Her collective had experienced threats from the public as well as the police, but she noted:

> happily, after a while in activism you achieve a certain resilience with the harassment in the networks above all. So what we do now is not read, to block, not to read, to block. We have learned to manage it, to take care of ourselves like this, because before it was like we read everything, but I tell them 'no, girls we are not going to read them, we are not going to fall like this'.

For one interviewee in Mexico, it was at in-person events that she experienced the most harassment. As she described:

> There was a demonstration a few years ago when the police went and, well, in a very violent way, they practically kidnapped people, didn't they? Because they just picked them up. So, a friend of mine was being taken away, and since then we've been more cautious, because it's not effective and it's a very big risk. We've already experienced these police abuses, haven't we, in a very close way, so we prefer to stop doing it.

This has not been entirely from conservative actors. One interviewee in Peru has experienced online harassment in the form of people cloning her group's

Facebook page and hacking their blog. They believe it 'has not even been the conservative groups'; she said: 'It has been the clandestine businesses that see us as a threat, so they impersonate us.' While she was unsure whether conservative groups could have been prompting the clandestine clinics to do it, it created extra work for her small and under-resourced group, who then had to set up an online presence again.

Given that most of this harassment stems from anti-abortion actors and their discourses, to understand the context of these threats and persecution, it is necessary to understand the current situation regarding anti-abortion debates in Latin America.

While anti-abortion discourses are far from new, the last two decades have seen the introduction of new actors and strategies, which have grown in strength in recent years. A large part of this is due to the growth in evangelical representatives in party politics over the past two decades, having gained positions in Argentina, Bolivia, Costa Rica, Brazil, Chile, Honduras, El Salvador, Mexico, and Peru, among others (Machado et al, 2022). Political candidates are expected to state their position on abortion, and those who stand on the pro-abortion side can suffer orchestrated political attacks. Standing as a pro-abortion candidate or party can mean serious electoral damage or even worse. In 2011, a public hearing on abortion in Argentina's legislature 'erupted in violence when abortion opponents physically attacked a member of the Chamber of Deputies, Victoria Donda of the Encuentro Social y Popular (Popular and Social Encounter)' (Marcus-Delgado, 2019, 21). While Donda was unharmed, this episode shows the gravity of even holding a meeting to discuss abortion rights.

Anti-abortion actors develop targeted strategies to influence political decision making. Cross-platform pro-life campaigning, such as the Vote for Life; Vote for a Candidate Who Defends Life campaign, has given anti-abortion discourses a new prominence, especially in Brazil and Peru (Machado et al, 2022). In the last few years, these actors have adapted their strategy, moving away from the overt criminalization of women who have abortions and instead claiming to be defending the rights of women and children through a discourse of 'protection'. This can be seen through the *salvemos las dos vidas* (let's save both lives) campaign that emerged in Argentina in 2018 and has since spread to other Latin American countries (Machado et al, 2022). Anti-abortion neo-conservative groups in Ecuador, for example, have also exploited the lack of data about abortion in order to manipulate their own facts and figures (Torres, 2022). Another strategy has been to step back from religious arguments and draw on research on genetics, embryology, and bioethics to root arguments in science and law (Machado et al, 2022).

Across Latin America, then, anti-abortion actors have been mobilizing and developing new strategies, often drawing on methods proven to be successful for progressive aims, in order to strengthen their hand in the political arena as well as in public discourse. On the one hand, this can fortify pro-abortion activism. As one interviewee in Costa Rica explained: 'It is true that we have a fairly large conservative movement that in the last few years, I think that also because of our counter-fight for legal abortion, has expanded more ... as a response.' On the other hand, it has emboldened anti-abortion harassment and led to the experiences narrated by the activists here.

Does the state care?

Much of this book has detailed the ways in which Latin American states have failed to provide abortions, even in the circumstances where they are permitted, leaving *acompañantes* to respond by developing their own feminist, empathetic approaches to supporting safe and effective abortion care. This section first explores why and how Latin American states have chosen to remain 'strategically ignorant' of the topic of abortion and then examines what happens when states do decide to take responsibility for abortion. The examples illustrate why and how states have shied away from tackling abortion as a legal issue and why some states choose to legislate abortion as their strategy of reproductive governance.

Across most of Latin America, abortion can be described as an 'open secret', as people generally know that abortions are possible and common, even where they are not permitted by law (Kimball, 2020). Shepard (2000, 111) terms this the 'double discourse system' – the maintenance of 'the status quo in repressive or negligent public policies while expanding private sexual and reproductive choices behind the scenes'. In this case, it is *acompañantes* who have worked to expand abortion access behind the scenes because of repressive and negligent abortion policies. The result is distance between abortion laws on paper and abortion access in practice.

The reason for this, Sandra Rodríguez and I argue (2024b), is that states choose 'strategic ignorance' to avoid the thorny political and public health issues around abortion. Strategic ignorance is a concept that has been mainly theorized within sociology to explore how ignorance is not an accidental fact or a neutral absence of knowledge; rather, ignorance is just as socially constructed as knowledge (Reser and Smithson, 1988; Sanabria, 2016). For the sociologist Linsey McGoey (2020, 198), strategic ignorance can be defined as 'the structural ability to exploit the unknowns in an environment in order to gain more power or resources', making it something that can be cultivated, including for nefarious political ends (Stankiewicz, 2009; Halliday, 2018). Latin American states have largely chosen to 'remain ignorant' about abortion and not address it as a public issue. This has happened in three ways: failing to provide legal routes to abortion through exceptions, not monitoring the true number of abortions in the country, and only prosecuting a relatively small number of abortions. As a result, states can claim 'wilful blindness' (McGoey, 2019) so that abortions that do not happen, are not measured, and are not prosecuted do not exist. If these abortions do not exist, then they are not a problem of governance and the risks of actively dealing with abortion can be avoided.

First, states give the illusion of meeting human rights needs while not delivering on them in practice. Most countries in Latin America allow abortions in specific circumstances, such as rape, foetal inviability, and risk to the health or life of the pregnant person, and that means these countries can avoid international scrutiny from groups such as the Inter-American Court of Human Rights. However, in reality, these exceptions are hard to access and most people who meet them will not know they exist, have time to apply for them, or have the desire to face the legal scrutiny and bureaucracy required when it does not even guarantee the abortion will be allowed or that there will be a medical professional willing to perform it (Pilecco et al, 2021). The states with these restrictions are failing to provide accessible information about legal routes for abortions, failing to provide legal and medical training on the procedure, and failing to provide clear regulations on abortion (Gianella and Álvarez, 2021). This creates confusion and misinformation about the legal position of abortion (Palomino et al, 2011). The result of the obfuscation is that fewer people are accessing these routes, which in turn makes it appear as though abortions are a form of healthcare that is not in high demand. States are able to produce their own strategic ignorance through creating ambiguity and demonstrating an apparent lack of need for abortions.

Second, states strategically remain ignorant on the true figures on abortion access in their countries. In contexts where abortion is completely criminalized or heavily restricted, the official abortion rate will be low, and the state can feign that abortions are rare and, therefore, do not need to be legislated on. Estimates on actual abortion rates are collated by non-governmental organizations and research centres, so these countries are not producing their own 'official' national data on abortion. They are therefore preventing themselves from knowing the state of abortion in their country as well as the severity of maternal mortality and health risks from abortions that are accessed unsafely. The 'dangerous' abortions that are known about can then be written off as deviance rather than situations that have been allowed to exist due to the failure of states and their (lack of) public health policy. Kumar et al (2009, 629) call this the 'prevalence paradox', meaning 'the social construction of deviance despite the high incidence of abortion'. In this way, stigma associated with abortion is reinforced, people are less likely to speak out in favour of abortion, and the state is less likely to be pushed to legislate on it.

Third, most states have relatively low prosecution rates for abortion. It is apparent from the abortion rate estimates that the criminalization of abortion does not prevent them from happening (Faúndes and Shah, 2015).

Acompañantes and activists evade detection to protect themselves and those they are supporting, but few states are actively pursuing and surveilling people who they suspect of having abortions. This is because if states were more actively pursuing cases, it would open a window on the true scale of abortion access, revealing that millions of abortions take place every year in the region. That would show that states were powerless to prevent abortions despite the restrictions put in place, and it would force states to reckon with the reality of abortion in their country. It would even likely reveal how it is the countries with the strictest abortion laws that have the highest mortality rates (Latt et al, 2019). By doing just enough abortion lawfare to uphold the need for (some) secrecy around abortion while also keeping the prosecution rate relatively low, the state can maintain the illusion that its surveillance mechanisms are effective.

These three failures mean that states are deliberately choosing to 'not know' about the problem of abortion. By choosing to remain ignorant, states can avoid having to legislate on abortion and all the political risks, loss of deep-pocketed funders, and controversy that come with that. Abortion is framed as an exceptional, deviant act which, in turn, justifies the need for it to be heavily regulated. The state continues to fail to provide access to safe abortions, so actors such as *acompañantes* step in to attend to this need. Ironically, these actors can flourish in the margins of the law that the state has left unattended, and the state remains largely blind to abortions that occur beyond state regulatory systems. The wielding of strategic ignorance means that abortion continues to be criminalized and clandestine while, at the same time, the conditions where those clandestine abortions can be made possible and kept hidden are cultivated.

However, this can make it seem that this cycle of state ignorance and enforced clandestinity is permanent. As recent legal changes in Argentina, Mexico, and Colombia have shown, states that previously shied away from looking at and discussing abortion can change their approach. But why do some states decide to take responsibility for abortion? As I argue here, this is not necessarily a feminist move, but one that governs abortion in new ways. Here, Argentina, which in December 2020 passed Law 27.610 to permit abortions within the first 14 weeks of pregnancy, can be seen as an example of a state that has chosen to take responsibility for abortion in new ways.

Before the 2020 ruling, abortions were only permitted in cases of rape or when the mother's health was at risk, but clandestine abortions still occurred at high rates. As one interviewee in Argentina described, the government did not want to discuss abortion, but it also did not want to prosecute it:

> It was more the idea of maintaining the stigma, of not discussing the stigma. That is, this society had decided that abortion was wrong and did not want to discuss it publicly. Now, there was total tolerance. There was practically no criminal prosecution. If there was, it was very little and the cases in which abortion was criminally prosecuted were

for … situations, well, maybe when there was a complication and the person who had an abortion had, well, she went to the hospital, it was seen that the abortion was done in bad conditions, maybe they tried to investigate, but in general not, almost none. But maybe a family member would file a complaint.

Argentina at this time was a clear example of a state employing strategic ignorance to look away from the realities of abortion.

Yet, in March 2018, then Argentine president Mauricio Macri surprised many when he publicly declared his support for a 'responsible and mature' national debate on the legal status of abortion (Daby and Moseley, 2022, 359). It is this framing of 'being responsible' that can be used to explore the move from ignorance to taking responsibility. This is not a 'turning off' of ignorance as such, but a reckoning with a societal issue. Scholars have been looking to Argentina to understand the path that took a Catholic country with a conservative government under Macri from highly restrictive abortion laws to Law 27.610. Policy reform is subject to numerous variables, such as executive branch preferences, how party systems function, and how activists form alliances with those in power (Fernández Anderson, 2020), but the implementation of pro-abortion rights is improbable without a broad ideological interparty coalition (Zaremberg and Rezende de Almeida, 2022, 70). This coalition is what got the law across the line, but Macri was forced to take responsibility for abortion in the first instance due to the immense pressure placed on him by the massive feminist mobilization that took place in the country from 2015 with the Ni Una Menos (Not One [Woman] Less) movement (Daby and Moseley, 2022).

The Ni Una Menos movement began in response to the murders of women in Argentina and mobilized substantial numbers of citizens to decry femicide and gender violence. This mass mobilization was extended to abortion, but predominantly through a social justice framing (Daby and Moseley, 2022). By highlighting the social inequities of the criminalization of abortion that disproportionately harm marginalized people, activists were able to transform the abortion debate in Argentina. But this was not a quick transformation. Earlier debates on abortion, in 2018, were rejected in the Senate, so what happened in the subsequent two years to lead to the legalization in 2020 of abortion on request up to 14 weeks of pregnancy? Interviewees in Argentina pointed to the feminist movement that: used a public health discourse based on the rates of maternal mortality related to unsafe abortions; included well-known celebrities, who set out why they were pro-abortion, in campaigns; and created a public spectacle of the legal debates by setting up large screens in public areas to broadcast the hearings. By bringing abortion into public consciousness, political candidates were pressured to 'come out' on the abortion issue. In this way, beginning with

Macri and up to the introduction of Law 27.610, immense pressure was put on politicians to take responsibility for abortion in Argentina and to reckon with the societal injustices wreaked by the criminalization of abortion.

States can, therefore, move away from criminalization as the primary mode of abortion governance. However, that does not mean that providers and individuals can cease their strategy of maintaining ignorance on the part of the authorities. Unless fully decriminalized, when abortion becomes sanctioned, it does so within the confines of the legal and medical sphere. Argentina's law allows voluntary abortion up to 14 weeks of gestation, and 'voluntary' was commonly read as meaning in any setting that the pregnant person chooses. This was shown not to be the case when the four activists in Villa Maria, Córdoba, were arrested in December 2022 on the charge of 'illegal practice of medicine'. Even when abortion itself is legal, adjacent laws can be used to criminalize activists. This case exemplifies the complexities that arise when the state directly addresses abortion. It took responsibility for abortion, but it did so on its own terms, and that resulted in increased attention and surveillance of those supporting autonomous abortions.

The case of Argentina also exemplifies that the legalization of abortion does not stop the (attempted) re-legislation of it. Libertarian and conservative president Javier Milei was elected to office in December 2023 on a platform that was explicitly anti-abortion. While at the time of writing there has been no formal legislation on the issue, he has been vocal in his belief that 'abortion is murder' and a politician from his party has introduced a bill in Congress that seeks to re-criminalize it (AFP, 2024).

State governance of abortion can change. When it is expedient to do so, states can move toward the liberalization of abortion and away from the enforced clandestinity and selective 'looking away' from it. The decision to 'take responsibility' for the harms of abortion criminalization was notably structured around social justice inequities in Argentina. But as the arrests in Córdoba illustrate, taking responsibility is also a paternalist act and the clandestinity that provided a shield of ignorance for abortion providers and those seeking abortions has been replaced by the eyes of the state. This is state governance, on the state's terms. This taking of responsibility can result in support and information for those wanting an abortion, but it can also lead to increased surveillance of abortions that occur outside the parameters set by the state. To genuinely address the harms and inequities of abortion criminalization, and stigma, then, full decriminalization and autonomy are necessary.

The law is the floor, not the ceiling

The law is ever-present in discussions of abortion in Latin America. Legal change is an important step towards the reduction of stigma, better conditions to guarantee rights, and more support for abortion providers (Fernández Vázquez and Brown, 2019). But legalization does not necessarily result in access for those who need abortions, it does not mean that all people understand the law or know about it, and it does not prevent the state from surveilling abortion seekers and activists (Drovetta et al, 2023; Ortiz et al, 2024). Legalization was frequently seen as a secondary issue for interviewees since they would continue to support people with their abortions regardless of the legal situation. They knew that abortions are necessary when abortion is criminalized, but they also knew that abortions are needed or desired outside the healthcare system even when abortion is legal. Legalization is, therefore, a positive step in most cases, but not the solution to all abortion needs. As one interviewee in Colombia put it, 'the law is the floor, not the ceiling'.

The strategies outlined in this chapter, of fighting for social decriminalization through prefigurative politics, of tactics employed to prevent detection, of use of the 'shield of healthcare' to legitimize abortion care, and ways to deal with the legal threats and harassment that come from this activism, are a result of being forced into clandestinity. For Shepard (2000, 115), such strategies can be seen as necessary 'escape valves', 'but because they are makeshift, illegal, or unofficial, neither availability, safety (in the case of services), nor protections of basic rights are guaranteed'. The criminalization of abortion forces it into the shadows. As one interviewee in Peru explained:

> I believe that one of the strategies – and it makes me angry to say it – has been to remain silent. That has been the unanimity of the group: shut up and deny. It makes me angry, really, but that has been the strategy. Because we couldn't put the noose around our necks.

As the final section in this chapter showed, states have often chosen not to explicitly address abortion because of the political risks of doing so. They claim 'wilful blindness' (McGoey, 2019) by not allowing abortions through legal routes, not measuring abortions, and not prosecuting them in large numbers. This approach allows the shadows of abortion to continue, and *acompañantes* take advantage of that. As one interviewee in Peru put it, 'being in the shadows allows us to continue operating quietly'. The shadows can become a space of survival in contexts that punish people for managing their own reproductive lives.

Even when states do take responsibility for abortion, it does not mean that abortion activists can come out of the shadows. The use of misoprostol outside clinical settings can still be targeted and adjacent laws can be used to prosecute activists. Nevertheless, abortion *acompañantes* will continue to provide safe, effective, feminist abortion care whatever the legal situation.

5

Misoprostol and Its Relations: In Search of a Gold Standard

As this book has explored so far, misoprostol is entangled with knowledge production, accompaniment practices, and socio-politico-legal discourses. But it is also entangled with other scientific developments and abortion techniques. This chapter explores the relations that misoprostol has with these objects and practices, primarily in pursuit of improving the efficacy of misoprostol. Recent studies have found that misoprostol-only regimens for abortion can reach efficacy rates as high as 100 per cent (Moseson et al, 2024), but typically failure rates are higher, causing abortion seekers and those who support abortions to search for ways to ensure effectiveness and improve the abortion experience in other ways.

One way has been to incorporate traditional knowledge about abortifacient herbs and plants, which has long circulated in Indigenous communities in Latin America. This can include using plants that are abortifacient themselves or plants that alleviate other symptoms as part of a 'hybrid' protocol with misoprostol. Another way is the use of mifepristone, the 'other' abortion pill, which is highly effective when used in combination with misoprostol. This regimen is commonly termed the 'gold standard' as it is effective in up to 97 per cent of abortions; it is how many first trimester abortions are practised in formalized medical spaces around the world (Kapp and Lohr, 2020). However, there is one problem. Because mifepristone is only used for abortions and, therefore, does not have the 'double life' that misoprostol has, access to mifepristone is far more challenging. This has led activists, researchers, and health providers to experiment with other medications, such as methotrexate, letrozole, and ulipristal acetate, which have other non-abortion indications, in order to improve access to medications that can increase the efficacy of misoprostol but without the obstacles to access that mifepristone has.

The chapter also explores how the development of misoprostol as an abortion medication has opened up knowledge of its other obstetric uses.

Misoprostol is effective in managing miscarriages, preventing and treating postpartum haemorrhage, and managing labour induction, and the increased access to misoprostol for abortions has also expanded its availability for these vital purposes (Stephenson and Wing, 2015). However, this has also had the inverse effect, and because of misoprostol's reputation as an abortion pill, anti-abortion regulation and stigma has hindered access to misoprostol for its other obstetric purposes. The chapter ends with a discussion of procedural abortions, which, while they are more expensive and have more potential for obstetric violence, are not necessarily antithetical to medical abortions with misoprostol. In some cases, a procedural abortion is the best choice for someone needing an abortion, and *acompañante* groups can help to facilitate access to safe abortion providers.

Misoprostol, therefore, does not exist in isolation. As Barry (2005, 52) argues, 'molecules should not be viewed as discrete objects, but as constituted in their relations to complex informational and material environments'. In this vein, misoprostol as a technology of abortion has been constituted by its relationship to the governing structures that regulate and facilitate access to abortion but also by other scientific developments and abortion techniques. Hardon and Sanabria (2017, 118) are interested in how care practices 'deactualize or reactualize pharmaceutical actions that may align with or disrupt the efficacies crafted in clinical trials', and abortion care practices and research, whether in activist collectives or clinical trials, illustrate attempts to increase the efficacy of misoprostol in ways that are attentive to contexts of Indigenous knowledge, regulatory barriers, and economic constraints. Therefore, 'pharmaceutical action is not reducible to the chemical properties of pharmaceuticals but is articulated, elicited, and informed within a meshwork of experimental, regulatory, and care settings' (Hardon and Sanabria, 2017, 126). This chapter seeks to survey this meshwork to better understand the far-reaching relations of misoprostol.

Ancestral abortions and the use of herbs

With a history recorded as far back as the ancient world, abortions have always taken place, though until relatively recently they occurred only in communities, not in medical environments (Riddle, 1992; 1997; Munson, 2018). Abortions were viewed within a wider strategy of 'regulating menses' and performed by midwives, wisewomen, healers, or women themselves, and evidence suggests that many were safe, effective, and widely known about (Gold and Cates, 1980; Van de Walle, 1997; Marcotte, 2016). There is a long history of using herbs and plants to terminate pregnancies. People seeking to end their pregnancies have historically used a variety of 'emmenagogues', plants that stimulate menstruation, such as tansy, rue, and pennyroyal. Other techniques have included inserting beeswax or lemon juice-soaked sponges into the vagina, soaking in hot baths, and giving abdominal massages (Petchesky, 1990; Roberts, 2017). Such knowledges circulated locally in communities but also through trade and other networks, including the slave trade (Perrin, 2001; Roberts, 2017). These were typically kept secret from men, up until the 17th century when male physicians became increasingly aware of practices of menstrual regulation (Marcotte, 2016).

It was only towards the end of the 19th century that abortion became 'medicalized', meaning that it was deemed to be a procedure that could only be performed by medical professionals. And with this came the implementation of laws prohibiting vernacular and non-clinical practice and the suppression of non-medical abortion methods (Reagan, 1997). Part of this medicalization process involved framing traditional abortion techniques as dangerous and 'backward', while physicians were positioned as the only people who had the necessary expertise to decide when an abortion was acceptable and how it should be practised (Munson, 2018). This medicalization did have clear benefits in creating access to safe abortions, reducing morbidity and mortality, and widening the options available to those terminating their pregnancies (Kapp and Lohr, 2020).

However, one consequence of medicalization has been that any other strategies to aid or complement surgical or medical abortions are seen as 'backward' and unnecessary, and, therefore, they have been 'wilfully forgotten' (Joffe, 2009). The medicalization of abortion reifies the doctor as the 'foetal protector', which entrenches power imbalances and the rule of law (Sheldon, 1997, 158). This has taken abortions out of communities, has made abortion an individualized 'problem' that is detached from its social context, and has constructed abortion as a controversial issue (Halfmann, 2012). As a result, the vast knowledge of abortifacient plants that existed throughout the ancient world was lost, and Europe, in particular, rejected knowledge of traditional abortifacient techniques (Schiebinger, 2004). Non-medical techniques remain untested and shrouded in stigma, and safe and effective techniques are indistinguishable from unsafe techniques, such as poisonous plants and drinks, and the insertion of foreign objects into the uterus.

In the Latin American context, herbs and plants have been described as being 'among the oldest and most widespread means used for inducing abortion' (Paxman et al, 1993, 208). While misoprostol has changed the landscape of abortion since the authors made that claim, many people still choose to use herbs and plants to end their pregnancy, either alone or supported by a traditional healer, a traditional medicine practitioner, an *acompañante*, or others. The variety of plants used and the knowledges about them are vast, with over 2,000 plant species used across Latin America, the Caribbean, sub-Saharan Africa, and South and Southeast Asia to treat menstrual disorders (Van Andel et al, 2014). Even in just one area of northern Peru, 105 plant species were documented and identified as herbal remedies for reproductive problems, and those that have been investigated for their efficacy have indicated positive results (Bussmann and Glenn, 2010).

The use of herbs and plants for abortions and other reproductive and menstrual issues needs to be understood under a broader umbrella of the use of traditional medicine. The World Health Organization (WHO) have found the use of traditional medicine to be widespread, with 71 per cent of Chileans and 40 per cent of Colombians reporting using it (Bussmann and Glenn, 2010). Under this umbrella, it is important to note the often-blurred lines between abortion and menstrual regulation, which do not correlate with Western medicine. Plants may well be used for menstrual regulation, to promote good health and fertility, or to time menstruation around cultural events, as in some contexts menstruating women cannot take part in certain events (Van Andel et al, 2014). Not everyone who uses plants and herbs to induce abortion would necessarily view themselves as doing so. Despite the evidence that suggests these herbs have abortifacient properties, the medicalization of abortion, and reproduction in general, means that 'folk methods' are regarded with superstition and discarded as absurd magical beliefs (O'Donnell, 2015). There has been a scholarly assumption that plants are no longer used because they are not effective, but evidence shows that they continue to be used with high levels of understanding about their benefits and risks (O'Donnell, 2015).

The knowledge about herbs and plants comes from multiple sources, including families and communities, healers and practitioners, and even pharmacy staff. One study in Colombia found some research participants had been told by drugstore vendors to use herbs in addition to misoprostol to facilitate abortion, and one interviewee reported: 'She didn't say which herbs they were, but she gave them to me and insisted that I should take them so that they clean everything that was going to come out' (Moore et al, 2021, 151). Nevertheless, it is primarily local healers who are viewed as possessing the deepest knowledge about the use of herbs, and research suggests their knowledge is indeed highly developed (Bussmann and Glenn, 2010). This information circulates primarily through word of mouth, and the local (re) development of this knowledge in local communities maintains its efficacy (O'Donnell, 2015). While this knowledge has typically been deemed to be 'women's knowledge', a study in an Indigenous Mexican community found that many men possessed empirical herbal knowledge of plants used for reproduction and reproductive health, challenging the assumptions that fertility management is a female affair (Browner, 1991).

Contemporary work on abortion in Latin America tends to be dismissive of the use of herbs, stating, for example, that people arrive at medical abortion after 'unsuccessfully trying other supposedly abortifacient methods such as herbal infusions' (Zamberlin et al, 2012, 5). However, greater attention should be paid to the use of medicinal plants in abortion practices in order to respect traditional knowledge and practices (Van Andel et al, 2014). In one example of this work, Bercu et al (2022, 133) argue that the incorporation of approaches such as herbal teas, 'may both have lower costs and be an additional point in care where the accompanied person has agency and choice, helping to empower them and improve their overall experience of care'. Interviewees in my own research sat at various points on the spectrum, with some disregarding herbs as inherently unsafe while others used them in their accompaniment practice.

Some interviewees were very sceptical about the use of plants, and one *acompañante* in Peru told me: 'There are also clandestine forms of abortion where we have heard ... with rue, for example, which is a plant. It is used for abortion. Obviously it is not safe.' Another, a doctor, explained that his motivation for supporting people to access abortions was the high number of deaths he saw when he was working in the 1980s and 1990s. He was attending women who experienced incomplete abortions or unsafe abortions and would present in septic shock from unclean equipment or instruments or the use of plants such as yucca. Some women would arrive at such as advanced stage of infection that they died almost immediately. His wariness of plants was, therefore, not unfounded, as plants and herbs can clearly be used in unsafe ways.

Other interviewees were aware of the use of herbs and plants but did not use them in their accompaniment practices themselves. Some had vague understanding, such as one interviewee in Mexico, who said: 'In other Latin American countries they use herbs, don't they. They use herbs, they use two misos, and a lot of herbs.' Another in Peru explained:

> I recently found out that in the jungle, in Asháninka communities, there are women who abort all the time with plants. I mean, there they abort with plants. And these are like data, statistics that we here in Lima do not have. So in this territory, there are other women who abort and not with pills, but in their community and with plants.

One medical practitioner in Peru recalled learning about the use of plants when she was working in a rural community: '[One woman] told me that there were some little plants, some herbs that she took, and that these were understood as a way "just to correct my period". It was the classic one.' Thus, knowledge that herbs could be successfully used for abortions had circulated among these interviewees but without the specifics on how this was possible in practice.

One *acompañante* in Venezuela was aware of herbs being used but understood this as something that required specialist knowledge. She explained that 'some abortion hotlines will recommend the use [of herbs] for pain management, or sometimes combinations', such as the integration of misoprostol with herbal teas. She continued: 'However, I think there's still a demonization of using herbs and plants because even some abortion hotlines will say this is unsafe, don't use it, rather than this is a very specific kind of knowledge, we have very few people who know [about] it.' She remarked: 'I know that you can have an abortion [but] I don't know how. I don't even know how to prepare it. ... You can find [herbs] in markets – the thing is that I have no idea how to use it.' For her, then, the use of herbs was a practice that some people could incorporate effectively but that, nonetheless, 'is still very demonized even within the safe abortion community'. Similarly, an interviewee in Peru explained: 'Our *curanderos* [traditional healers] have been doing abortions all their lives. ... People already had plants not only to prevent pregnancy, [but also] they had plants, concoctions, and techniques to interrupt it.' She described the *curanderos'* approach to 'menstrual regulation': '[If] you ask them if they do abortions, they say they don't. But if you say I haven't got my period, can I get something to regulate it, they say yes.' So 'that's why when we women have a delay, we go to the *yerbera* [herbalist], to the *curandero*, to the *curandera*, and we say we have a delay. And the *yerbera* does not tell you "you are pregnant". She gives you some *ruda* [rue].' These interviewees emphasized that there are certain members of the community who hold the knowledge of how to abort with herbs.

Some interviewees had little current knowledge of the use of herbs themselves but were either considering using them or worked with others who did incorporate them. One collective in Mexico saw the use of herbs as a way of reclaiming autonomy and one member said: 'Maybe we will go back to ancestral knowledge or other options, which are things that are beginning to be discussed among the *compañeras*.' An *acompañante* in Colombia explained that her collective had a biologist as part of the team and she gave 'a workshop on the use of aromatic herbs that are very easy to get in Colombia to deal with pain and things like that', so people within the group could tell people who were having an abortion 'how much rue they could take because, of course, if they took too much rue it could hurt them. But rue, in sufficient quantity, will help everything to come out faster.' Another *acompañante*, in Peru, had heard about 'a whole cool activist movement that is using herbs. *Yerbateras* from Colombia, people in Chile. Colombian women using herbs not to abort but to accompany the abortion.' This led her to contact the Peruvian Ministry of Health for 'information on complementary medicine and reproductive health protocols for herbs'. They referred her to someone to speak to rather than being able to supply her with information, and she was keen 'to ask the state for information about complementary medicine in reproductive health to have official information'. The perspectives of these interviewees illustrate that rather than *acompañantes* rejecting ancestral knowledges now that misoprostol is well known, they are seeking ways to incorporate them to improve abortion experiences.

One interviewee I spoke to in Mexico had extensive experience of using herbs in supporting abortions, so I turn to her case at length. This *acompañante*, who I will call Juana, is part of a feminist collective of Mayan women who work on women's wellbeing and combating violence. As part of their activism, the collective practices 'abortion accompaniment with medicines in combination with medicinal plants', trains others with this knowledge, and has created a workshop – Herbolaria para enriquecer abortos con medicamentos [Herbalism to Enrich Medical Abortions]. She began using plants to deal with people's specific circumstances. For instance, one woman was experiencing anxiety and Juana found that she could alleviate this with herbs. She also used them where other methods were not easily available – for example, she used plants to help treat infections in a context where antibiotics are not freely available. This led her to do more research and gradually incorporate plants into her accompaniment practice more and more.

Juana explained that when she began using plants for abortions, she was wary of using them to induce the abortion for fear of causing haemorrhaging. She explained: 'the first plants that I began to incorporate were to alleviate the emotional situation – that is, the anxiety, the anguish, the insomnia of the women' who were going to have an abortion with misoprostol. She then found that the pain that people were experiencing during the abortion could be alleviated through plants and also that some plants were helping with the dilation of the cervix, so she 'began to gradually incorporate other ... plants depending on the problems that arose'. She described the precise balance of plants she would use, as some could only be used in certain quantities – for example, parsley, which, 'although it is a very good abortifacient' thins the blood, which can increase the risk of a haemorrhage.

She described her approach as follows: 'I do not give the herbs from the beginning, but rather I give all the indications for misoprostol and then I mention, if you like, you can complement it with plants.' So she explains to people that plants can be used in a complementary way, but if they do not feel comfortable with the use of plants, then she can support them with the use of misoprostol, in combination with mifepristone if she is able to access it. She has found that some people are really happy to be able to incorporate plants and some people have contacted her wanting to have an abortion exclusively with plants. She has had to tell them that she doesn't have an 'infallible' regimen of using plants, but she is keen to develop one to reduce the dependency on medications and to support people who contact the collective with a pregnancy so early that misoprostol would not be effective.

In terms of the herbs that Juana incorporates, she chooses 'plants that can be found in the supermarket, anywhere' in order to facilitate access. As she explained: 'Obviously, if I were to give a workshop based on wild plants ... it would be useful to very few people.' So she only recommends plants that can be bought in a supermarket or in 'every market [that] has its section of medicinal plants, sometimes combined with issues that have to do with magic, witchcraft, but there are medicinal plants'. She herself also buys rolls of plants from markets that can be used to make tinctures, meaning that the active properties of the plants can last for longer. Using tinctures also gives greater standardization 'because with tinctures the plant is weighed', and the most ideal plants can be selected because 'the plants, from the time they are planted or from where they are collected, there are many things that can vary, whether they have pesticides or fertilizers, the time of collection, how they are moved during the collection, how they are dried' – all these factors influence the abortifacient properties of the plant. So she ideally creates her own tinctures from plants that she has grown, so that she can have full control over the strength of the herbal tinctures.

Juana's knowledge emerged from a mixture of sources. She explained: 'My family has always used medicinal plants – that is, my mother, my grandmother are Mayan, and plants have always been present.' However, as she entered education systems, particularly university, she found that medicinal plants were seen as 'herbalist stuff, superstitions and things like that. She said: 'well, for me, plants have always solved a lot of things'. So she has developed knowledge on the use of plants for abortions. She explained how she gathers information: 'I talk to my mom, I talk to my grandmother, I talk to other people that work with plants, that they are medical, traditional [healers], on the one hand. On the other hand, I go looking for information' through university resources, scientific journals, libraries 'and things like that, complementing the traditional knowledge'. Juana's experience shows how the intersection of Indigenous ancestral knowledge and medical abortion techniques can support the development of abortion care that is attentive to the needs of the community she works with.

A more mature approach to the use of plants and herbs for abortions acknowledges that for many people this is a preferred approach and recognizes the 'hybrid' techniques that are being developed in Latin America to bring together the use of misoprostol with other ancestral knowledges. The bringing together of techniques such as misoprostol with plants and herbs can be used as an example of 'how scientific knowledge in Latin America has been creatively and critically forged at the intersections between Indigenous and foreign cultures and put to use in projects of a political or cultural nature, often with emancipatory ends' (del Pilar Blanco and Page, 2023, 2). While it is clear that the use of herbs and plants can have dangerous results, by dismissing *all* use of herbs and plants as backward and dangerous, important knowledge is being eradicated and people are being denied the culturally sensitive abortion care that they desire. Greater research in this area could unpick the rejection of all abortion methods outside medical or procedural approaches to better explore which approaches can be incorporated safely and effectively and which are overly dangerous.

Mifepristone and the 'famous combo'

The administration of mifepristone, followed by a prostaglandin, usually misoprostol, is the 'gold standard' for medical abortions (Winikoff and Sheldon, 2012). This is because the combined regimen of mifepristone and misoprostol has been shown to be more effective than the misoprostol-only regimen (Abubeker et al, 2020). While efficacy rates vary between clinical studies, misoprostol-only regimens end in the successful termination of a pregnancy in around 87 per cent of cases, but this rises to 97 per cent when used in combination with mifepristone (Veldhuis et al, 2022b). Mifepristone reduces the availability of progesterone, the hormone required for a successful pregnancy, while misoprostol induces uterine contractions to expel the pregnancy (Winikoff and Sheldon, 2012). While early scholars were sceptical of its capabilities, with one writing that '[r]ather than being a "wonder drug", mifepristone may instead be simply a harbinger of better medications to come', mifepristone has been proven to be a highly effective and well-tolerated medication (Klitsch, 1991, 280). The success of the mifepristone-misoprostol combination, or what one interviewee in Peru called 'the famous combo', means that people who access a medical abortion in a healthcare setting where abortion is legal will receive mifepristone with misoprostol as the standard medical abortion regimen (Johnson, 2023).

Mifepristone was developed in the 1980s by French endocrinologists who demonstrated that when used with a prostaglandin, it was remarkably effective at inducing an abortion (Löwy and Dias Villela Corrêa, 2020). It was first licensed in 1988 in France and China with other countries such as Sweden, the United Kingdom, and Germany following suit (Creinin, 2000; Rowlands, 2012), and then included on the WHO's List of Essential Medicines for its use in early abortions (Harvey, 2015). The original name for mifepristone, RU-486, refers to the French pharmaceutical company who developed it, Roussel Uclaf, and it was Étienne-Émile Baulieu, a scientist in the company, who has been lauded as 'the father of the pill' (Johnson, 2023, 140). Baulieu hailed mifepristone as 'the "second-generation" pill', and its use for the safe termination of millions of pregnancies around the world attests to this (Clarke and Montini, 1993, 67). In contrast to misoprostol, then, which was designed for one purpose but then 'rescripted' as an abortion pill, mifepristone was developed precisely to terminate pregnancies.

This explicit development as an abortion medication has caused controversy with its introduction into healthcare systems hampered by political opposition and regulatory controls (Assis and Erdman, 2022). Roussel Uclaf even suspended their production of mifepristone due to concerns about the boycotting of their other products that was being orchestrated by anti-abortion groups (Rowlands, 2012). This resulted in outcry, particularly by the World Congress of Gynecologists and Obstetricians, and the French government ordered Roussel Uclaf to resume marketing and distribution (Rowlands, 2012). In the United States, however, governments were less favourable to mifepristone: US Presidents Ronald Reagan and George Bush Senior prohibited any research on the drug and the US Food and Drug Administration (FDA) banned its importation for personal use in 1989 under the claim that it was a 'threat to public health' (Rowlands, 2012, 118). These delays resulted in a slower global uptake of mifepristone, particularly in the global South, but as of 2024, 103 countries have approved its use (Dzuba et al, 2013; Gynuity Health Projects, 2024).

The safety of mifepristone is well established, with over 100 studies proving it to be safe (Rowlands and Harrison-Woolrych, 2023). The medication has been used by millions of people worldwide and the mortality rate is estimated at less than 1 per 100,000, making it far safer than the continuation of pregnancy and childbirth (Henderson et al, 2005). Interviewees reported on their preference for supporting people with mifepristone-misoprostol abortions rather than misoprostol alone because of the higher efficacy and the reported lower levels of pain with the combination regimen. One interviewee in Argentina stated that 'obviously the effectiveness of misoprostol is very high, but it is not the best' and 'mifepristone is better than misoprostol: to perform the treatment means less pain, less time'. Another explained: 'We have known about mife for several years and this has also changed the way we accompany, and we have had to learn how to use it, the symptoms.' She described how the combination regimen meant using less misoprostol overall so that the uterine contractions brought on by the prostaglandin are over more quickly. Because the mifepristone has already been taken, the misoprostol starts the contractions when 'the walls are already weakened … and in general the bleeding starts very quickly with misoprostol, and it usually hurts less'. An *acompañante* in Mexico explained that in her collective, they aim to use mifepristone when they can 'because there is less medication. And that is also one of our working premises – that is, the less medicine you consume, the better.' Mifepristone is, therefore, often desired by those having or supporting abortions in Latin America, but the challenge comes it accessing the medication.

Misoprostol is available across Latin American precisely because of its 'double life' as a stomach ulcer medication. Mifepristone, having been developed as an abortion medication, is harder to move under other guises. An *acompañante* in Mexico explained that with 'mifepristone, there is no way for the women who are accompanied to get it in a pharmacy'… 'so we have an agreement with another collective that does have access to this medicine, so they send it to different parts of the country', but this still comes at a higher price than misoprostol with the cost of postage. This collective reserves mifepristone shipments 'only for cases in which the pregnancies are advanced, for example, or that the girls have some special condition'. This led her to remark that 'mifepristone is very precious, it's very difficult to get it'. An interviewee in Costa Rica found that mifepristone was completely inaccessible in her country. Therefore, it is frequently regulatory controls around mifepristone that prevent it from being accessible in Latin America.

Another issue with accessing mifepristone is its cost. While misoprostol is relatively inexpensive, mifepristone is much more expensive, and the high cost of registering it means that for-profit companies have little incentive to take it to market in contexts where there is a small population of reproductive age women (Winikoff and Sheldon, 2012). In contexts where abortion is criminalized, mifepristone can only be legally used under exceptions, such as rape or risk to the health of the pregnant person, and given the challenges of accessing these exceptions, legal use and, therefore, the motivation for companies to register mifepristone in these contexts is low (Dzuba et al, 2013). One interviewee in Peru explained that public health facilities in the country struggle to access mifepristone because of these barriers to its entry. For those outside health facilities who wish to self-manage abortions using mifepristone, the obstacles are even greater. As one *acompañante* explained, 'of course, it is not sold here because it does not have a sanitary registration, right? There is no sanitary registration so if someone sells it, you know perfectly well that it is illegal.' Where people are selling mifepristone on the black market, the pills are, 'I suspect, from places like India, where it is very cheap and they bring them here.'

When people are able to access mifepristone, the cost is high. As an interviewee in Mexico told me: 'It's more expensive, isn't it? I mean, one pill, I don't know, costs about 700 pesos [US$36] as opposed to a box of misoprostol with 28 pills that costs 500 [US$26], right? So, it's a big difference.' An interviewee in Mexico believed that it is the higher cost of mifepristone that makes it more attractive to scammers on the black market. They are able to advertise a 'combi-pack' at a low price, but when the abortion seeker arrives, they are told that the mifepristone will cost extra, often an unaffordable price. An interviewee in Peru recalled a young woman who had got in touch after buying pills from a man and although she said she only wanted to buy misoprostol, 'he told her "you asked for miso, but I sell mife". He took the mife out of his pocket, he was selling it for 10 soles [US$2.66]. Either it is a miracle and we are in paradise or it is a *bamba* [knock-off].' Another interviewee in Peru had received a supply of mifepristone from a source she trusted only to find the pills were counterfeit. She spoke to others who had also encountered fake mifepristone that was actually a placebo pill. She thought the anti-abortion movement might be behind it, but the problem was so widespread that her collective had to keep their misoprostol-only regimen due to their concerns about the quality of the mifepristone that was circulating in Peru.

Mifepristone is becoming easier to access, especially as the legalization of abortion in some countries is creating opportunities for national production, as has happened recently in Argentina. Other groups exploit loopholes where it is legal to send prescription medicines for personal use. One interviewee explained that mifepristone is undergoing research for its use for other indications, such as for prostate cancer, as an antidepressant, and for urinary tract cysts, so it can be moved for these purposes. As the interviewee elaborated: 'It's legal to send it. It's legal to receive it. What is not legal is to take it, right, for an abortion. But who's going to know that you took it for an abortion?' Given the desire to use the mifepristone-misoprostol combination regimen, groups develop strategies to access mifepristone despite the challenges and higher cost.

Nevertheless, the challenges of accessing mifepristone mean that even if the combination regimen is the gold standard medical abortion regimen, the misoprostol-only regimen is the one most commonly used worldwide (Johnson, 2023). The lower price of misoprostol and the ability to buy it over the counter in pharmacies means that people can begin the abortion process sooner and feel that they have greater autonomy in the process (Belfrage, 2023). So although the misoprostol-only regimen does not have efficacy rates as high as the combination regimen, it is still the desired route for many. It may even become increasingly common in contexts such as the United States because misoprostol is not restricted by the US FDA Risk Evaluation and Mitigation Strategy, which widens the group of people who are permitted to administer it (Moseson et al, 2024). While mifepristone is important, it is not the only medication used in combination with misoprostol.

Experimentation with other medications

Since the self-experimentation with misoprostol that began in the 1980s, it has long been used in combination with other medications. This, however, was often out of necessity rather than for any practical reason. Due to its creation as a stomach ulcer medication, it is frequently manufactured with other pharmaceuticals that are designed to support that medical indication. For example, in Argentina, there used to be just one commercially available brand, Oxaprost, which was a pill that combined misoprostol with the non-steroidal anti-inflammatory drug diclofenac (Fernández et al, 2009). The diclofenac part of the medication treats rheumatoid arthritis or osteoarthritis, while the misoprostol part is used to prevent ulcers caused by the use of the diclofenac. Despite being designed for the treatment of joint pain, it is still effective as an abortifacient and a report by the College of Pharmacists of Buenos Aires revealed that approximately 80 per cent of all Oxaprost prescriptions in Argentina are written by obstetrician-gynaecologists (Fernández et al, 2009). One interviewee in Argentina recalled that when her group began supporting abortions using Oxaprost, they found that the misoprostol part of the pill was on the outside, wrapped around the diclofenac, so, as she explained: 'What we did was to break the medication, so that the part in the middle was not consumed and the part on the outside, which was the misoprostol, was consumed.' Another interviewee had the same experience and noted that the separation of misoprostol from diclofenac was 'something that became known over time'. This was a type of 'hacking' that provided access to the abortifacient properties of misoprostol.

Other medications have also been purposefully used in combination with misoprostol. Medications have long been experimented with to induce abortions, and this has been done in medical research since the 1950s (Creinin, 2000), with more recent testing exploring what can be used alongside misoprostol. One medication that has been tested is methotrexate, an immunosuppressant that is used to treat rheumatoid arthritis, psoriasis, and Crohn's disease and which can be prescribed for cancer. Pilot studies testing the efficacy of methotrexate in combination with misoprostol for abortions began as early as 1993, with efficacy in trials ranging between 91 per cent and 98 per cent (Creinin and Darney, 1993; Aldrich and Winikoff, 2007). Methotrexate-misoprostol was seen at this time as a promising medical abortion regimen, as mifepristone had not been licensed in many countries, including the United States, and methotrexate is much cheaper than mifepristone (Creinin and Darney, 1993; Rowlands, 2012). However, bleeding was shown to last longer with a methotrexate-misoprostol regimen compared to a mifepristone-misoprostol one, and methotrexate is a teratogen, a substance or agent that can cause or increase the risk of birth defects in a developing foetus, which means that if an abortion fails with this regimen, the person requires careful follow-up (Creinin and Darney, 1993; Aldrich and Winikoff, 2007). Nevertheless, methotrexate continued to be used in Canada as late as 2012 because mifepristone had not been approved there (Rowlands, 2012). The case of methotrexate shows the innovative use of additional techniques to increase the efficacy of misoprostol, particularly with medications that, like misoprostol, are cheap and accessible due to their other, 'legitimate' uses.

Another medication that has been experimented with in combination with misoprostol more recently is letrozole. Letrozole is an aromatase inhibitor, which is a type of hormone therapy used to treat breast cancer. While its exact mechanism in inducing abortion is unknown (Biswas et al, 2024), the WHO states that it suppresses estrogen levels, which then leads to pregnancy loss (WHO, 2022), while other researchers say that it softens the cervix and increases the uterus' responsiveness to misoprostol (Mohamed et al, 2024). In a recent study comparing the use of misoprostol-letrozole with misoprostol-only regimens in abortions under 12 weeks of pregnancy, the administration of letrozole for three days prior to using misoprostol 'leads to a considerably greater rate of complete abortion than misoprostol alone' (Nofal et al, 2024, 2112). In addition to improving the rate of complete expulsion, the use of letrozole also appears to reduce the time to complete expulsion and the likelihood of requiring a procedural intervention (Bahaa et al, 2022; Biswas et al, 2024; Mohamed et al, 2024). Letrozole is, therefore, a relative newcomer, mentioned to me by just one interviewee in Peru, but one that appears to be promising as an effective medication that is available for its other uses and can improve the efficacy of abortions as well as people's experiences of the abortion.

Even more recently, a 2025 proof of concept study has shown the potential benefits of ulipristal acetate in combination with misoprostol (Winikoff et al, 2025). Ulipristal acetate has a similar chemical profile to mifepristone and is registered and available in 74 countries for emergency contraception, including in countries where mifepristone is not available. While the clinical study was small, at 133 patients, the efficacy rate of 97 per cent is highly promising and suggests that ulipristal acetate could become a safe, effective, and more accessible alternative to mifepristone pending further research. However, ulipristal acetate is currently approved by the US FDA for use in the United States as an emergency contraceptive, which creates the risk that the medication may become a target for anti-abortion politicians. Any restrictions placed on ulipristal acetate would, therefore, impact people requiring emergency contraception as well as abortions (Grossman, 2025). Nevertheless, finding cheaper and more accessible alternatives to mifepristone, such as letrozole or ulipristal acetate, could be particularly valuable in Latin America and other low-income contexts where regulations on mifepristone exist, as well as in contexts such as the United States, where mifepristone access is under attack.

The examples of diclofenac, methotrexate, letrozole, and ulipristal acetate show that pharmaceuticals are 'informed' materials that can be understood through their far-reaching relations (Barry, 2005). The scientists who developed these non-abortion drugs likely could not have foreseen the hacking of diclofenac or the use of arthritis and cancer drugs to create more effective abortion regimes. As medical anthropologists have shown, the effects that pharmaceuticals go on to have reach far beyond the laboratory (Hardon and Sanabria, 2017). These reinscription processes exemplify how the scientific experimentation of misoprostol for abortions that began in Brazil in the 1980s will likely continue into the future as the quest for abortions that best suit the physical and contextual needs of those who need them keeps going.

Misoprostol's other uses

While misoprostol was designed as a stomach ulcer drug and is now used most commonly as an abortion medication, it has other uses as well. It is particularly important for its use in managing miscarriages, preventing and treating postpartum haemorrhage, and making labour easier by softening the cervix (Stephenson and Wing, 2015). For Assis (2021, 2), it was precisely the experimentation with misoprostol for abortions that 'led to extensive research on the several uses of misoprostol in the fields of gynecology and obstetrics'. The off-label and formal testing of misoprostol for additional uses exemplifies the ongoing reformulation of the 'biography of pharmaceuticals' (Van der Geest et al, 1996). Pharmaceuticals are never 'finished', but rather always on the way to becoming something else.

The use of misoprostol in labour induction, for the treatment of incomplete or missed abortion, and for the prevention and treatment of postpartum haemorrhage has been particularly noted for its significance in low-resource settings, where it is 'potentially lifesaving' (Fernández et al, 2009, 180). Providing access to misoprostol for haemorrhaging and pregnancy termination specifically 'would do more than any other realistically achievable, sustainable, large-scale intervention to save the lives of women at risk for death by maternal causes' (Fernández et al, 2009, 180). These other uses of misoprostol have become recognized over time, with the WHO putting misoprostol on its List of Essential Medications for labour induction in 2005, for the treatment of incomplete or missed abortion in 2010, for preventing postpartum haemorrhage in 2011, and for treating postpartum haemorrhage in 2015 (Suh, 2021). However, as with the incorporation of misoprostol and mifepristone on WHO lists for the treatment of abortion, being labelled as 'essential' for a specific indication does not guarantee that states, healthcare providers, and pharmacy staff will provide access to it.

The discovery that misoprostol had other benefits beyond abortion came quickly after its development as an abortifacient. By 1999, misoprostol had 'been used so frequently and effectively' for cervical ripening as a prelude to induction of labour 'that it has become the treatment of choice' and the American College of Obstetricians and Gynecologists published guidelines on how to use it effectively (Hale and Zinberg, 2001, 59). The effects of cervical ripening (the softening and dilatation of the cervical os) were also soon recognized for their support in procedural abortions by reducing the risk of cervical lacerations or uterine perforation during the procedure (Goldberg et al, 2001). In addition, given that labour induction is a common practice, and increasingly so, wider access to misoprostol would fulfil a still unmet need in many parts of the world (Handal-Orefice et al, 2019). Misoprostol also has clear benefits in the treatment of incomplete miscarriage, because traditionally the two methods of treatment have been expectant observation or surgical curettage (Murchison and Duff, 2004). These are not ideal options because expectant observation can provoke uncertainty and trauma for the patient waiting for the miscarriage to complete, while curettage is more expensive and can come with the risk of uterine perforation. Misoprostol, then, is a safe, effective, and cheap way to treat an incomplete abortion. An obstetrician in Peru explained that as she began using misoprostol, she was impressed by the range of its uses, whether to support a procedural abortion, treat an incomplete abortion, or induce an abortion. This means that when she trains people in how to accompany abortions, she teaches 'them all the aspects that this product can have and its benefits'.

The effectiveness of misoprostol for these obstetric uses beyond abortion have led global reproductive health experts to recommend its integration 'into national maternal mortality reduction strategies because it can be effectively administered by clinicians at lower levels of the health system' (Suh, 2019, 32). The problem has been that as registration for misoprostol for abortions has been blocked, this has had downstream implications for the registering of misoprostol for obstetric-gynaecologic indications more broadly (Fernández et al, 2009). This is exacerbated by restrictions on its use, such as in Brazil where misoprostol's distribution is restricted by law to hospitals for approved indications only (Fernández et al, 2009). This makes it highly challenging to access in smaller healthcare settings that would still greatly benefit from using misoprostol in labour induction, the treatment of incomplete or missed abortion, and the prevention and treatment of postpartum haemorrhage. The outcome is that the revolutionary, life-saving potential of misoprostol is stymied because of fears that it will lead to unregulated abortion and increased involvement of traditional birth attendants in obstetric care (Suh, 2021).

Misoprostol's reinscription as an abortifacient had the consequence of highlighting its additional obstetric uses. For Suh (2021, 6), '[t]hrough its multiple "lives," misoprostol is anchored in multiple global regimes of maternal and reproductive health governance' that incorporate the life-saving potential of misoprostol, especially in low-income settings, but also in the anti-abortion regulations that have prevented this potential from being fully realized. The call, therefore, to increase access to misoprostol for abortions would also create pathways to access for misoprostol's use in labour induction, the treatment of incomplete or missed abortion, and the prevention and treatment of postpartum haemorrhage. Pharmaceuticals are 'always-emergent' (Hardon and Sanabria, 2017, 126), and the continued experimentation with misoprostol for purposes beyond stomach ulcer treatment and abortions illustrates its ongoing reformulation.

Procedural abortions

The focus on misoprostol throughout this book could give the impression that procedural abortions are in opposition to medical abortions with misoprostol. This is certainly not the case, and while this book takes as its focus misoprostol and the accompaniment practices surrounding it to show how they have transformed the landscape of abortion access in Latin America, that does not mean that procedural abortions are not important, necessary, or intertwined with misoprostol. Many *acompañante* groups will help people to access a procedural abortion when it is the optimal or preferred route for them. One study of *acompañantes* in Mexico found that respondents reported women lacking information about abortion accompaniment with medications and were also concerned about reliable access to mifepristone, making procedural abortions an important alternative (Larrea et al, 2024). An *acompañante* I interviewed in Mexico explained that while they accompany abortions with pills, for a range of reasons they help some people who contact them to have a surgical abortion. This may be because the person is one of the rare cases with an allergy to prostaglandins, they have attempted an abortion with pills but not had success, or they simply want to have a very rapid abortion and to know immediately that it was complete. Similarly, an *acompañante* in Peru found that some people she supported to have an abortion preferred to access a procedural abortion, if they could afford it, because 'it takes less time, and sometimes they are anesthetized if they wish, and they don't have to go through the whole 12-hour process'. Another described a recent case of someone who came to them for abortion support but 'didn't want to take pills'; she explained: 'we referred her to a place that we know they don't victimize. It is the least we can do.'

Procedural abortions can be associated with 'curettage' techniques, a procedure that involves scraping the uterine lining, but first trimester abortions are almost always performed through manual vacuum aspiration (MVA), a simple, well-received hand-held technique than can be performed outside hospitals with simple equipment (Rowlands and Wale, 2020). This equipment, or what Murphy (2012) calls a 'device for not performing abortions', has similarities with 'menstrual extraction kits', which were used by feminists in the United States in the 1970s, and 'menstrual regulation kits', which have been deployed in the 'third world', along with contraceptives, as part of non-governmental organizations' (NGOs') 'family planning' initiatives. By the 1990s, the MVA abortion became standard when NGOs conducted research on its efficacy in relation to curettage. They found that MVA was 60 per cent cheaper, quicker, did not require general anaesthesia, meant less time spent in the clinical setting and had fewer complications (Chinchilla et al, 2014). MVA equipment was quickly taken up, and in the 1970s, even before abortion was legalized, kits were mass produced for 'menstrual regulation' in the United States, and then in the 1990s, it was lauded as the technology of choice for post-abortion care in the developing world (Suh, 2015). Curettage, meanwhile, plays an important role in second trimester abortions, but it is more expensive, requires anaesthesia, and comes with the (rare) risk of uterine perforation and other complications (Murchison and Duff, 2004).

As MVA equipment and training on how to perform the procedure spread, an extensive network of healthcare providers who could offer procedural abortions expanded across Latin America. Throughout the 1990s, these networks trained up doctors but also midwives, nurses, nurse technicians, and traditional midwives, who were all qualified to perform MVAs, even though these were not legal for elective abortions. These networks began in large cities, but training quickly spread to smaller cities and rural areas, where those newly trained could then share that knowledge, expanding the network across the region. The result was a cadre of health professionals who increased access to safe abortion services and decentralized the sites where that care could take place (Duffy et al, 2023). One interviewee in Peru recalled the feelings she had when she was trained in MVA use in the 1990s. She was angry at the lack of political will to address the situation of unsafe abortion; she said, 'when I saw the MVA, I felt more rebellious', and this was because she realized that 'it is something so simple, so basic and why is there this ignorance or this desire, this bad intention of torturing women and not allowing [MVA]'. The low-cost, safe, and easy-to-use nature of MVA sat at odds with states' refusals to provide safe abortion access, in the way that misoprostol has done more recently.

A key actor in the rollout of MVA provision in Latin America has been US-based Ipas (International Projects Assistance Service), an international NGO that works to increase access to safe abortions and contraception. Using a post-abortion care approach, they developed MVA techniques and training that could replace curettage as a treatment for incomplete abortions or miscarriages (Kulczycki, 2011). The original MVA device was designed by Ipas in the 1970s and remains the most widely used version, with the rights now owned by DKT International, who distribute the device in over 100 countries. The kit is approved for use 25 times but, particularly in low-resource contexts, reports suggest that they can be used effectively up to 100 times (Clark et al, 2017). These kits are relatively inexpensive at approximately US$10.52, and they are predominantly purchased by international donors at an estimated 200,000 units annually (Clark et al, 2017).

Ipas may have an explicit mission to increase safe access to abortions, but that has not prevented governments that criminalize abortion from openly collaborating with them. The reason for this is that Ipas offers training for post-abortion care, which responds to deaths from incomplete abortions or miscarriages, a leading cause of maternal mortality. Because of this, the Peruvian Ministry of Health requested the assistance of Ipas in developing a hospital-based model of post-abortion care with the aim of disseminating it in regional health centres, and the Honduran Ministry of Health has worked with Ipas to train healthcare providers in MVA for post-abortion care (Chinchilla et al, 2014). Since the same equipment and techniques are used to treat incomplete abortions or miscarriages and to perform abortions, Ipas and other networks can legitimately train healthcare providers in MVA.

Another key actor in the expansion of MVA proficiency in Latin America is Fundación ESAR (Education for Reproductive Health), trained by Oriéntame in Colombia. Like Ipas, ESAR is located within the NGO sphere, and such providers are estimated to provide the majority of private sector abortion care (Bower et al, 2021). One interviewee who was trained by ESAR during the 'boom' in MVA training in the 1990s and early 2000s estimated that in Peru, 70 doctors and 230 midwives have been trained by ESAR and they perform 80,000 abortions per year, accounting for roughly 20 per cent of the country's total abortions. The interviewee continued: 'and that means almost 80,000 women that are not going to die from abortion … because abortion is still the third cause of maternal death in the country, in Peru, so how many women's lives have we saved because they are not going to go somewhere else'.

These NGO actors also played an important role in developing teaching aids to roll out the ability to perform abortions using MVA. In 1996, for example, Dr Miguel Gutierrez wanted to give people being trained in MVA techniques a better way to gain experience before attempting the procedure on a real patient. Gutierrez, part of the Pathfinders NGO, created an anatomical model, made from materials easily accessible from a hardware store, that gave an experience of using the equipment that was as realistic as possible (Webb, 2000). This model has been used by organizations such as Ipas and ESAR for their training in Latin America. While this may seem prosaic, it is these types of teaching aids that have resulted in tens of thousands of safe abortions. However, we can also read the development of MVA and the aids to teach it through what Murphy (2012, 174) terms 'NGO-ized feminist health care'. These tools actively reshape healthcare, policy, and discourses of 'family planning' in ways that can have uneven and inequitable global effects.

While misoprostol activism has been explicitly associated with feminist political praxis, MVA abortions can be articulated as feminist activism too. One obstetrician who also accompanies abortions in Peru found that in the 1990s there were more men trained in MVA abortions than women, so she always 'looked for alliances, trying to make a difference'… 'always trying to give it a feminist approach, which is not only the technical, the procedure, but with a reflection on autonomy'. For her, the high number of men performing MVA abortions with a medicalized perspective contrasts with feminist approaches and is 'a clearly patriarchal, sexist issue'. Another interviewee in Peru said that she asked for training from a doctor in one of the networks that trained people to use MVA. She felt that MVA practice needed to be taken out of the hands of male doctors. Also she wanted to be able to practice a technique that didn't require the use of general anaesthetic because 'sometimes the use of anaesthesia is used as a very punitive issue, because they [medical professionals] don't give you anaesthesia and people complain a lot about the pain'. For this interviewee, broadening the scope of who had the knowledge to perform MVA abortions was a way to reduce obstetric violence.

Despite these feminist MVA practitioners, issues with overmedicalization and obstetric violence in procedural abortion remain. One *acompañante* in Peru remarked that there is a culture of obstetric violence even among those who are willing to perform abortions, with many believing that 'if you got pregnant and you didn't want to, you put up with it. And if you need an abortion, I'll perform a curettage without anaesthesia as a punishment. There is this culture of punishment with respect to women's sexuality.' Another ensures that if she does support someone to access a procedural abortion, it is at a 'place that guarantees that she will not be re-victimized. Because we have all met, and several of our colleagues who have had abortions have told us about re-victimizing clinics, obstetricians who are abusive.' These clinics can also charge vast sums, as one interviewee reported, and they even conceal information about medical abortion with pills in order to charge extra for the MVA procedure. This interviewee was sceptical about how many of these procedures in the Peruvian context were carried out by trained medical providers, estimating that 'almost 70 per cent are not'. Therefore, while some 'clandestine abortion clinics … are run by very well-meaning doctors', as one interviewee in Venezuela put it, others practice procedural abortions for the money and are not feminist or care-full in their provision.

The *acompañante* networks that facilitate abortion care with medications in the present can be seen as an extension of the feminist activist groups that supported access to procedural abortions, such as the Jane Collective, which operated in Chicago between 1969 and 1973, and networks in Italy in the 1960s. While not all MVA training networks in Latin America have been developed from this feminist activist positioning, the development of MVA techniques and the rollout of training to a broad cadre of practitioners led to the increased availability of procedural abortions across the region. These were not technically permitted by states that criminalized abortion, but NGO training networks were often able to work with states, as part of post-abortion care training, to expand knowledge and access to equipment. This training could be applied to induced abortions as well as the management of incomplete abortions or miscarriages, which resulted in the expansion of MVA provision. Like misoprostol, MVA sits in an in-between space, as it can be legally distributed and used for post-abortion care, which then unlocks its use for abortions (Suh, 2015). This provision is important because, even with the advent of medical abortion, a procedural abortion is still the optimal or preferred route for some abortion seekers. Future abortion access should retain procedural abortions for a range of reasons, including for those who have had a negative experience with a medical abortion, for certainty that the abortion is complete, for speed, and for those not wanting to have the abortion at home (Hoggart and Berer, 2022). Misoprostol can be understood in its relations to procedural abortions, as it can be administered to soften the cervix before the insertion of the MVA equipment, but procedural and medical abortions are also entangled as different techniques that can support both bodily autonomy and reproductive justice.

Misoprostol and its entanglements

Misoprostol, as a pharmaceutical product, has been mobilized in ways that have centred its use in the expansion of safe abortion care across Latin America and the world. This book has primarily focused on the role of *acompañante* groups, who have generated knowledge and information on how to effectively use misoprostol as well as strategies to disseminate both the medication itself and the knowledge about its use. Misoprostol is a 'thing-in-itself', but it would be remiss to desuture it 'from the practices and social dynamics within which objects come into being and through which they are made meaningful' (Hardon and Sanabria, 2017, 126). Chemical matter is inherently relational (Barry, 2005), and by directly looking at misoprostol's relations with other techniques or medications and use for non-abortion indications, its technoscientific entanglements in terms of material, technical, and social relations come to the fore (Murphy, 2012).

This chapter shows that misoprostol does not exist in isolation and that how it is understood as a chemical can never be a finished product; rather, it can be brought into 'hybrid' relationships with already-existing knowledges, such as ancestral understandings of the abortifacient properties of plants, and reconceptualized in terms of efficacy through its experimentation with other medications, such as methotrexate, letrozole, and ulipristal acetate. Misoprostol is also entangled with the politics of its 'other uses' – for managing miscarriages, preventing and treating postpartum haemorrhage, and labour induction – which both expand and restrict access to the medication. Finally, it is also entangled with other technologies of abortion, such as MVA techniques, because medical and procedural abortions are not in opposition to one another but offer different approaches to terminating pregnancies depending on the needs of the abortion seeker.

It is also imperative to note that misoprostol's relationships with other techniques go beyond using it in combination with other technologies. For many people seeking to end their pregnancy, misoprostol is just one tool among a constellation of others. As Bury et al (2012, S7) found in their research on abortion in Bolivia: 'More often than not, the first attempt at abortion failed for women who drank herbs, roots, salts or other substances; deliberately incurred falls or lifted heavy objects; or had intramuscular injections.' Misoprostol may be the solution that provides them with a safe and effective abortion, but they may have attempted other solutions on the way.

Hardon and Sanabria (2017, 118) ask 'what can be gained by breaking open the pharmaceutical object and examining efficacy as a processual, relational, and situated event, as well as a pharmacological one[?]' What I hope this chapter has shown is that the efficacy of misoprostol is mediated through its relations with alternative knowledges, techniques, medications, and indications. For Murphy (2012, 12), entanglements refer to 'recursive loops, sideways movements, circuits of appropriation, and other vectors of connection within the past', and by beginning with misoprostol and exploring these entanglements, it can be seen how this medication in particular constitutes 'a nexus of social and cultural processes including knowledge, symbols and beliefs, politics, profit-making, trust and conflict' (van der Geest, 2011, 9). In all, understanding misoprostol can never just be about misoprostol.

For Abortion Liberation: A Conclusion

Misoprostol and the people who have mobilized it in Latin America have transformed abortion safety, knowledge, and practices. This book has focused on Latin America as the site where misoprostol 'became' an abortion medication and where *acompañantes* have developed new formations of abortion care, but the impacts of these developments have changed abortion access across the world. To end the book, I want to bring together all the threads – of the biography of misoprostol as a pharmaceutical, of the *acompañantes* who have facilitated access to misoprostol, of the mobility strategies to ensure it reaches those who need it, of the legal challenges and opportunities of misoprostol, and of its far-reaching relations – to theorize misoprostol and the activism underpinning it as a tool for abortion liberation.

By abortion liberation, I refer to the full separation of abortion from the state, with autonomy given to pregnant people to manage their reproductive lives in the ways that work best for them. While Western understandings of abortion centre on it being highly medicalized (that is, only to be performed by a medical professional), liberation allows for the conceptualization of other practices and understandings. As we can see from the abortion care practices that have developed in Latin America, radically different ways of conceptualizing abortion access are possible in the present. My thinking about abortion liberation here has been strongly informed by literature and activism on prison abolition. Just as Angela Davis (2011) writes of prisons being 'obsolete' and therefore in need of being abolished, I argue that the medicalization and legal control of abortion is obsolete and must be abolished.

I argue that abortion governance is obsolete because strategies to control bodily autonomy have no basis given the evidence on safe medical abortions. Whereas previous laws sought to regulate abortion in order to safeguard people from 'dangerous' practices, the advent of self-managed medical abortions shows that these laws are archaic. Misoprostol is safe, and accompaniment practices have proven that supported, empathetic abortion care is more than possible beyond medicalized frameworks. Abortion governance seeks to impose rules on who can access abortion, when, and in what circumstances, but this imposition has no place in self-managed medical abortions.

If abortion governance is obsolete and the answer is to abolish it, then what should exist in its place? Prevailing public discourse posits prison abolition as unthinkable, implausible, unrealistic, and even mystifying and foolish (Davis, 2011). Davis argues that the question of what will replace prisons 'is the puzzling question that often interrupts further consideration of the prospects for abolition. Why should it be so difficult to imagine alternatives to our current system of incarceration?' (Davis, 2011, 105). She expounds that we need to envision an array of radical alternatives, and I want to argue in this chapter that the answer to what must replace abortion governance is the radical alternative of abortion liberation.

Liberal approaches can call for an expansion of the 'exceptions' when abortions are permitted, a loosening of the gestational age at which an abortion can be accessed, and training to reduce obstetric violence and harm in abortion care. Yet tinkering with these regulations and provisions will never lead to reproductive justice. As Gilmore (2022, 195) writes, 'it is perhaps time to pause and consider how the unfinished work of radical abolition might help in practical as well as theoretical ways to get out of the trap of reformist reform'. These liberal approaches are simple 'reformist reform' and do not adequately deal with the power structures that have constrained abortion access and enacted harms.

Abolishing abortion governance does not mean abolishing abortion support. Instead, it means opening up pathways to support and valuing the strategies that have been so carefully developed to ensure access to safe and effective abortions. Abolishing regulations does not prevent people from accessing an abortion through a medicalized framework if they so choose, but it does mean that they would no longer be constrained by 'acceptable reasons' to have an abortion, gestational time frames, or rules about where their abortion takes place. Taking laws out of abortion access would eliminate the possibility of people being imprisoned for managing their own abortion, or even for experiencing a miscarriage, and would allow people who facilitate access to safe abortions to do so openly.

The growth of accompaniment groups reflects 'a critical transnational and abolition feminist mode of resistance' (Krauss, 2023, 409) that is actively creating a world where abortion liberation is possible. Self-managed abortions using abortion pills will continue to expand across Latin America because regulating the use of them is a huge legal and practical headache for states regardless of whether abortion is legal or illegal. The work of *acompañantes* and other activists to increase knowledge of and access to these pills will continue to facilitate abortions and lead to greater social decriminalization of abortion. Abortions with pills are not a second-best option or merely the solution in a context where no other safe method of accessing an abortion is possible. Abortions with pills are safe and cheap, and they have a high level of acceptability among users and have transformed the process of having an abortion. Far from having to obtain a medical appointment, fulfil any legal hoops such as mandatory waiting periods or counselling, and then booking in a procedure, people seeking to end their pregnancy can purchase pills and manage their abortion when and where suits them.

The chapter proceeds by exploring this idea of abortion liberation through three themes that draw on the Latin American abortion accompaniment practices detailed in this book: reproductive justice, the expansion of knowledges, and a new vision of abortion. It then ends by detailing what this vision of abortion liberation from Latin America can mean for the rest of the world.

Abortion liberation as reproductive justice

Reproductive justice as a movement has called for and works towards bodily autonomy through three primary tenets: the right to have children, the right not to have children, and the right to parent children with safety and dignity. This involves analysing how power systems function, examining the effects of intersecting oppressions, and putting the most marginalized people at the centre of any activism. Abortion liberation is, therefore, an extension of reproductive justice that puts these concepts into practice to realize bodily autonomy. Work and activism on reproduction in Latin America has shown the myriad ways in which the most marginalized communities are the ones who bear the brunt of death, harm, criminalization, stigma, and surveillance (Sutton, 2024). Reproductive justice is well placed to provide tools to explore the injustices that arise at certain intersections and organize for a vision that abolishes them.

Reproductive justice advocates can fall into a pattern of defining reproductive justice as what it is *not* – *not* just about rights, *not* about 'choice', and *not* only about abortion (Thomsen, 2015). Thomsen (2015, 18) argues that this 'discursive distancing from abortion, a method used to mark the concerns of reproductive justice as distinct from reproductive rights, has harmful consequences for how we conceptualize reproduction and organize for justice'. Abortion is a common and material issue in people's lives, and activism in support of it should not be written off as liberal, White women's campaigning. Reproductive justice must take a broad approach to people's reproductive lives and the contexts they live in, but that does not make abortion any less important as a reproductive justice issue. The global North critiques of abortion activism as excessively pro-choice are far less relevant in contexts, such as in parts of Latin America, where there are no legal routes to an abortion and, therefore, not even an illusion of choice (Rowlands and Wale, 2020). I hope this book has offered a contribution here in illustrating the intersectional politics of abortion access and care in Latin America. Reproductive justice must go beyond abortion, but it must recognize it as a core issue too.

While reproductive justice was formulated in the context of the United States, although born from transnational connections, it can be fruitful to travel with the concept to other contexts. For Suh and McReynolds-Pérez (2023, 400): 'If the reproductive justice approach can be expanded to include the global South, then a serious consideration of abortion is merited as we focus on countries where the consequences of unsafe abortion routinely impact the life and health of women.' The reproductive justice lens chimes well with activism in the global South that has always encompassed inclusive demands around population control, holistic strategies regarding reproductive health, and avoidance of obstetric violence (Suh and McReynolds-Pérez, 2023; Searcy et al, 2024). Abortion is just one issue within this, but one that is connected to multiple other reproductive issues, and more global analyses of abortion can support a critical interrogation of reproductive governance through the reproductive justice framework (Suh and McReynolds-Pérez, 2023). This does not mean dismissing the decades of feminist organizing in Latin America around abortion and other reproductive issues that have primarily taken a rights-based and public health approach (Morgan and Roberts, 2012; Sutton, 2020; Encarnación, 2022). This organizing has led to material wins, such as lower mortality rates, improved access to reproductive health services, and a reduction in obstetric violence. However, the rights angle and public health angle result in reproductive *rights* and reproductive *healthcare*, not reproductive *justice*.

The overarching aim of reproductive justice is to fight for bodily autonomy, and this is central to abortion liberation. Autonomy means respecting people's own decisions about their reproductive lives and rejecting discourses that frame *acompañamiento* as a second-best option that steps in to provide abortion care until the state can do it. *Acompañante* groups are sometimes defined as 'autonomous health movements', which is a form of direct action rooted in social justice movements and the specific contexts of the community (Braine, 2020). *Acompañantes* are, therefore, autonomous in their own activism, but they are also working towards the autonomy of others through their activism. Through facilitating what they term *aborto autónomo* (autonomous abortions), a new form of abortion care that rejects the patriarchal governance controlling people's bodies is possible (Fernández Vázquez and Szwarc, 2018). This 'praxis invites a retheorizing of bodily autonomy beyond hegemonic concepts of "choice" that are necessarily dictated by state-controlled rights', particularly in contexts where 'choice' is a concept that does not reflect the constraints that people live under (Belfrage, 2024, 537). A core component to realizing this autonomy is the decriminalization of abortion.

I talk about decriminalization rather than legalization because the legalization of abortion keeps it within the judicial frame and expands the circumstances under which the state permits an abortion. This means that abortion remains as a stigmatized, exceptional act that has to be 'permitted'. The formalization and regulation of abortion in this way does not adequately challenge inequalities in access and continues to create situations of vulnerability and risk (Nandagiri and Berro Pizzarossa, 2023; Duffy, 2024). Decriminalization, then, removes criminal sanctions against abortion from the law entirely and means that people cannot be punished for having or providing access to a safe abortion, it takes the police and courts out of abortion, and it means that abortion is treated like every other form of healthcare (Berer, 2017). This doesn't prevent the law from being used as a tool to deal with issues such as coercing someone to have an abortion or practising unsafe abortions under grievous bodily harm, assault, or manslaughter laws, but it does mean removing criminal sanctions against the act of abortion itself (Berer, 2017).

Decriminalization does not immediately resolve all issues of abortion access. For example, following the decriminalization of abortion in Northern Ireland, it took nearly two years for abortion services to be actually commissioned (Duffy, 2024). Nevertheless, it is a fundamental step on the path to equitable abortion access. The criminalization of abortion is correlated with increases in mortality and morbidity but does not reduce the number of abortions happening, while decriminalization results in significantly fewer abortion-related deaths but does not increase the number of abortions happening (Faúndes and Shah, 2015). The decriminalization of abortion is, therefore, quite literally a matter of life and death.

The decriminalization of abortion is essential to realizing abortion liberation. Abortion is a safe and common medical procedure that has no business being governed by criminal laws that were often written in previous centuries. We need to stop treating abortion as exceptional, and instead must practise it in the same way as other medical procedures. Abortion liberation, through focusing on bodily autonomy and removing abortion entirely from judicial frameworks, reimagines abortion as care that everybody has free and equal access to.

Abortion liberation as expanding knowledges

Abortion criminalization is heavily intertwined with abortion medicalization. Legal structures govern the conditions under which abortions can be practised, and that means practising them under the authority of medical professionals. Early scholarship seeking to understand medicalization defined it 'as a medical problem or illness' and advocated 'mandating or licensing the medical profession to provide some sort of treatment for it' (Conrad, 1975, 12). Abortion liberation, however, expands the scope of who is seen as a legitimate 'performer' of an abortion as well as what types of abortion knowledge are valued.

In the last 150 years, abortion has been seen a practice that must be performed under certain circumstances and by a trained medical professional. However, the medicalization of abortion can preclude reproductive autonomy, and abortion accompaniment has shown how abortion knowledges can be expanded beyond the narrow, medicalized framework to include everyone. For Mines et al (2013, 155) '[o]ver-medicalizing abortion is violence', but misoprostol has opened up new possibilities for people to manage their own abortions. Self-managed abortions with misoprostol show that the person having the abortion can legitimately 'perform' the abortion themselves 'because by having the correct information for its use they can manage and handle the entire abortion process, which, among many other disruptive characteristics, makes the practice of abortion less unequal' (Mines et al, 2013, 155). This is an expansion of abortion knowledge to value how abortions can be *self*-determined and *self*-administered.

Across the mid to late 19th century, abortion began to be framed in scientific discourses, and this created a distinction between, on the one hand, legitimate physicians who could diagnose a pregnancy, decide whether an abortion would be permissible, and dictate how it should be performed and, on the other, the traditional understandings of early abortion and alleviating 'menstrual blockages' that had prevailed for thousands of years (Reagan, 1997). The self-management of abortion and the accessing of an abortion outside a medicalized space were framed as both physically and morally dangerous. This transformed abortion from being a common and community-based practice into one that was a moral 'bad' that could only be practised in exceptional circumstances by a doctor. By treating abortion as something 'exceptional', it is framed as something in need of being medicalized, and this only reinforces the apparent need for its exceptionalism (Nandagiri and Berro Pizzarossa, 2023).

The de-medicalization of abortion, with an emphasis on self-managed abortions with pills, does not mean rejecting the formal healthcare system. More effective collaborative between medical systems and autonomous health movements is an important way to recognize the value of self-managed abortion and to expand access and enhance the empowerment of people who want to be in control of their own abortion (Yanow et al, 2021). Therefore, de-medicalization does not preclude people from accessing abortion care in institutional medical systems, but it does give them greater options for blending the type of care that best suits them. This may entail, for example, receiving support from an *acompañante* group when they are making the decision to have an abortion, accessing the pills through a doctor, or taking the pills with support from an *acompañante* and then attending post-abortion care at a clinic to confirm that the abortion was complete.

Neither does the de-medicalization of abortion mean an end to demanding that the state recognizes and provides the need for access to safe abortion services. As I argued in the previous section, the state should not penalize people for managing their own bodily autonomy, but they should offer information and access on how to safely have an abortion, whether in a medicalized context or not. As Mines et al (2013, 156) argue, '[w]e need to think about the resources that are effectively needed to guarantee the safety of an abortion [and demand that the state] guarantees universal access to information and medication'. However, the de-medicalization of abortion does expand who it is that can provide access to safe abortion services beyond the state.

Abortion liberation as expanding knowledges entails broadening understandings of who is seen as a legitimate 'performer' of an abortion as well as what types of abortion knowledge are valued. The arrival of medical abortions has meant that the knowledge of how to use medications to complete a safe and effective abortion can be widely shared. The case of misoprostol in Latin America, from women in Brazil experimenting on their own bodies to the *acompañantes* generating and sharing knowledge on its use, has shown that the medicalized framework is not necessary. *Acompañantes* have not replaced the doctor; rather, they have 'used expertise about pharmaceutical abortion, along with peer education, to position themselves as lay experts on safe abortion in a context of illegality' (McReynolds-Pérez, 2017, 371). People do not need to expose themselves to a biomedical gaze to confirm the expertise that they already have about their own bodies (Murphy, 2012). Their expertise is deeply attuned to their own contexts, which calls for situating misoprostol knowledge in people's daily lives and recognizing that the people who get in touch with *acompañantes* are experts in their own circumstances (McReynolds-Pérez, 2017). Abortion liberation means taking seriously these forms of knowledge developed by *acompañantes*.

Abortion liberation also stresses the importance of the person having the abortion being at the centre of their narrative and abortion journey. The power over all decisions about the abortion must be located with the pregnant person (Larrea et al, 2024), and *acompañantes* provide the level of support that best suits the needs of that person. As Maffeo et al (2015) reiterate, it is the pregnant person who is 'aborting'; the *acompañantes* do the accompanying. This was echoed by an interviewee in Mexico who stated: 'It always comes from the women. I mean, we have to understand that women have all this knowledge. ... So, we're basically just a tool. We're just serving them. ... They're the only ones that are experts in their body and their lives.' Another, in Argentina, told me: 'Abortion belongs to the one who aborts. That is something we are also very clear about – we are not the protagonists. Doctors are not the protagonists. The person is going to have an abortion under the conditions he/she wants to have it. We want to facilitate that.'

The example of misoprostol and the accompaniment practices around it position Latin America as the centre of knowledge production, not somewhere that has imported knowledge from the global North. This contributes to scholarship rethinking the place of Latin America in the history of science and the scientific imagination and takes seriously the knowledge that has been produced and generated there (del Pilar Blanco and Page, 2023). This knowledge making focuses on themes that have too often been sidelined, 'including social justice, Indigenous identities and Indigenous rights, the causes and effects of economic dependency, neoliberalism, and human rights—themes central to a full understanding of technology and its role in society' (Lemon and Medina, 2014, 112). Latin America is not at the 'periphery' of science and knowledge generation – it is central to understandings of abortion technologies, forms of abortion care, and, therefore, abortion liberation.

Abortion liberation as a new vision of abortion

Accompaniment practices facilitating access to abortions with misoprostol and other medications are not copying a medicalized approach to abortion provision; instead, they are formulating a new vision of what abortion care can be. This vision is not necessarily 'new' for those who have been supporting access to abortions in community contexts for centuries, but it is new in contrast to prevailing medicalized and criminalizing discourses on abortion. In order to avoid the pitfall of defining abortion liberation by what it is *not*, I wish to provide a hopeful vision of what abortion liberation can be and, in fact, *already is*. *Acompañante* activism is a form of 'prefigurative politics' that does not accept the status quo and instead creates 'what could be' (Lin et al, 2016, 302). Abortion activist groups 'have developed utopian visions of reproductive justice that sometimes go beyond what can be codified by the law and state institutions' (Sutton and Vacarezza, 2023, 383).

Acompañantes are not waiting for laws to change or asking for 'reformist reform'; rather, they act as if abortion liberation already exists and build their own 'just and inclusive systems of care' in the present (Assis and Erdman, 2022, 2243). For Krauss (2019, 37), this doesn't necessarily entail creating new worlds, but it prompts her to ask the question: 'What is it to make a new world versus to make *this* world livable?' As an approach to glimpsing prefigurative abortion politics in *this* world, we can see how abortion activism isn't always something that takes place completely outside health services; rather, we can see the possibilities of collaboration with those who work in healthcare and understand abortion activism as a broader political project rather than a specific and bounded 'thing' (Duffy, 2024).

A vision of abortion through abortion liberation reaches for the possibilities of what could be. Accompaniment groups have refused to parrot a medical model and instead have developed around their commitment to providing abortions outside medical contexts, autonomy, holistic care, and collective care. This means that the care that they provide is focused on that person's autonomy and needs, can be quickly accessed, and is 'horizontal', thereby challenging the power dynamics of medicalized abortion care (Rowlands and Wale, 2020; Vacarezza and Burton, 2023). Such visions of abortion are not utopian; they have been proven to be effective and well-functioning in the here and now. One interviewee in Argentina described the significant fall in maternal mortality as a result from unsafe abortions when *acompañantes* began facilitating access to misoprostol, saying 'that was not because of state action but because of the action of organized feminism'. These visions are building on long histories of both ancestral techniques of abortion in Latin America and activism that has sought to seize control of people's own reproductive lives (Murphy, 2012).

Bringing new visions of abortion into being is of course not without its challenges. From the re-criminalization of abortion, the social criminalization of abortion, and renewed attacks from anti-abortion actors, creating 'what could be' can still come under fire. This can be seen through the arrests of the Socorristas in Argentina and in the harassment and intimidation outlined in this book. Moreover, as Murphy (2012) writes of the feminist self-help movement of the 1970s and 1980s, despite fighting for control over their own bodies, activists were not necessarily implicated in a biomedical regime that is tied to 'broader historical formations of technoscience, public health, neoliberalism, racial formations, and family planning' (Murphy, 2012, 5). In a similar vein, abortion pills have created possibilities for new forms of abortion care, but they are also entwined with neoliberal discourses of 'responsible' reproductive behaviour and the individualization of reproductive lives (Belfrage, 2023). It is important, therefore, that these visions of abortion liberation are not viewed uncritically.

Nevertheless, scholars and activists have proposed ways to further visions of abortion liberation. Rowlands and Harrison-Woolrych (2023) argue that abortion everywhere should be self-managed, with medications available over the counter and support as needed. They go further, stating that restrictions on abortion pills are unnecessary and only deprive people of access to safe abortion, so authorities must increase accessibility to medications in order to allow people to control their fertility in the ways that best suit them (Rowlands and Harrison-Woolrych, 2023). Others argue that there should be even fewer restrictions on abortion pills and that they, along with other products like tampons and aspirin, should be made available in public bathrooms and convenience stores for people who need them (Yanow et al, 2021). The activists in this book exemplify how bringing a new vision of abortion into being is not only possible but already being practised with world-changing effects.

Abortion liberation from Latin America to the world

The challenge of writing a book about Latin America is sufficiently addressing the heterogeneity of the region. Misoprostol is not readily accessible in all Latin American countries, and not all areas have *acompañante* groups working to facilitate access to it. Not all countries have been swept up in the progressive *marea verde*, as shown by the abortion restrictions in Honduras and El Salvador and the evidence that deaths from self-induced abortions have been increasing in recent years in Suriname (Kodan et al, 2021). Interviewees in Peru frequently spoke of the *marea verde* in Argentina, and for some it was a hopeful beacon, with one telling me: 'I feel that we are like Argentina. In that direction. I need that hope. Sometimes I fool myself.' Another said that 'definitely what happened in Argentina has been a great fuel for women, like, in our country, right, they are expecting to want to make changes' but that was all dependent on the Peruvian political context where 'things are not looking very good, to tell the truth'. A third emphatically told me that 'Latin America is not Argentina'.

Many interviewees were hopeful about the future of abortion access in Latin America, pointing to the strength of feminist organizing and believing that abortion liberalization is inevitable, even if not in the immediate future. Some saw the possibility of the legalization of abortion, within prescribed circumstances, as more realistic than full decriminalization in the short term in countries such as Peru. Others who saw abortion liberalization as inevitable believed that, in the words of one interviewee, 'the slogans and the perspective have changed' since events in Argentina; she said that while, until recently, 'it was about abortion in cases of rape or the issue of grounds … now it seems … that now, for example, the slogan this year was *libre* [free], safe and *gratuito* [monetarily free] abortion'. Likewise, another told me that she, with her fellow organizers in Peru, 'said "let's not go for the rape cause because we are wearing ourselves out and it will surely be a difficult battle, so let's go all out [for full decriminalization]"'. Others viewed their work through a prefigurative politics lens, stating that whatever happens in terms of the legal situation, they will continue to support people to access medical abortions. Whether in contexts of extreme criminalization or places where abortion is legal, *acompañantes* continue to be crucial in facilitating access for those who face barriers to access, for whatever reason (Sutton and Vacarezza, 2023).

The *acompañante* model developed in Latin America cannot be simply transplanted to other places in the world. *Acompañamiento* is a deeply contextual, relational practice that is rooted in Latin America. However, it can be useful to consider alternatives to medicalized abortion provision that can likewise work towards abortion liberation. One example is abortion doulas. Doulas are trained lay support people who have typically been involved in supporting the labour process in physical, emotional, and educational ways across many different cultures (Chor et al, 2012; Searcy et al, 2024). This focus on labour has expanded to what has been termed the 'full spectrum doula movement', which can 'echo the full-service midwives of previous centuries' (Mahoney and Mitchell, 2016, xv). Abortion is one aspect that can be supported by a doula, and they may be able to provide support through techniques such as massage, reassurance, breathing guidance, conversation, joking, and listening (Chor et al, 2012). People who have been supported through their abortion with a doula have reported that it gave them comfort, control, and a more secure sense of safety (Chor et al, 2012). It also has a wider political imperative by shifting abortion from being an individualized, private event to being a collective act (Mahoney and Mitchell, 2016). In terms of the support they offer and the political project of doula work, which is intertwined with the reproductive justice movement, linkages with *acompañante* activism can be seen.

Having support structures in place, whatever form those take, is essential given the deliberate or unintended misinformation about abortion available online, in communities, and in spaces such as crisis pregnancy centres. An emerging challenge is the use of artificial intelligence (AI) in supporting abortion access. In a recent study, McMahon and McMahon (2024) used the AI 'virtual assistant' ChatGPT to find out what information it would provide about medical abortions. While it did produce mostly accurate responses, it stated that 'misoprostol is typically taken orally or inserted into the vagina', while in fact it is most effective when used buccally, sublingually, or vaginally (McMahon and McMahon, 2024, 3). It also stressed the need to use misoprostol under the supervision of a qualified healthcare provider and overstated the potential risks of self-managed medical abortions. Existing and emerging forms of inaccurate and misleading information on abortion can be combated through easy access to accurate information and support. *Acompañantes,* doulas, and other sources of support can be a crucial way to prevent this misinformation.

Acompañante activism is also part of a global abortion solidarity movement. The safe abortion possibilities developed by *acompañantes* in Latin America are relevant to the other parts of the world where mortality from unsafe abortions remains acute. Latin America, for instance, technically has a higher rate of 'unsafe' abortion than Africa, but the risk of dying from an unsafe abortion is roughly 15 times higher in Africa than in Latin America (Faúndes and Shah, 2015). There are also other health and social implications, such as infertility and chronic pelvic pain, all of which disproportionately impact the poorest and most marginalized in society but are entirely preventable with access to safe abortion (Faúndes and Shah, 2015). Moreover, between 2015 and 2019, over half of all estimated unsafe abortions globally were in Asia, and there were also high rates of mortality and other risks to health and wellbeing (WHO, 2021b). The ways in which *acompañantes* in Latin America have created pathways to safe abortion access and drastically reduced the deaths and health impacts from unsafe abortions are highly relevant to these contexts.

However, this solidarity is relevant in places where abortion rights are seen as having been 'won' as well as in more restrictive contexts. For example, in England, from where I write this, abortion is still criminalized under the Offences Against the Person Act 1861. The Abortion Act 1967 was introduced to provide legal exceptions as long as two doctors certify that the reason for the abortion is covered by the Act, that the abortion is carried out by a registered medical practitioner, and that it is performed at an approved premise (Nandagiri and Berro Pizzarossa, 2023). Abortion here is, therefore, highly medicalized, and anyone who wishes to self-manage their abortion – for example, by purchasing misoprostol and following the WHO guidelines – can be prosecuted and face life imprisonment. Other examples such as abortion criminalization in Poland and Malta and the repeal of *Roe v Wade* in the United States, show that the global North is far from a paradise of abortion access. In the context of anti-abortion discourses in certain parts of the world, namely the United States and Europe, an appreciation of misoprostol-only abortions may become increasingly relevant. Misoprostol, due to its indication for stomach ulcers, is not restricted by the US FDA, and this means that the role of misoprostol may become increasingly prominent if access to mifepristone becomes restricted (Moseson et al, 2024). Global connections of abortion activism, then, are not about liberal saviourism, but are central to all of our lives and reproductive futures. There is no abortion liberation without abortion liberation everywhere.

I want to end by offering a hopeful vision of abortion liberation, one that is robust and clear-eyed regardless of the states that seek to restrict abortion access or the anti-abortion actors who attack it. Abortion liberation means fighting for abortion to be taken out of the state's law books and away from the imposed gaze of the medical practitioner. Abortions can clearly be accessed in unsafe ways, and an abortion liberation approach is certainly not advocating for those methods. This vision of abortion puts it more in line with other health issues that are self-managed, such as diabetes, mental health, epilepsy, and arthritis. Too often, abortion pills are presented as risky and transgressive, but misoprostol and the accompaniment practices that support access to it have shown that autonomous, safe, empathetic, feminist, care-full abortion futures are possible in the present. This abortion liberation should be available to all.

References

Abubeker, F.A., Lavelanet, A., Rodriguez, M.I. and Kim, C. (2020) 'Medical termination for pregnancy in early first trimester (≤ 63 days) using combination of mifepristone and misoprostol or misoprostol alone: a systematic review', *BMC Women's Health*, 20(1): 142. doi: 10.1186/s12905-020-01003-8

Acre, V.N., Küng, S.A., Arce, C., Yapu, A., Iriondo, D. and Morales, M. (2023) 'Reach, experience, and acceptability of an abortion self-care intervention in Bolivia: a mixed-methods evaluation', *Sexual and Reproductive Health Matters*, 31(1): 2139888. doi: 10.1080/26410397.2022.2139888

AFP (2024) 'Argentina's Milei tells school kids abortion is "murder"', *France 24* [online], 6 March. Available at: www.france24.com/en/live-news/20240306-argentina-s-milei-tells-school-kids-abortion-is-murder

Aldrich, T. and Winikoff, B. (2007) 'Does methotrexate confer a significant advantage over misoprostol alone for early medical abortion? A retrospective analysis of 8678 abortions', *BJOG: An International Journal of Obstetrics & Gynaecology*, 114(5): 555–562.

Alfirevic, Z. and Weeks, A. (2006) 'Oral misoprostol for induction of labour', *Cochrane Database of Systematic Reviews*, 2: CD001338. doi: 10.1002/14651858.CD001338.pub2

Algora, R.G. (2021) 'Advancing reproductive justice in Latin America through a transitional justice lens', *Michigan Journal of Gender & Law*, 28(2): 155–194.

Anderson, W. (2002) 'Introduction: postcolonial technoscience', *Social Studies of Science*, 32(5–6): 643–658.

Arango, D.A., Cartwright, A.F., Braccia, A., Moore, A. and Vivas, M.M. (2025) 'Seeking abortion medications online: experiences from a mystery client study in Colombia', *BMJ Open*, 15(1): e086404. doi: 10.1136/bmjopen-2024-086404

Arguedas-Ramírez, G. and Wenner, D.M. (2023) 'Reproductive justice beyond borders: global feminist solidarity in the post-Roe era', *Journal of Law, Medicine & Ethics*, 51(3): 606–611.

Assis, M.P. (2020) 'Liberating abortion pills in legally restricted settings: activism as public criminology', in K. Henne and R. Shah (eds) *Routledge Handbook of Public Criminologies*, New York: Routledge, pp 120–130.

Assis, M.P. (2021) 'Misoprostol on trial: a descriptive study of the criminalization of an essential medicine in Brazil', *Cadernos de Saúde Pública*, 37(10): e00272520. doi: 10.1590/0102-311X00272520

Assis, M.P. and Erdman, J.N. (2021) 'In the name of public health: misoprostol and the new criminalization of abortion in Brazil', *Journal of Law and the Biosciences*, 8(1): 1–20.

Assis, M.P. and Erdman, J.N. (2022) 'Abortion rights beyond the medico-legal paradigm', *Global Public Health*, 17(10): 2235–2250.

Atienzo, E.E., Cruz, V., Garduño, S., Lomelí, S., Meza, M., Zurbriggen, R. et al (2023) 'Safe abortion in Latin America: a look at abortion accompaniment collectives from the perspective of their activists', *Culture, Health & Sexuality*, advance online publication. doi: 10.1080/13691058.2023.2233589

Atukunda, E.C., Brhlikova, P., Agaba, A.G. and Pollock, A.M. (2015) 'Civil Society Organizations and medicines policy change: A case study of registration, procurement, distribution and use of misoprostol in Uganda', Social Science & Medicine, 130: 242–249.

Bahaa, H.A., Ahmed, A.A., El Amen, A.E.H. and Manran, A.E. (2022) 'A comparative study between methotrexate versus letrozole prior to misoprostol in induction of first trimester missed miscarriage', *Minia Journal of Medical Research*, 33(4): 177–184.

Barbieri, C.H.C., Gianella, C., Defago, M.A.P. and Machado, M.R. (2021) 'Abortion lawfare in Latin America: some reading keys for a changing scenario', *Revista Direito GV*, 17(3): 1–6.

Barbosa, R.M. and Arilha, M. (1993) 'The Brazilian experience with cytotec', *Studies in Family Planning*, 24(4): 236–240.

Barry, A. (2005) 'Pharmaceutical matters: the invention of informed materials', *Theory, Culture & Society*, 22(1): 51–69.

Bastian Duarte, Á.I. (2012) 'From the margins of Latin American feminism: Indigenous and lesbian feminisms', *Signs: Journal of Women in Culture and Society*, 38(1): 153–178.

Belfiori, D. (2021) *Código rosa. Relatos sobre abortos* (2nd edn), Buenos Aires: Ediciones La parte maldita.

Belfrage, M. (2023) 'Revolutionary pills? Feminist abortion, pharmaceuticalization, and reproductive governance', *International Feminist Journal of Politics*, 25(1): 6–29.

Belfrage, M. (2024) 'Reclaiming autonomy: the changing landscape of Mexican abortion activism', *Signs: Journal of Women in Culture and Society*, 49(3): 535–556.

Bercu, C., Moseson, H., McReynolds-Pérez, J., Wilkinson Salamea, E., Grosso, B. Trpin, M. et al (2022) 'In-person later abortion accompaniment: a feminist collective-facilitated self-care practice in Latin America', *Sexual and Reproductive Health Matters*, 29(3): 121–143.

Berer, M. (2017) 'Abortion law and policy around the world: in search of decriminalization', *Health and Human Rights*, 19(1): 13–27.

Bergallo, P., Sierra, I.C.J. and Vaggione, J.M. (eds) (2018) *El aborto en América Latina: estrategias jurídicas para luchar por su legalización y enfrentar las resistencias conservadoras*, Madrid: Siglo XXI Editores.

Berro Pizzarossa, L. and Nandagiri, R. (2021) 'Self-managed abortion: a constellation of actors, a cacophony of laws?', *Sexual and Reproductive Health Matters*, 29(1): 23–30.

Billings, D.L., Walker, D., del Paso, G.M., Clark, K.A. and Dayananda, I. (2009) 'Pharmacy worker practices related to use of misoprostol for abortion in one Mexican state', *Contraception*, 79(6): 445–451.

Biswas, S., Sengupta, M., Ghosh, D. and De Rajesh, R. (2024) 'Induction of abortion in the first trimester of pregnancy using letrozole and misoprostol combination versus misoprostol alone – a comparative observational study', *Asian Journal of Medical Sciences*, 15(1): 94–101.

Blofield, M. and Ewig, C. (2017) 'The left turn and abortion politics in Latin America', *Social Politics: International Studies in Gender, State & Society*, 24(4): 481–510.

Bloomer, F., Pierson, C. and Estrada-Claudio, S. (2020) *Reimagining Global Abortion Politics*, Bristol: Bristol Policy Press.

Borboleta, H., Cisneros García, K.N. and Llanes Granillo, M.R. (2022) 'Modelo de partería, justicia reproductiva y atención de aborto en México', *Iberoforum*, 2(1): e000198. doi: 10.48102/if.2022.v2.n1.198

Bower, J., Romero, M. and Chinery, L. (2021) *Market Assessment for Medical Abortion Drugs in Argentina*, Buenos Aires: CEDES.

Bower, J., Chinery, L., Fleurent, A., Gülmezoglu, A.M., Im-Amornphong, W., Kilfedder, C. et al (2024) 'Quality testing of mifepristone and misoprostol in 11 countries', *International Journal of Gynecology & Obstetrics*, 165(2): 405–415.

Braine, N. (2020) 'Autonomous health movements: criminalization, de-medicalization, and community-based direct action', *Health and Human Rights Journal*, 22(2): 85–97.

Braine, N. (2023) *Abortion Beyond the Law: Building a Global Feminist Movement for Self-Managed Abortion*, London: Verso Books.

Braine, N. and Velarde, M. (2022) 'Self-managed abortion: strategies for support by a global feminist movement', *Women's Reproductive Health*, 9(3): 183–202.

Briggs, L. (2022) 'Reproductive justice: born transnational', *Gender, Work & Organization*, 29(1): 1–7.

Browner, C.H. (1991) 'Gender politics in the distribution of therapeutic herbal knowledge', *Medical Anthropology Quarterly*, 5(2): 99–132.

Bugalho, A., Bique, C., Almeida, L. and Faúndes, A. (1993) 'The effectiveness of intravaginal misoprostol (Cytotec) in inducing abortion after eleven weeks of pregnancy', *Studies in Family Planning*, 24(5): 319–323.

Burke, P. (2023) *Ignorance: A Global History*, New Haven, CT: Yale University Press.

Burton, J. (2017a) 'De la comisión al socorro: trazos de militancia feminista por el derecho al aborto en Argentina', *Descentrada*, 1(2): 1–17.

Burton, J. (2017b) 'Invenciones feministas en la lucha por el aborto legal', *Bordes: Revista de Política, Derecho y Sociedad*, 157–164.

Burton, J. (2017c) 'Prácticas feministas en torno al derecho al aborto en Argentina: aproximaciones a las acciones colectivas de Socorristas en Red', *Revista Punto Género*, 7: 91–111.

Burton, J. (2021) 'La legitimidad de abortar', *Descentrada*, 5(1): 1–5.

Burton, J. and Peralta, G. (2016) 'Redes en torno al aborto clandestino: vínculos de socorristas y sistema de salud en Neuquén, Argentina', *Clivajes. Revista de Ciencias Sociales*, 6: 158–181.

Burton, J. and Peralta, G. (2021) 'Un aborto feminista es un aborto cuidado. Prácticas de cuidado en el socorrismo patagónico', *Revista Estudos Feministas*, 29(2): e70809. doi: 10.1590/1806-9584-2021v29n270809

Bury, L., Aliaga Bruch, S., Machicao Barbery, X. and Garcia Pimentel, F. (2012) 'Hidden realities: what women do when they want to terminate an unwanted pregnancy in Bolivia', *International Journal of Gynecology & Obstetrics*, 118(S1): S4–S9.

Bussmann, R.W. and Glenn, A. (2010) 'Medicinal plants used in northern Peru for reproductive problems and female health', *Journal of Ethnobiology and Ethnomedicine*, 6: 30. doi: 10.1186/1746-4269-6-30

Calkin, S. (2019) 'Towards a political geography of abortion', *Political Geography*, 69: 22–29.

Calkin, S. (2021) 'Transnational abortion pill flows and the political geography of abortion in Ireland', *Territory, Politics, Governance*, 9(2): 163–179.

Calkin, S. (2023) *Abortion Pills Go Global: Reproductive Freedom Across Borders*, Berkeley: University of California Press.

Calkin, S. (2024) '"It's not mifepristone, but it's not poison": finding fakes in Poland's abortion underground', *The Cambridge Journal of Anthropology*, 42(2): 47–64.

Calkin, S. and Freeman, C. (2019) 'Trails and technology: social and cultural geographies of abortion access', *Social & Cultural Geography*, 20(9): 1325–1332.

Calkin, S., Freeman, C. and Moore, F. (2022) 'The geography of abortion: discourse, spatiality and mobility', *Progress in Human Geography*, 46(6): 1413–1430.

Cammarota, K., Romero, M. and Szwarc, L. (2022) 'Barreras al acceso al aborto legal después de las 13 semanas de gestación: estudio cualitativo con profesionales de la salud en ciudades seleccionadas de Argentina', *Derecho y Ciencias Sociales*, 26: 1–23.

Cely-Andrade, L., Cárdenas-Garzón, K., Enríquez-Santander, L.C., Saavedra-Avendano, B., Ortiz-Avendano, G.A., Betancourt-Rojas, L.A. et al (2024) 'Effectiveness and safety of medication abortion via telemedicine versus in-person: a cohort of pregnant people in Colombia', *Contraception*, 138: 110514. doi: 10.1016/j.contraception.2024.110514

Centro Las Libres and Ipas (2014) Accompaniment [documentary], YouTube. Available at: www.youtube.com/watch?v=MC8jxYGzdWQ

Chambers, D.W. and Gillespie, R. (2000) 'Locality in the history of science: colonial science, technoscience, and Indigenous knowledge', *Osiris*, 15: 221–240.

Chaneton, J. and Vacarezza, N. (2011) *La intemperie y lo intempestivo. Experiencias del aborto voluntario en el relato de mujeres y varones*, Buenos Aires: Marea Editorial.

Chia, E. (2018) 'Aborto farmacológico y libertad de información en Chile', in P. Bergallo, I.C. Jaramilo Sierra and J.M. Vaggione (eds) *El aborto en América Latina: estrategias jurídicas para luchar por su legalización y enfrentar las resistencias conservadoras*, Madird: Siglo XXI Editores, pp 271–296.

Chinchilla, A.L., Flores, I.F., Morales, A.F. and de Gil, M.P. (2014) 'Changes in the use of manual vacuum aspiration for postabortion care within the public healthcare service network in Honduras', *International Journal of Gynecology & Obstetrics*, 126(S1): S24–S27.

Chor, J., Goyal, V., Roston, A., Keith, L. and Patel, A. (2012) 'Doulas as facilitators: the expanded role of doulas into abortion care', *Journal of Family Planning and Reproductive Health Care*, 38(2): 123–124.

Clark, H., RamaRao, S. and Townsend, J. (2017) *Ensuring Access to Safe Abortion Supplies*, New York: Population Council. Available at: www.rhsupplies.org/uploads/tx_rhscpublications/Safe_Abortion_Supplies_Landscaping_Report.pdf

Clarke, A. and Montini, T. (1993) 'The many faces of RU486: tales of situated knowledges and technological contestations', *Science, Technology, & Human Values*, 18(1): 42–78.

Coêlho, H.L., Misago, C., Da Fonseca, W.C., Sousa, D.C. and De Araujo, J.L. (1991) 'Selling abortifacients over the counter in pharmacies in Fortaleza, Brazil', *The Lancet*, 338(8761): 247. doi: 10.1016/0140-6736(91)90379-4

Coêlho, H.L.L., Teixeira, A.C., Santos, A.P., Forte, E.B., Morais, S.M., LaVecchia, C. et al (1993) 'Misoprostol and illegal abortion in Fortaleza, Brazil', *The Lancet*, 341(8855): 1261–1263.

Cohen, J., Ortiz, O., Llaguno, S.E., Goodyear, L., Billings, D. and Martinez, I. (2005) 'Reaching women with instructions on misoprostol use in a Latin American country', *Reproductive Health Matters*, 13(26): 84–92.

Collins, F.S. and Mahoney, M.J. (1983) 'Hydrocephalus and abnormal digits after failed first-trimester prostaglandin abortion attempt', *The Journal of Pediatrics*, 102(4): 620–621.

Colón Warren, A. (2023) 'Hacia la justicia reproductiva en Puerto Rico: de la eugenesia al siglo XXI', *Revista IusGénero América Latina*, 1(2): 7–24.

Conrad, P. (1975) 'The discovery of hyperkinesis: notes on the medicalization of deviance', *Social Problems*, 23(1): 12–21.

Correa, S. and Petchesky, R. (1994) 'Reproductive and sexual rights: a feminist perspective', in G. Sen, A. Germain and L. Chen (eds) *Population Policy Reconsidered: Health, Empowerment and Rights*, Cambridge, MA: Harvard University Press, pp 107–126.

Costa, S.H. (1998) 'Commercial availability of misoprostol and induced abortion in Brazil', *International Journal of Gynecology & Obstetrics*, 63(S1): S131–S139.

Costa, S.H. and Vessey, M.P. (1993) 'Misoprostol and illegal abortion in Rio de Janeiro, Brazil', *The Lancet*, 341(8855): 1258–1261.

Creinin, M.D. (2000) 'Medical abortion regimens: historical context and overview', *American Journal of Obstetrics and Gynecology*, 183(S2): S3–S9.

Creinin, M.D. and Darney, P.D. (1993) 'Methotrexate and misoprostol for early abortion', *Contraception*, 48(4): 339–348.

Creinin, M.D. and Vittinghoff, E. (1994) 'Methotrexate and misoprostol vs misoprostol alone for early abortion: a randomized controlled trial', *JAMA*, 272(15): 1190–1195.

Curiel, O., Borzone, M. and Ponomareff, A. (2016) 'Rethinking radical anti-racist feminist politics in a global neoliberal context', *Meridians*, 14(2): 46–55.

Cusicanqui, S.R. (2010) 'The notion of "rights" and the paradoxes of postcolonial modernity: Indigenous peoples and women in Bolivia', *Qui Parle: Critical Humanities and Social Sciences*, 18(2): 29–54.

Cusicanqui, S.R. (2018) *Un mundo ch'ixi es posible. Ensayos desde un presente en crisis*, Buenos Aires: Tinta Limón.

Daby, M. and Moseley, M. (2022) 'Feminist mobilization and the abortion debate in Latin America: lessons from Argentina', *Politics & Gender*, 18(2): 359–393.

Daigle, M., Duffy, D.N. and Castañeda, D.L. (2022) 'Abortion access and Colombia's legacy of civil war: between reproductive violence and reproductive governance', *International Affairs*, 98(4): 1423–1448.

Das, V. and Poole, D. (2004) *Anthropology in the Margins of the State*, Santa Fe, NM: School of American Research Press.

Davis, A.Y. (2011) *Are Prisons Obsolete?* New York: Seven Stories Press.

del Pilar Blanco, M. and Page, J. (2023) 'Introduction: reimagining science in Latin America in geopolitics, culture, and the scientific imaginary in Latin America', in M. del Pilar Blanco and J. Page (eds) *Geopolitics, Culture, and the Scientific Imaginary in Latin America*, Gainesville: University Press of Florida.

De Zordo, S. (2016) 'The biomedicalisation of illegal abortion: the double life of misoprostol in Brazil', *História, Ciências, Saúde-Manguinhos*, 23(1): 19–36.

Downie, W.W. (1991) 'Misuse of misoprostol', *The Lancet*, 338(8761): 247.

Drovetta, R.I. (2015) 'Safe abortion information hotlines: an effective strategy for increasing women's access to safe abortions in Latin America', *Reproductive Health Matters*, 23(45): 47–57.

Drovetta, R., Freeman, C. and Agustina R. (2023) 'Self-care for abortion activists and providers: lessons of law and risk from Argentina', *BMJ Sexual & Reproductive Health*, 49(4): 308–309.

Duffy, D. (2024) *Abortion Trail Activism: The Global Infrastructures for Abortion Access*, London: Bloomsbury.

Duffy, D., Freeman, C. and Rodríguez, S. (2023) 'Beyond the state: abortion care activism in Peru', *Signs: Journal of Women in Culture and Society*, 48(3): 609–634.

Dzuba, I.G., Winikoff, B. and Peña, M. (2013) 'Medical abortion: a path to safe, high-quality abortion care in Latin America and the Caribbean', *The European Journal of Contraception & Reproductive Health Care*, 18(6): 441–450.

Elati, A. and Weeks, A.D. (2009) 'The use of misoprostol in obstetrics and gynaecology', *BJOG: An International Journal of Obstetrics & Gynaecology*, 116: 61–69.

El-Refaey, H. and Templeton, A. (1994) 'Early abortion induction by a combination of mifepristone and oral misoprostol: a comparison between two dose regimens of misoprostol and their effect on blood pressure', *BJOG: An International Journal of Obstetrics & Gynaecology*, 101(9): 792–796.

Encarnación, O.G. (2022) 'Latin America's abortion rights breakthrough', *Journal of Democracy*, 33(4): 89–103.

Engle, O. (2022) 'Abortion mobilities', *Geography Compass*, 16(9): e12656. doi: 10.1111/gec3.12656

Engle, O. (2025) '"Everything I can do at home, I will do it at home": the materialities, temporalities, and spatialities of telemedicine abortion care', *Social & Cultural Geography*, 1–19. doi: 10.1080/14649365.2024.2441774

Erdman, J.N. (2011) 'Access to information on safe abortion: a harm reduction and human rights approach', *Harvard Journal of Law and Gender*, 34: 413–462.

Erdman, J.N. (2012) 'Harm reduction, human rights, and access to information on safer abortion', *International Journal of Gynecology & Obstetrics*, 118(1): 83–86.

Erdman, J.N., DePiñeres, T. and Kismödi, E. (2013) 'Updated WHO guidance on safe abortion: health and human rights', *International Journal of Gynecology & Obstetrics*, 120(2): 200–203.

Erdman, J.N., Jelinska, K. and Yanow, S. (2018) 'Understandings of self-managed abortion as health inequity, harm reduction and social change', *Reproductive Health Matters*, 26(54): 13–19.

Etkin, N.L. (1992) '"Side effects": cultural constructions and reinterpretations of western pharmaceuticals', *Medical Anthropology Quarterly*, 6(2): 99–113.

Facioli, L.R.R., da Costa, A.J. and Zimkovicz, R. (2024) '"No one wants to go to hospital" – moral grammars and abortion networks among women in Brazil', *Mediações*, 29(1): 1–22.

Faúndes, A. and Shah, I.H. (2015) 'Evidence supporting broader access to safe legal abortion', *International Journal of Gynecology & Obstetrics*, 131: S56–S59.

Fernández, M.M., Coeytaux, F., de León, R.G.P. and Harrison, D.L. (2009) 'Assessing the global availability of misoprostol', *International Journal of Gynecology & Obstetrics*, 105(2): 180–186.

Fernández Anderson, C. (2016) 'Reproductive inequalities: as Latin America's pink tide recedes, the struggle for reproductive health reform continues', *NACLA Report on the Americas*, 48(1): 15–17.

Fernandez, M., Fernandes, L.M. and de Amorim, M.M. (2025) 'Total criminalisation of abortion is a threat to sexual and reproductive health in Brazil', *British Medical Journal*, 388: r52. doi: 10.1136/bmj.r52. PMID: 39794001

Fernández Anderson, C. (2020) *Fighting for Abortion Rights in Latin America: Social Movements, State Allies, and Institutions*, London: Routledge.

Fernández Romero, F. (2020) '"Podemos concebir otra historia": Activismo trans, derecho al aborto y justicia reproductiva', *XIV Jornadas Nacionales de Debate Interdisciplinario en Salud y Población*, Instituto de Investigaciones Gino Germani, Facultad de Ciencias Sociales, Universidad de Buenos Aires.

Fernández Vázquez, S. and Szwarc, L. (2018) 'Aborto medicamentoso: transferencias militantes y transnacionalización de saberes en Argentina y América Latina', *RevIISE: Revista de Ciencias Sociales y Humanas*, 12(12): 163–177.

Fernández Vázquez, S. and Brown, J. (2019) 'From stigma to pride: health professionals and abortion policies in the Metropolitan Area of Buenos Aires', *Sexual and Reproductive Health Matters*, 27(3): 65–74.

Fonseca, W., Alencar, A.J.C., Mota, F.S.B. and Coelho, H.L.L. (1991) 'Misoprostol and congenital malformations', *The Lancet*, 338(8758): 56.

Freeman, C. (2017) 'The crime of choice: abortion border crossings from Chile to Peru', *Gender, Place & Culture*, 24(6): 851–868.

Freeman, C. (2020) 'Viapolitics and the emancipatory possibilities of abortion mobilities', *Mobilities*, 15(6): 896–910.

Freeman, C. and Rodríguez, S. (2024a) 'The chemical geographies of misoprostol: spatializing abortion access from the biochemical to the global', *Annals of the American Association of Geographers*, 114(1): 123–138.

Freeman, C. and Rodríguez, S. (2024b) 'The making of clandestinity: "strategic ignorance" in abortion practices in Latin America', *International Feminist Journal of Politics*, 26(3): 633–656.

Frohlick, S., Lozanski, K., Speier, A. and Sheller, M. (2019) 'Mobilities meet reproductive vibes…', *Transfers*, 9(1): 95–102.

Gago, V. and Mason-Deese, L. (2019) 'Rethinking situated knowledge from the perspective of Argentina's feminist strike', *Journal of Latin American Geography*, 18(3): 202–209.

García, E., Lozano, G. and Arias, M. (2020) 'La criminalización de mujeres por el delito de aborto en Honduras'. Available at: www.clacaidigital.info/bitstream/handle/123456789/1315/La%20Criminalizacio%CC%81n%20de%20las%20Mujeres%20por%20el%20Delito%20de%20Aborto%20en%20Honduras.pdf?sequence=1&isAllowed=y

Gemzell-Danielsson, K., Fiala, C. and Weeks, A. (2007) 'Misoprostol: first-line therapy for incomplete miscarriage in the developing world', *BJOG: An International Journal of Obstetrics and Gynaecology*, 114(11): 1337–1339.

Gianella, C. and Álvarez, B. (2021) 'Lawfare judicial: análises dos argumentos jurídicos contra os direitos ao aborto nas cortes Peruanas', *Revista Direito GV*, 17: e2146. doi: 10.1590/2317-6172202146

Gilmartin, M. and White, A. (2011) 'Interrogating medical tourism: Ireland, abortion, and mobility rights', *Signs: Journal of Women in Culture and Society*, 36(2): 275–280.

Gilmore, R.W. (2022) *Abolition Geography: Essays towards Liberation*, London: Verso Books.

Gloppen, S. (2021) 'Conceptualizing abortion lawfare', *Revista Direito GV*, 17(3): e2143. doi: 10.1590/2317-6172202143

Gold, J. and Cates, W. (1980) 'Herbal abortifacients', *JAMA*, 243(13): 1365–1366.

Goldberg, A.B., Greenberg, M.B. and Darney, P.D. (2001) 'Misoprostol and pregnancy', *New England Journal of Medicine*, 344(1): 38–47.

González, A.C. (2012) '"The health exception": a means of expanding access to legal abortion', *Reproductive Health Matters*, 20(40): 22–29.

González, C.H., Vargas, F.R., Perez, A.B.A., Kim, C.A., Brunoni, D., Marques-Dias, M.J. et al (1993) 'Limb deficiency with or without Möbius sequence in seven Brazilian children associated with misoprostol use in the first trimester of pregnancy', *American Journal of Medical Genetics*, 47(1): 59–64.

González, D.J. (2005) 'Marianismo', in S. Oboler and D.J. González (eds) *The Oxford Encyclopedia of Latinos and Latinas in the United States*, Oxford: Oxford University Press.

Greene, J.A. and Sismondo, S. (2015) 'Introduction', in S. Sismondo and J.A. Greene (eds) *The Pharmaceutical Studies Reader*, Hoboken, NJ: John Wiley & Sons, pp 1–16.

Greenhouse, S. (1985) Special to the New York Times 'Monsanto to aquire G. D. Searle', *The New York Times*, 19 July. ISSN 0362-4331.

Grossman, D. (2025) 'New data on ulipristal acetate and misoprostol for medication abortion—a step forward?', *NEJM Evidence*, advance online publication. Available at: https://evidence.nejm.org/doi/full/10.1056/EVIDe2400460#body-ref-r1

Grupo De Información en Reproductión Elegida (2018) '*Maternidad o Castigo. La criminalización del aborto en México*', GIRE, August. Available at: https://gire.org.mx/wp-content/uploads/2019/11/Maternidad_o_castigo.pdf

Gudiño Bessone, P. (2023) 'Prácticas feministas en salud y acceso al aborto en Argentina (2018–2021)', *Iztapalapa: Revista de ciencias sociales y humanidades*, 44(95): 379–419.

Guedes, A.C. (2000) 'Abortion in Brazil: legislation, reality and options', *Reproductive Health Matters*, 8(16): 66–76.

Gurr, B. (2014) *Reproductive Justice: The Politics of Health Care for Native American Women*, New Brunswick: Rutgers University Press.

Gynuity Health Projects (2007) *Choices for Medical Abortion Introduction in Brazil, Colombia, Mexico, and Peru*, New York: Gynuity. Available at: https://gynuity.org/assets/resources/workpap_ma_lac_en.pdf

Gynuity Health Projects (2024) *Mifepristone Approved List*, New York: Gynuity. Available at: https://gynuity.org/assets/resources/mife_by_country_and_year_en.pdf

Hale, R.W. and Zinberg, S. (2001) 'Use of misoprostol in pregnancy', *New England Journal of Medicine*, 344(1): 59–60.

Halfmann, D. (2012) 'Recognizing medicalization and demedicalization: discourses, practices, and identities', *Health*, 16(2): 186–207.

Halliday, T.C. (2018) 'Plausible folk theories: throwing veils of plausibility over zones of ignorance in global governance', *The British Journal of Sociology*, 6(4): 936–961.

Handal-Orefice, R.C., Friedman, A.M., Chouinard, S.M., Eke, A.C., Feinberg, B., Politch, J. et al (2019) 'Oral or vaginal misoprostol for labor induction and cesarean delivery risk', *Obstetrics & Gynecology*, 134(1): 10–16.

Harding, S. (2009) 'Postcolonial and feminist philosophies of science and technology: convergences and dissonances', *Postcolonial Studies*, 12(4): 401–421.

Harding, S. (2014) 'Beyond postcolonial theory: two undertheorized perspectives on science and technology', in M. Wyer, M. Barbercheck, D. Cookmeyer, H. Ozturk and M. Wayne (eds) *Women, Science, and Technology* (3rd edn), London: Routledge.

Harding, S. (2016) 'Latin American decolonial social studies of scientific knowledge: alliances and tensions', *Science, Technology, & Human Values*, 41(6): 1063–1087.

Harding, S. (2017) 'Latin American decolonial studies: feminist issues', *Feminist Studies*, 43(3): 624–636.

Hardon, A. and Sanabria, E. (2017) 'Fluid drugs: revisiting the anthropology of pharmaceuticals', *Annual Review of Anthropology*, 46: 117–132.

Harvey, P. (2015) 'Medical abortion: the hidden revolution', *Journal of Family Planning and Reproductive Health Care*, 41(3): 193–196.

Hawkey, C.J., Karrasch, J.A., Szczepañski, L., Walker, D.G., Barkun, A., Swannell, A.J. et al (1998) 'Omeprazole compared with misoprostol for ulcers associated with nonsteroidal antiinflammatory drugs', *New England Journal of Medicine*, 338(11): 727–734.

Henderson, J.T., Hwang, A.C., Harper, C.C. and Stewart, F.H. (2005) 'Safety of mifepristone abortions in clinical use', *Contraception*, 72(3): 175–178.

Hernandez, P.M. (2002) 'The myth of machismo: an everyday reality for Latin American women', *St. Thomas Law Review*, 15(4): 859–882.

Hernández Castillo, R.A. (2010) 'The emergence of Indigenous feminism in Latin America', *Signs: Journal of Women in Culture and Society*, 35(3): 539–545.

Ho, P.C. and Ngai, S.W. (1999) 'Mifepristone and misoprostol', *Current Obstetrics & Gynaecology*, 9(1): 29–33.

Hoevels-Guerich, H., Haferkorn, L., Persigehl, M., Hofstetter, R. and von Bernuth, G. (1984) 'Widening of cranial sutures after long-term prostaglandin E2 therapy in two newborn infants', *The Journal of Pediatrics*, 105(1): 72–74.

Hoggart, L. and Berer, M. (2022) 'Making the case for supported self-managed medical abortion as an option for the future', *BMJ Sexual & Reproductive Health*, 48(2): 146–148.

Hulme, S., Hughes, C.E. and Nielsen, S. (2020) 'The price and mark up of pharmaceutical drugs supplied on the black market', *International Journal of Drug Policy*, 76: 102626. doi: 10.1016/j.drugpo.2019.102626

Hyman, A., Blanchard, K., Coeytaux, F., Grossman, D. and Teixeira, A. (2013) 'Misoprostol in women's hands: a harm reduction strategy for unsafe abortion', *Contraception*, 87(2): 128–130.

Jarman, M. (2015) 'Relations of abortion: crip approaches to reproductive justice', *Feminist Formations*, 27(1): 46–66.

Jelinska, K. and Yanow, S. (2018) 'Putting abortion pills into women's hands: realizing the full potential of medical abortion', *Contraception*, 97(2): 86–89.

Joffe, C. (2009) 'Abortion and medicine: a sociopolitical history', in M. Paul, E. Lichtenberg, L. Borgatta, D. Grimes, P. Stubblefield and M. Creinin (eds) *Management of Unintended and Abnormal Pregnancy*, Oxford: Blackwell, pp 1–9.

Joffe, C. and Schroeder, R. (2021) 'COVID-19, health care, and abortion exceptionalism in the United States', *Perspectives on Sexual and Reproductive Health*, 53(1–2): 5–12.

Joffe, C. and Weitz, T.A. (2003) 'Normalizing the exceptional: incorporating the "abortion pill" into mainstream medicine', *Social Science & Medicine*, 56(12): 2353–2366.

Joffe, C.E., Weitz, T.A. and Stacey, C.L. (2004) 'Uneasy allies: pro-choice physicians, feminist health activists and the struggle for abortion rights', *Sociology of Health & Illness*, 26(6): 775–796.

Johnson, D.M. (2023) 'The promise of abortion pills: evidence on the safety and effectiveness of self-managed medication abortion and opportunities to expand access', *SMU Law Review*, 76(1): 135–162.

Juarez, F., Bankole, A. and Palma, J.L. (2019) 'Women's abortion seeking behavior under restrictive abortion laws in Mexico', *PLoS One*, 14(12): e0226522. doi: 10.1371/journal.pone.0226522

Kapp, N. and Lohr, P.A. (2020) 'Modern methods to induce abortion: safety, efficacy and choice', *Best Practice & Research Clinical Obstetrics & Gynaecology*, 63: 37–44

Karlin, J. and Joffe, C. (2023) 'Self-sourced medication abortion, physician authority, and the contradictions of abortion care', *Journal of Health Politics, Policy and Law*, 48(4): 603–627.

Keefe-Oates, B. (2021) 'Transforming abortion access through feminist community-based healthcare and activism', in B. Sutton and N.L. Vacarezza (eds) *Abortion and Democracy: Contentious Body Politics in Argentina, Chile, and Uruguay*, Abingdon: Routledge, pp 190–204.

Keefe-Oates, B., Filippa, S., Janiak, E., Zurbriggen, R., Grosso, B., Chen, J.T. et al (2024) 'Seeking abortion accompaniment: experiences and self-managed abortion preferences of hotline callers after abortion legalisation in Argentina', *BMJ Sexual & Reproductive Health*, 18: bmjsrh-2023-202209. doi: 10.1136/bmjsrh-2023-202209

Kimball, N.L. (2020) *An Open Secret: The History of Unwanted Pregnancy and Abortion in Modern Bolivia*, New Brunswick: Rutgers University Press.

Kimport, K., McReynolds-Pérez, J., Bercu, C., Cisternas, C., Wilkinson Salamea, E., Zurbriggen, R. et al (2023) 'The pleasure, joy and positive emotional experiences of abortion accompaniment after 17 weeks' gestation', *Culture, Health & Sexuality*, 26(8): 1028–1043.

Klitsch, M. (1991) 'Antiprogestins and the abortion controversy: a progress report', *Family Planning Perspectives*, 23(6): 275–282.

Knopes, J. (2019) 'Science, technology, and human health: the value of STS in medical and health humanities pedagogy', *Journal of Medical Humanities*, 40(4): 461–471.

Kodan, L.R., Verschueren, K.J.C, Paidin, R., Paidin, R., Browne, J.L., Bloemenkamp, K.W.M. et al (2021) 'Trends in maternal mortality in Suriname: 3 confidential enquiries in 3 decades', *AJOG Global Reports*, 1(1): 100004. doi: 10.1016/j.xagr.2021.100004

Krauss, A. (2019) 'The ephemeral politics of feminist accompaniment networks in Mexico City', *Feminist Theory*, 20(1): 37–54.

Krauss, A. (2021) 'Legal guerilla: jurisdiction, time, and abortion access in Mexico City', *Revista Direito GV*, 17: e2139. doi: 10.1590/2317-6172202139

Krauss, A. (2023) 'Archaeologies of the body: imagining abortion care with feminist acompañantes in Mexico', *South Atlantic Quarterly*, 122(2): 407–416.

Kreimer, P. (2007) 'Social studies of science and technology in Latin America: a field in the process of consolidation', *Science, Technology & Society*, 12(1): 1–9.

Kreimer, P. and Vessuri, H. (2018) 'Latin American science, technology, and society: a historical and reflexive approach', *Tapuya: Latin American Science, Technology and Society*, 1(1): 17–37.

Kulczycki, A. (2011) 'Abortion in Latin America: changes in practice, growing conflict, and recent policy developments', *Studies in Family Planning*, 42(3): 199–220.

Kumar, A., Hessini, L. and Mitchell, E. (2009) 'Conceptualizing abortion stigma', *Culture, Health, and Sexuality*, 11(6): 625–639.

Küng, S.A., Darney, B.G., Saavedra-Avendaño, B., Lohr, P.A. and Gil, L. (2018) 'Access to abortion under the heath exception: a comparative analysis in three countries', *Reproductive Health*, 15(1): 107. doi: 10.1186/s12978-018-0548-x

Lafaurie, M.M., Grossman, D., Troncoso, E., Billings, D.L. and Chávez, S. (2005) 'Women's perspectives on medical abortion in Mexico, Colombia, Ecuador and Peru: a qualitative study', *Reproductive Health Matters*, 13(26): 75–83.

LaMarre, A., Rice, C., Cook, K.M. and Friedman, M. (2020) 'Fat reproductive justice: navigating the boundaries of reproductive health care', *Journal of Social Issues*, 76(2): 338–362.

Lara, D., García, S.G., Ellertson, C., Camlin, C. and Suárez, J. (2006) 'The measure of induced abortion levels in Mexico using random response technique', *Sociological Methods & Research*, 35(2): 279–301.

Lara, D., García, S.G., Wilson, K.S. and Paz, F. (2011) 'How often and under which circumstances do Mexican pharmacy vendors recommend misoprostol to induce an abortion?', *International Perspectives on Sexual and Reproductive Health*, 75–83.

Larrea, S., Palència, L. and Borrell, C. (2024) 'Medical abortion provision and quality of care: what can be learned from feminist activists?', *Health Care for Women International*, 45(1): 47–66.

Latt, S.M., Milner, A. and Kavanagh, A. (2019) 'Abortion laws reform may reduce maternal mortality: an ecological study in 162 countries', *BMC Women's Health*, 19(1): 1–9.

Lemon, M. and Medina, E. (2014) 'Technology in an expanded field: a review of history of technology scholarship on Latin America in selected English-language journals', in E. Medina, I.C. Marques and C. Holmes (eds) *Beyond Imported Magic. Essays on Science, Technology and Society in Latin America*, Cambridge, MA: MIT Press, pp 111–136.

Lesbianas y Feministas por la Descriminalización del Aborto (2010) Todo lo que querés saber sobre cómo hacerse un aborto con pastillas, Buenos Aires: Editorial del Collective.

Liboiron, M. (2016) 'Redefining pollution and action: The matter of plastics', *Journal of Material Culture*, 21(1): 87–110.

Liboiron, M. (2021) *Pollution is Colonialism*, Durham, NC: Duke University Press.

Liboiron, M., Tironi, M. and Calvillo, N. (2018) 'Toxic politics: acting in a permanently polluted world', *Social Studies of Science*, 48(3): 331–349.

Lin, C.S., Pykett, A.A., Flanagan, C. and Chávez, K.R. (2016) 'Engendering the prefigurative: feminist praxes that bridge a politics of prefigurement and survival', *Journal of Social and Political Psychology*, 4(1): 302–317.

Lockwood, C.J. (2001) 'Editorial: into the vortex', *Contemporary OB/GYN*, 46(8): 8.

Lockwood, C.J. (2002) 'Editorial: here we go again', *Contemporary OB/GYN*, 47(7): 11.

Löwy, I. and Dias Villela Corrêa, M.C. (2020) 'The "abortion pill" misoprostol in Brazil: women's empowerment in a conservative and repressive political environment', *American Journal of Public Health*, 110(5): 677–684.

Lugones, M. (2007) 'Heterosexualism and the colonial/modern gender system', *Hypatia*, 22(1): 186–219.

Lugones, M. (2010) 'Toward a decolonial feminism', *Hypatia*, 25(4): 742–759.

Luigi-Bravo, G. and Gill, R.K. (2022) 'Safe abortion within the Venezuelan complex humanitarian emergency: understanding context as key to identifying the potential for digital self-care tools in expanding access', *Sexual and Reproductive Health Matters*, 29(3): 20–27.

MacDonald, M.E. (2021) 'Misoprostol: the social life of a life-saving drug in global maternal health', *Science, Technology, & Human Values*, 46(2): 376–401.

Machado, M.R., Peñas-Defago, M.A. and Gianella, C. (2022) 'Anti-abortion mobilization in Latin America: signs of a field in transformation', *Revista Direito GV*, 18(3): e2234. doi: 10.1590/2317-6172202234

Maffeo, F., Santarelli, N., Satta, P. and Zurbriggen, R. (2015) 'Parteras de nuevos feminismos. Socorristas en Red (feministas que abortamos): una forma de activismo corporizado y sororo', *Revista Venezolana de Estudios de la Mujer*, 20: 217–227.

Mahoney, M. and Mitchell, L. (2016) *The Doulas: Radical Care for Pregnant People*, New York: The Feminist Press at CUNY.

Marcotte, J. (2016) 'The agnotology of abortion: a history of ignorance about women's knowledge of fertility control', *Outskirts: Feminisms Along the Edge*, 34: 1–21.

Marcus-Delgado, J. (2019) *The Politics of Abortion in Latin America: Public Debates, Private Lives*, Boulder, CO: Lynne Rienner Publishers.

Martin, P. (2023) 'Poner la cuerpa: the body as a site of reproductive rights activism in Peru', *Bulletin of Latin American Research*, 42(1): 21–35.

Martin, Z.C., Riedl, M.J. and Woolley, S.C. (2023) 'How pro-and anti-abortion activists use encrypted messaging apps in post-Roe America', *Big Data & Society*, 10(2): 20539517231221736. doi: 10.1177/2053951723122

Mateo, N. (2024) '"Poner el cuerpo": primeras experiencias de abortos ambulatorios con misoprostol en Argentina', *Íconos-Revista de Ciencias Sociales*, 80: 53–72.

McGoey, L. (2019) *The Unknowers: How Strategic Ignorance Rules the World*, London: Zed Books.

McGoey, L. (2020) 'Micro-ignorance and macro-ignorance in the social sciences', *Social Research: An International Quarterly*, 87(1): 197–217.

McMahon, H.V. and McMahon, B.D. (2024) 'Automating untruths: ChatGPT, self-managed medication abortion, and the threat of misinformation in a post-*Roe* world', *Frontiers in Digital Health*, 6: 1287186. doi: 10.3389/fdgth.2024.1287186

McReynolds-Pérez, J. (2017) 'No doctors required: lay activist expertise and pharmaceutical abortion in Argentina', *Signs: Journal of Women in Culture and Society*, 42(2): 349–375.

Medina, E., Marques, I.C. and Holmes, C. (eds) (2014) *Beyond Imported Magic: Essays on Science, Technology, and Society in Latin America*, Cambridge, MA: MIT Press.

Millar, E. (2023) 'Abortion stigma, abortion exceptionalism, and medical curricula', *Health Sociology Review*, 32(3): 261–276.

Miller, L. and Alcoba, N. (2024) 'Argentina's leader takes ax to program that drove down teen pregnancy', *The New York Times*, 8 November. Available at: www.nytimes.com/2024/11/08/world/americas/argentina-javier-milei-abortion-access.html

Mines, A. (2011) *Lesbianas y Feministas por la Descriminalización del aborto-Aborto-traducción cultural-lesbianas-poder*, Actas de las IX Jornadas de Sociología, Buenos Aires: Facultad de Ciencias Sociales, Universidad Nacional de Buenos Aires.

Mines, A., Villa, G.D., Rueda, R. and Marzano, V. (2013) '"El aborto lesbiano que se hace con la mano": Continuidades y rupturas en la militancia por el derecho al aborto en Argentina (2009–2012)', *Bagoas-Estudos gays: gêneros e sexualidades*, 7(9): 134–160.

Mohamed, A.A.B., Badawy, A. and Fahmy, S.S.E. (2024) 'Improved effectiveness of medical management of missed abortion in second trimester with letrozole-misoprostol combination: a prospective cohort study', *African Journal of Biological Sciences*, 6(9): 3450–3459.

Molina, V. (2022) 'Abortion, same-sex marriage, and gender identity during the Pink Tide: Venezuela compared to Latin American trends', *The International Journal of Human Rights*, 26(7): 1293–1312.

Montanaro Mena, A.M. (2017) *Una mirada al feminismo decolonial en América Latina*, Madrid: Dykinson, S.L.

Moore, A.M., Ortiz, J., Blades, N., Whitehead, H. and Villarreal, C. (2021) 'Women's experiences using drugs to induce abortion acquired in the informal sector in Colombia: qualitative interviews with users in Bogotá and the Coffee Axis', *Sexual and Reproductive Health Matters*, 29(1): 146–161.

Morgan, L.M. (2015) 'Reproductive rights or reproductive justice? Lessons from Argentina', *Health and Human Rights Journal*, 17: 136–147.

Morgan, L.M. (2019) 'Reproductive governance, redux', *Medical Anthropology*, 38(2): 113–117.

Morgan, L.M. (2021) 'Costa Rica's oversized role in Latin American sexual and reproductive rights lawfare', *Revista Direito GV*, 17: e2137. doi: 10.1590/2317-6172202137

Morgan, L.M. and Roberts, E.F.S. (2012) 'Reproductive governance in Latin America', *Anthropology & Medicine*, 19(2): 241–254.

Moseson, H., Jayaweera, R., Raifman, S., Keefe-Oates, B., Filippa, S., Motana, R. et al (2020) 'Self-managed medication abortion outcomes: results from a prospective pilot study', *Reproductive Health*, 17(1): 1–12.

Moseson, H., Jayaweera, R., Baum, S.E. and Gerdts, C. (2024) 'How effective is misoprostol alone for medication abortion?', *NEJM Evidence*, 3(6): EVIDccon2300129. doi: 10.1056/EVIDccon2300129

Munson, Z. (2018) *Abortion Politics*, Hoboken, NJ: John Wiley & Sons.

Murchison, A. and Duff, P. (2004) 'Misoprostol for uterine evacuation in patients with early pregnancy failures', *American Journal of Obstetrics and Gynecology*, 190(5): 1445–1446.

Murphy, M. (2012) *Seizing the Means of Reproduction: Entanglements of Feminism, Health, and Technoscience*, Durham, NC: Duke University Press.

Murphy, M. (2017) *The Economization of Life*, Durham, NC: Duke University Press.

Murray, L. and Khan, N. (2020) 'The im/mobilities of "sometimes-migrating" for abortion: Ireland to Great Britain', *Mobilities*, 15(2): 161–172.

Murtagh, C., Wells, E., Raymond, E.G., Coeytaux, F. and Winikoff, B. (2018) 'Exploring the feasibility of obtaining mifepristone and misoprostol from the internet', *Contraception*, 97(4): 287–291.

Nandagiri, R. and Berro Pizzarossa, L. (2023) 'Transgressing biomedical and legal boundaries: the "enticing and hazardous" challenges and promises of a Self-Managed Abortion multiverse', *Women's Studies International Forum*, 100: 102799. doi: 10.1016/j.wsif.2023.102799

Nations, M. K., Misago, C., Fonseca, W., Correia, L. L. and Campbell, O. M. (1997) 'Women's hidden transcripts about abortion in Brazil' *Social Science & Medicine*, 44(12): 1833–1845.

Necochea López, R. (2014) *A History of Family Planning in Twentieth-Century Peru*, Chapel Hill, NC: UNC Press Books.

Nofal, A.M., Abd El All, N.K., El Halaby, A.E.F., Mahmoud, F.F. and El-Kelani, O.A. (2024) 'Efficacy of adjunctive use of letrozole and misoprostol in the medical induction of first trimester abortion', *The Egyptian Journal of Hospital Medicine*, 95(1): 2112–2118.

Nolan, R. (2022) 'Reproductive justice in Latin America', *Latin American Research Review*, 57(4): 948–959.

Norman, J.E., Thong, K.J. and Baird, D.T. (1991) 'Uterine contractility and induction of abortion in early pregnancy by misoprostol and mifepristone', *The Lancet*, 338(8777): 1233–1236.

Oberman, M. (2018) *Her Body, Our Laws: On the Frontlines of the Abortion War from El Salvador to Oklahoma*, Boston, MA: Beacon Press.

O'Donnell, R. (2015) 'Biotechnology and biopiracy: plant-based contraceptives in the Americas and the (mis) management of nature', *Canadian Woman Studies*, 31(1/2): 76.

Orr, J. (2017) *Abortion Wars: The Fight for Reproductive Rights*, Bristol: Policy Press.

Ortiz, J., Blades, N. and Prada, E. (2024) 'Motivations for using misoprostol for abortion outside the formal healthcare system in Colombia: a qualitative study of women seeking postabortion care in Bogotá and the Coffee Axis', *Reproductive Health*, 21(1): 76. doi: 10.1186/s12978-024-01814-0

Palomino, N., Padilla, M.R., Talledo, B.D., Mazuelos, C.G., Carda, J. and Bayer, A.M. (2011) 'The social constructions of unwanted pregnancy and abortion in Lima, Peru', *Global Public Health*, 6(1): S73–S89.

Paxman, J.M., Rizo, A., Brown, L. and Benson, J. (1993) 'The clandestine epidemic: the practice of unsafe abortion in Latin America', *Studies in Family Planning*, 24(4): 205–226.

Pecheny, M., Lucaccini, M., Zaidan, L. and Szwarc, L. (2022) 'Movilizaciones por la interrupción voluntaria del embarazo en Argentina y Uruguay: esperas que no son dulces', *Canadian Journal of Latin American and Caribbean Studies*, 47(3): 390–414.

Perrin, L.M. (2001) 'Resisting reproduction: reconsidering slave contraception in the Old South', *Journal of American Studies*, 35(2): 255–274.

Petchesky, R. (1990) *Abortion and Woman's Choice*, Boston, MA: Northeastern University Press.

Pheterson, G. and Azize, Y. (2005) 'Abortion practice in the northeast Caribbean: "just write down stomach pain"', *Reproductive Health Matters*, 13(26): 44–53.

Philip, N.M., Winikoff, B., Moore, K. and Blumenthal, P. (2004) 'A consensus regimen for early abortion with misoprostol', *International Journal of Gynecology & Obstetrics*, 87(3): 281–283.

Pilecco, F.B., Mccallum, C.A., Da Conceição Chagas De Almeida, M., Alves, F.J.O, Dos Santos Rocha, A., Ortelan, N. et al (2021) 'Abortion and the COVID-19 pandemic: insights for Latin America', *Cadernos de Saúde Pública*, 37(6): 1–13.

Potts, M. and Hemmerling, A. (2006) 'The worldwide burden of postpartum haemorrhage: policy development where inaction is lethal', *International Journal of Gynecology & Obstetrics*, 94: S116–S121.

Radi, B. (2020) 'Reproductive injustice, trans rights, and eugenics', *Sexual and Reproductive Health Matters*, 28(1): 1824318. doi: 10.1080/26410397.2020.1824318

Radiolab (2023) 'Ukraine: under the counter' [podcast episode]. Available at: https://radiolab.org/podcast/ukraine-under-counter

Rajão, R., Duque, R.B. and De', R. (2014) 'Introduction: voices from within and outside the South—defying STS epistemologies, boundaries, and theories', *Science, Technology, & Human Values*, 39(6): 767–772.

Ramos, S., Romero, M. and Aizenberg, L. (2014) 'Women's experiences with the use of medical abortion in a legally restricted context: the case of Argentina', *Reproductive Health Matters*, 22(44): 4–15.

Reagan, L.J. (1997) *When Abortion Was a Crime: Women, Medicine, and Law in the United States, 1867–1973*, Berkeley: University of California Press.

Reser, J.P. and Smithson, M.J. (1988) 'When ignorance is adaptive: not knowing about the nuclear threat', *Knowledge in Society*, 1(4): 7–27.

Riddle, J. (1992) *Contraception and Abortion from the Ancient World to the Renaissance*, Cambridge, MA: Harvard University Press.

Riddle, J. (1997) *Eve's Herbs: A History of Contraception and Abortion in the West*, Cambridge, MA: Harvard University Press.

Ringel, R.E., Haney, P.J., Brenner, J.I., Mancuso, T.J., Roberts, G.S., Moulton, A.L. et al (1983) 'Periosteal changes secondary to prostaglandin administration', *The Journal of Pediatrics*, 103(2): 251–253.

Rivera Berruz, S. (2023) 'Latin American feminism', in E.N. Zalta and U. Nodelman (eds) *The Stanford Encyclopedia of Philosophy*, Standford, CA: The Metaphysics Research Lab.

Roberts, D.E. (2017) *Killing the Black Body: Race, Reproduction, and the Meaning of Liberty* (2nd edn), New York: Vintage.

Roberts-Ganim, M. (2023) *Medicine on the Margins: Sex Workers, Abortion, and Scientific Knowledge in Chicago, 1867–1912*, Unpublished thesis, University of Chicago.

Rojas, V.R., Morales, M.D.R.R., Martín, M.B.H., Pedraza, Y.R. and Falcón, M.R. (2022) 'Aborto, una mirada desde los activismos feministas', *Iberoforum. Revista de Ciencias Sociales*, 2(1): 1–8.

Ross, L.J. (2017) 'Reproductive justice as intersectional feminist activism', *Souls*, 19(3): 286–314.

Ross, L. and Solinger, R. (2017) *Reproductive Justice: An Introduction*, Berkeley: University of California Press.

Roth, C. (2020) *A Miscarriage of Justice: Women's Reproductive Lives and the Law in Early Twentieth-century Brazil*, Stanford, CA: Stanford University Press.

Roth, C. (2023) 'Abortion access in the Americas: a hemispheric and historical approach', *Frontiers in Public Health*, 11: 1284737. doi: 10.3389/fpubh.2023.1284737

Rowlands, S. (2012) 'Abortion pills: under whose control?', *Journal of Family Planning and Reproductive Health Care*, 38(2): 117–122.

Rowlands, S. and Wale, J. (2020) 'A constructivist vision of the first-trimester abortion experience', *Health and Human Rights*, 22(1): 237–249.

Rowlands, S. and Harrison-Woolrych, M. (2023) 'Improving access to medicines for early medical abortion: learning from experiences of medicines licensing and service delivery', *BMJ Sexual & Reproductive Health*, 49(4): 234–237.

Ruibal, A. and Fernandez Anderson, C. (2020) 'Legal obstacles and social change: strategies of the abortion rights movement in Argentina', *Politics, Groups, and Identities*, 8(4): 698–713.

Ruibal, A. (2021) 'Using constitutional courts to advance abortion rights in Latin America', *International Feminist Journal of Politics*, 23(4): 579–599.

Ruiz, S.R. (2023) 'Apuntes hacia la justicia reproductiva en el Estado de México', *Revista Filosofía en la Red*, 4: 62–72.

Salazar, E. (2019) 'Abortar en Perú: cuando víctima y familiares son llevados a cárcel', Ojo Público, 22 October. Available at: https://ojo-publico.com/1411/abortar-en-peru-victima-y-familiares-son-llevados-carcel

Sanabria, E. (2016) 'Circulating ignorance: complexity and agnogenesis in the obesity epidemic', *Cultural Anthropology*, 31(1): 131–158.

Sang, G.W., Weng, L.J., Shao, Q.X., Du, M.K., Wu, X.Z., Lu, Y.L. et al (1994) 'Termination of early pregnancy by two regimens of mifepristone with misoprostol and mifepristone with PG05—a multicentre randomized clinical trial in China', *Contraception*, 50(6): 501–510.

Schiebinger, L. (2004) *Plants and Empire*, Cambridge, MA: Harvard University Press.

Schonhofer, P.S. (1991) 'Brazil: misuse of misoprostol as an abortifacient may induce malformations', *The Lancet*, 337(8756): 1534–1535.

Schwartz Marin, E. and Fiske, A. (2022) 'The frog and the vine: Indigenous knowledge, biomedical innovation, and biopiracy in Latin America', in A. Barahona (ed) *Handbook of the Historiography of Latin American Studies on the Life Sciences and Medicine*, Cham: Springer International Publishing, pp 487–503.

Searcy, J.J., Block, E. and Castañeda, A.N. (2024) 'Strategic advocacy: doula care, liminality, and reproductive justice', *Studies in Comparative International Development*, advance online publication. doi: 10.1007/s12116-024-09431-5

Segato, R.L. (2021) *La guerra contra las mujeres*, Buenos Aires: Prometeo Editorial.

Sethna, C. and Davis, G. (eds) (2019) *Abortion Across borders: Transnational Travel and Access to Abortion Services*, Baltimore: JHU Press.

Sheldon, S. (1997) *Beyond Control: Medical Power and Abortion Law*, London: Pluto Press.

Sheldon, S. (2016) 'How can a state control swallowing? The home use of abortion pills in Ireland', *Reproductive Health Matters*, 24(48): 90–101.

Sheller, M. and Urry, J. (2006) 'The new mobilities paradigm', *Environment and Planning A*, 38(2): 207–226.

Sheller, M. (2011) 'Sustainable mobility and mobility justice: towards a twin transition', in M. Grieco and J. Urry (eds) *Mobilities: New Perspectives on Transport and Society*, London: Routledge, pp 289–304.

Sheller, M. (2018a) *Mobility Justice: The Politics of Movement in an Age of Extremes*, London: Verso.

Sheller, M. (2018b) 'Theorising mobility justice', *Tempo Social*, 30(2): 17–34.

Shenkin, E.N. and Abee, M. (2024) 'International spaces for feminist cross-border resistance', *Political Geography*, 112: 103111. doi: 10.1016/j.polgeo.2024.103111

Shepard, B. (2000) 'The "double discourse" on sexual and reproductive rights in Latin America: the chasm between public policy and private actions', *Health and Human Rights*, 4(2): 110–143.

Shochet, T., Pizzarossa, L.B., Larrea, S., Blum, J., Jelinska, K., Comendant, R. and Sagaidac, I. (2023) 'Self-managed abortion via the internet: analysis of one year of service delivery data from Women Help Women', *Gates Open Research*, 7: 41.

Side, K. (2016) 'A geopolitics of migrant women, mobility and abortion access in the Republic of Ireland', *Gender, Place & Culture*, 23(12): 1788–1799.

Side, K. (2020) 'Abortion im/mobility: spatial consequences in the Republic of Ireland', *Feminist Review*, 124(1): 15–31.

Sieder, R. and Espinosa, Y.B. (2021) 'Abortion lawfare in Mexico's supreme court: between the right to health and subnational autonomy', *Revista Direito GV*, 17(3): e2138. doi: 10.1590/2317-6172202138

Singer, E.O. (2019) 'Realizing abortion rights at the margins of legality in Mexico', *Medical Anthropology*, 38(2): 167–181.

Singer, E.O. (2022) *Lawful Sins: Abortion Rights and Reproductive Governance in Mexico*, Redwood City, CA: Stanford University Press.

Singh, S., Remez, L., Sedgh, G., Kwok, L. and Onda, T. (2018) *Abortion Worldwide 2017: Uneven Progress and Unequal Access*, New York: Guttmacher Institute.

Siskindovich, J. (2018) 'La experiencia de aborto como apertura política imaginativa. Lugares del deseo y la esperanza', *Crítica y Resistencias: Revista de conflictos sociales latinoamericanos*, 7: 122–136.

Sodero, S. (2019) 'Vital mobilities: circulating blood via fictionalized vignettes', *Cultural Geographies*, 26(1): 109–125.

Soto Laveaga, G. (2009) *Jungle Laboratories: Mexican Peasants, National Projects, and the Making of the Pill*, Durham, NC: Duke University Press.

Speier, A., Lozanski, K. and Frohlick, S. (2020) 'Reproductive mobilities', *Mobilities*, 15(2): 107–119.

Stankiewicz, P. (2009) 'The role of risks and uncertainties in technological conflicts: three strategies of constructing ignorance', *Innovation*, 22(1): 105–124.

Statista (2024) 'Average monthly net salary in selected countries in Latin America and the Caribbean as of 2024'. Available at: www.statista.com/statistics/950903/average-salary-latin-america-by-country/

Stephenson, M. and Wing, D. (2015) 'Misoprostol for induction of labor', *Seminars in Perinatology*, 39(6): 459–462.

Stern, A.M. (2016) 'Zika and reproductive justice', *Cadernos de saude publica*, 32: e00081516. doi: 10.1590/0102-311X00081516

Subramaniam, B., Foster, L., Harding, S., Roy, D. and TallBear, K. (2016) 'Feminism, postcolonialism, technoscience', in U. Felt, R. Fouché, C.A. Miller and L. Smith-Doerr (eds) *The Handbook of Science and Technology Studies* (4th edn), Cambridge, MA: MIT Press, pp 407–434.

Suh, S. (2015) '"Right tool," wrong "job": manual vacuum aspiration, post-abortion care and transnational population politics in Senegal', *Social Science & Medicine*, 135: 56–66.

Suh, S. (2019) 'Post-abortion care in Senegal: a promising terrain for medical sociology research on global abortion politics', *Reproduction, Health, and Medicine: Advances in Medical Sociology*, 20: 19–43.

Suh, S. (2021) 'A stalled revolution? Misoprostol and the pharmaceuticalization of reproductive health in francophone Africa', *Frontiers in Sociology*, 6: 590556. doi: 10.3389/fsoc.2021.590556

Suh, S. and McReynolds-Pérez, J. (2023) 'Subversive epidemiology in abortion care: reproductive governance from the global to the local in Argentina and Senegal', *Signs: Journal of Women in Culture and Society*, 48(2): 395–421.

Sunder Rajan, K. (2017) *Pharmocracy: Value, Politics, and Knowledge in Global Biomedicine*, Durham, NC: Duke University Press.

Sutton, B. (2020) 'Intergenerational encounters in the struggle for abortion rights in Argentina', *Women's Studies International Forum*, 82: 102392. doi: 10.1016/j.wsif.2020.102392

Sutton, B. (2024) 'Abortion rights in the crosshairs: a transnational perspective on resistance strategies', *Journal of Lesbian Studies*, 28(3): 525–532.

Sutton, B. and Borland, E. (2013) 'Framing abortion rights in Argentina's Encuentros Nacionales de Mujeres', *Feminist Studies*, 39(1): 194–234.

Sutton, B. and Vacarezza, N.L. (2023) 'Introduction: abortion rights strategies in Argentina, Colombia, and Mexico', *South Atlantic Quarterly*, 122(2): 378–385.

Szwarc, L. (2024) 'Los aportes de las luchas por el aborto legal en Argentina: para un enfoque feminista de la salud', *Critical Times*, 7(1): 26–45.

Taylor, L. (2022) 'How South America became a global role model for abortion rights', *BMJ*, 378: 1908. doi: 10.1136/bmj.o1908

Taylor, L. (2023) 'Abortion is decriminalised in Mexico as "green wave" sweeps the region', *BMJ*, 382: 2060. doi: 10.1136/bmj.p2060

Templeton, A. (1998) 'Misoprostol for all?', *British Journal of Obstetrics and Gynaecology*, 105(9): 937–939.

Thakur, N. (2023) 'Sub-standard or sub-legal? Distribution, pharma dossiers, and fake-talk in India', *Medicine Anthropology Theory*, 10(3): 1. doi: 10.17157/mat.10.3.7279

Thiel, D. (2015) *Criminal ignorance. In Routledge international handbook of ignorance studies*, Routledge, pp 256–265.

Thomsen, C. (2015) 'The politics of narrative, narrative as politic: rethinking reproductive justice frameworks through the South Dakota abortion story', *Feminist Formations*, 27(2): 1–26.

Thong, K.J. and Baird, D.T. (1992) 'Medical abortion', *British Medical Journal*, 305: 187–188.

Torres, M.E. (2022) 'Neoconservative camouflage: the datafication of abortion debates in Ecuador', *Tapuya: Latin American Science, Technology and Society*, 5(1): 2110356. doi: 10.1080/25729861.2022.2110356

Tsing, A. (2005) *Friction: An Ethnography of Global Connection*, Princeton, NJ: Princeton University Press.

Unnithan, M. and Pigg, S.L. (2014) 'Sexual and reproductive health rights and justice–tracking the relationship', *Culture, Health & Sexuality*, 16(10): 1181–1187.

Vacarezza, N.L. (2021) 'Aborto, experiencia, afectos', in D. Belfiori (ed) *Código rosa. Relatos sobre abortos* (2nd edn), Buenos Aires: Ediciones La parte maldita, pp 121–128.

Vacarezza, N.L. and Burton, J. (2023) 'Transformar los sentidos y el sentir: El activismo cultural de las redes de acompañantes de abortos en América Latina', *Debate Feminista*, 66: 1–30.

Van Andel, T., de Boer, H.J., Barnes, J. and Vandebroek, I. (2014) 'Medicinal plants used for menstrual disorders in Latin America, the Caribbean, sub-Saharan Africa, South and Southeast Asia and their uterine properties: a review', *Journal of Ethnopharmacology*, 155(2): 992–1000.

Van der Geest, S. (2011) 'The urgency of pharmaceutical anthropology: a multilevel perspective', *Curare*, 34(1): 9–15.

Van der Geest, S., Whyte, S.R. and Hardon, A. (1996) 'The anthropology of pharmaceuticals: a biographical approach', *Annual Review of Anthropology*, 25(1): 153–178.

Van de Walle, E. (1997) 'Flowers and fruits: two thousand years of menstrual regulation', *The Journal of Interdisciplinary History*, 28(2): 183– 203.

Vázquez, S., Gutiérrez, M.A. Calandra, N. and Berner, E. (2006) 'El aborto en la adolescencia: investigación sobre el uso de misoprostol para la interrupción del embarazo en adolescentes', in S. Checa (ed) *Realidades y coyunturas del aborto: entre el derecho y la necesidad*, Buenos Aires: Paidós, pp 277–297.

Vasquez Del Aguila, E. (2022) 'Precarious lives: forced sterilisation and the struggle for reproductive justice in Peru', *Global Public Health*, 17(1): 100–114.

Veldhuis, S., Sánchez-Ramírez, G. and Darney, B.G. (2022a) '"Becoming the woman she wishes you to be": a qualitative study exploring the experiences of medication abortion *acompañantes* in three regions in Mexico', *Contraception*, 106: 39–44.

Veldhuis, S., Sánchez-Ramírez, G. and Darney, B.G. (2022b) 'Locating autonomous abortion accompanied by feminist activists in the spectrum of self-managed medication abortion', *Studies in Family Planning*, 53(2): 377–387.

Veldhuis, S., Sánchez-Ramírez, G. and Darney, B.G. (2022c) '"Sigue siendo un sistema precario": barreras de acceso a abortos clínicos: la experiencia de acompañantes en tres regiones mexicanas', *Cadernos de Saúde Pública*, 38: ES124221. doi: 10.1590/0102-311XES124221

Verza, M. and Riquelme, G. (2023) 'Burner phones, aliases, code words: the secret networks that women use to circumvent Honduras' abortion ban', *CBS News*, 20 May. Available at: www.cbsnews.com/news/burner-pho nes-aliases-code-words-how-secret-networks-help-women-circumvent-honduras-abortion-ban

Vivaldi, L. and Stutzin, V. (2021) 'Exploring alternative meanings of a feminist and safe abortion in Chile', in B. Sutton and N.L. Vacarezza (eds) *Abortion and Democracy: Contentious Body Politics in Argentina, Chile, and Uruguay*, Abingdon: Routledge, pp 226–245.

Wainwright, M., Colvin, C.J., Swartz, A. and Leon, N. (2016) 'Self-management of medical abortion: a qualitative evidence synthesis', *Reproductive Health Matters*, 24(47): 155–167.

Walsh, A. (2020) 'Feminist networks facilitating access to misoprostol in Mesoamerica', *Feminist Review*, 124(1): 175–182.

Walt, R.P. (1992) 'Misoprostol for the treatment of peptic ulcer and antiinflammatory-drug–induced gastroduodenal ulceration', *New England Journal of Medicine*, 327(22): 1575–1580.

Watkins, E.S. (1998) *On the Pill: A Social History of Oral Contraceptives, 1950–1970*, Baltimore, MD: JHU Press.

Weaver, G., Schiavon, R., Collado, M.E., Küng, S. and Darney, B.G. (2020) 'Misoprostol knowledge and distribution in Mexico City after the change in abortion law: a survey of pharmacy staff', *BMJ Sexual & Reproductive Health*, 46(1): 46–50.

Webb, S. (2000) *Addressing the Consequences of Unsafe Abortion*, Watertown, MA: Pathfinder International.

Weeks, A.D., Fiala, C. and Safar, P. (2005) 'Misoprostol and the debate over off-label drug use', *BJOG: An International Journal of Obstetrics & Gynaecology*, 112(3): 269–272.

WHO (World Health Organization) (2012) *Safe Abortion: Technical and Policy Guidance for Health Systems* (2nd edn), Geneva: WHO.

WHO (World Health Organization) (2021a) *World Health Organization Model List of Essential Medicines: 22nd List (2021)*, Geneva: WHO.

WHO (World Health Organization) (2021b) *Access to Medical Abortion Medicines in the South-East Asia Regio: A Status Report*, New Delhi: World Health Organization, Regional Office for South-East Asia.

WHO (World Health Organization) (2022) 'Medical management of induced abortion: recommendations 27–30 (3.4.2)'. Available at: https://srhr.org/abortioncare/chapter-3/abortion-3-4/medical-management-of-induced-abortion-recommendations-27-30-3-4-2/

WHO (World Health Organization) (2024) 'Substandard and falsified medical products' 3 December 2024. Available at: www.who.int/news-room/fact-sheets/detail/substandard-and-falsified-medical-products

Whyte, S.R., Van der Geest, S. and Hardon, A. (2002) *Social Lives of Medicines*, Cambridge: Cambridge University Press.

Wilson, T.D. (2014) 'Violence against women in Latin America', *Latin American Perspectives*, 41(1): 3–18.

Winikoff, B. and Sheldon, W. (2012) 'Use of medicines changing the face of abortion', *International Perspectives on Sexual and Reproductive Health*, 38(3): 164–166.

Winikoff, B., Bousiéguez, M., Salmerón, J., Robles-Rivera, K., Hernández-Salazar, S., Martínez-Huitrón, A. et al (2025) 'A proof-of-concept study of ulipristal acetate for early medication abortion', *NEJM Evidence*, 4(2). doi: 10.1056/EVIDoa2400209

Wollum, A., Huerta, S.G., Uribe, O.L., Garnsey, C., Gaddis, S.M., Baum, S.E. et al (2022) 'The influence of feminist abortion accompaniment on emotions related to abortion: a longitudinal observational study in Mexico', *SSM-Population Health*, 19: 101259. doi: 10.1016/j.ssmph.2022.101259

Women Resisting Violence Collective (2022) *Women Resisting Violence: Voices and Experiences from Latin America*, Rugby, UK: Practical Action Publishing.

Wurtz, H. (2012) 'Indigenous women of Latin America: unintended pregnancy, unsafe abortion, and reproductive health outcomes', *Pimatisiwin*, 10(3): 271–82.

Yanow, S., Pizzarossa, L.B. and Jelinska, K. (2021) 'Self-managed abortion: exploring synergies between institutional medical systems and autonomous health movements', *Contraception*, 104(3): 219–221.

Zamberlin, N., Romero, M. and Ramos, S. (2012) 'Latin American women's experiences with medical abortion in settings where abortion is legally restricted', *Reproductive Health*, 9(1): 1–11.

Zaremberg, G. and Rezende de Almeida, D. (2022) *Feminisms in Latin America: Pro-Choice Nested Networks in Mexico and Brazil*, Cambridge: Cambridge University Press.

Zurbriggen, R., Keefe-Oates, B. and Gerdts, C. (2018) 'Accompaniment of second-trimester abortions: the model of the feminist Socorrista network of Argentina', *Contraception*, 97(2): 108–115.

Zurbriggen, R. (2019) 'Abortar y acompañar a abortar: armándonos vidas activistas feministas afectadas', in S. Balaña, A. Finielli, C. Giuliano, A. Paz, C. Ramírez, D. Barrancos et al (eds) *Salud feminista: Soberanía de los cuerpos, poder y organización*, Buenos Aires: Tinta Limón, pp 199–218.

Index

A

abortifacients *see* abortion pills; herbs/plants; mifepristone; misoprostol
abortion accompaniment process *see acompañamiento*
Abortion Act 166
abortion doulas 164–165
abortion exceptionalism 4, 124, 160
abortion governance 155–156
abortion hotlines 13, 43–45, 47, 57–58, 64, 80, 121, 137–138
abortion lawfare 105–106, 109, 124, 129
abortion laws
  author's overview of 5–7, 5n1, 103–104, 155–156, 166
  challenging of 13–14
  healthcare and 117–123
  impacts of 8, 104–105
  information on, access to 117–118, 128
  legal persecution 123–127, 129
  misoprostol, and 20, 79
  strategic ignorance 103, 127–128, 129–130
  see also criminalization of abortions; decriminalization of abortions; re-criminalization of abortions
abortion liberation
  abortion care, rethinking 162–163
  abortion governance and 155–156
  author's overview of 155
  global context, in a 164–166
  knowledge expansion, and 159–162
  reproductive justice, as 157–159
abortion mobilities 12–14 *see also* mobility justice
abortion pills 133, 144–146, 156–157 *see also* dosages; medical abortions; mifepristone; misoprostol; self-managed abortions
abortion rates 5, 129, 151
abortions
  author's overview of 3–4
  de-medicalization of 33, 41, 160–161
  medicalization of 111, 135, 136, 152, 155, 159–160
  person-centred care 161
  religion and 5
  social decriminalization of 109–110, 132, 156
  therapeutic abortions 6, 119
  uterine contractions 2, 24, 27, 141, 142
  see also abortion laws; herbs/plants; medical abortions; mifepristone; misoprostol; procedural abortions; safe abortions; self-managed abortions; unsafe abortions
ACOG *see* American College of Obstetricians and Gynecologists (ACOG)
acompañamiento
  feminists, between 74–75
  history of 51
  as holistic support 53
  impacts of 68–69, 77, 164–165
  political motivations of 50, 72–73
  support provision, types of 56–65
  virtual accompaniment 50, 58–61, 100
acompañante groups
  activism by 54–55, 162–163
  author's overview of 51
  increase in 51–52, 156
  medical professionals in 66
  roles of 50, 52–54
  solidarity within 74–75
  see also *acompañantes*; collectives
acompañantes
  abortion laws and 109–110, 118–123
  activism by 52, 162–163, 165–166
  author's overview of 19–20, 51, 158
  concealment strategies of 103–104, 111–117
  experiences of 63–64
  harassment of 125–127, 132, 163
  healthcare and 118–123
  herbs/plants, and 137–139
  knowledge building by 39–40, 73–76
  legal persecution of 124–126
  mobility of misoprostol 80, 82, 83–84, 87, 89, 90–91, 91–94, 96–98, 102
  motivations of 69–73
  reproductive justice and 51, 55, 77–78
  roles of 1, 50, 52–54, 77–78, 83–84, 156, 161
  safe abortions 53, 99–101, 127–129, 134, 149

INDEX

strategies for women from 37–39
support provided by 55–56, 98, 161
the term *acompañar* 50
virtual accompaniment 50, 58–61, 100
see also collectives; interviewees
Africa 7, 33, 135, 165
American College of Obstetricians and Gynecologists (ACOG) 32, 147
ancestral knowledge *see* herbs/plants; traditional medicine
anti-abortion actors/movement
  abortion lawfare 105–106, 109
  misinformation by 3, 4
  misoprostol access and 85, 96, 134, 148, 166
  politics and 131, 146
  religion and 5, 59
  tactics of 125, 126–127
Argentina
  abortion accompaniment in 39, 40, 54, 57
  abortion laws in 6, 103, 104, 106, 107, 108, 118–119, 129–131
  abortion liberation in 161, 164
  abortion restrictions in 8
  acompañantes in 2, 40, 51, 64, 70–71, 142
  anti-abortion movement in 126, 131
  concealment strategies in 112, 114, 115
  experiences of abortion in 42–43
  information access in 44, 45–46, 47
  La Revuelta 50
  legal persecution in 124
  misoprostol in 81–82, 86, 107, 144–145
  movement of misoprostol in 25–26, 92
  reproductive justice in 10–11
  social decriminalization in 109
  see also Socorristas en Red
Asia 7, 135, 165–166
Assis, M.P. 26, 49, 78, 109, 147
author's research *see* interviewees; research by author
autonomy
  abortions and 54, 73, 144
  acompañantes and 19, 52–53, 162–163
  bodily autonomy 6, 20–21, 155, 158–159, 160, 161
  herbs/plants, and 138
  information access and 44, 65
  the term *autonomy* 52
  WHO guidelines and 39

B

Baird, D.T. 28
Barry, A. 16, 134
Baulieu, É.-É. 141
Belfiori, D. 36
Belfrage, M. 2, 98
Bercu, C. 137

Biolab 23, 31
black market
  mifepristone access from 143
  misoprostol access from 32, 79, 84–87, 95–96, 101
bodily autonomy *see* autonomy
Bogotá 119
Bolivia 26, 68, 86, 90, 153
Braine, N. 52
Brazil
  abortion laws in 6, 22, 23, 105
  anti-abortion movement in 126
  misoprostol access in 87, 96
  misoprostol history in 1, 19, 22, 24, 25–26
  restrictions on misoprostol in 31–32, 49, 81, 148
  scholarship on misoprostol from 27, 28, 85
Briggs, L. 10
Burton, J. 39, 74, 106
Bury, L. 153
Bush, George 142

C

Calkin, S. 13–14, 102
the Caribbean 5, 6, 7, 39, 49, 75, 135
  see also specific countries (e.g. Cuba, Dominican Republic)
casuistic knowledge 40, 41
Catholicism 5, 59, 75, 105, 130
Catholics for Choice 5
Central America 6, 123 *see also specific countries (e.g. El Salvador, Honduras)*
Chile
  abortion laws in 6
  information access in 44
  misoprostol access in 79, 81, 95
  traditional medicine use in 136, 138
coagulation of misoprostol 91–92, 102
code words 111–112, 117
Código rosa (Belfiori) 36
Coêlho, H.L. 27
Colectiva por la Libre Información para las Mujeres (CLIM) 44–45, 46, 120
collectives
  acompañamiento practices in 56–57, 74–75
  concealment strategies 112–113
  harassment of 125
  herbs/plants, and 138–139
  horizontal approach to 53–54
  Jane Collective 51, 152
  knowledge building 70, 73–77, 120
  medical professionals in 66
  mifepristone access 142–143
  misoprostol mobilities, and 82–84, 87, 91, 98
  political values of 55
  Red Compañera 75–76
  reproductive justice and 9, 55

193

rise in 51
see also *acompañante* groups
Collins, F.S. 26–27
Colombia
  abortion laws in 6, 103, 105, 106, 108, 118, 119
  acompañantes in 38, 54, 61, 72, 74, 100
  concealment strategies in 113, 115–116
  counselling model in 68
  herbs/plants, use of in 136, 138
  manual vacuum aspiration (MVA) 151
  misoprostol access in 81–82, 87, 90, 96, 97
concealment strategies 111–117
Costa, S.H. 27
Costa Rica 81, 85–86, 95, 101, 105, 127, 143
costs
  of manual vacuum aspiration (MVA) kits 150
  of medical abortions 28
  of mifepristone 143, 144
  of misoprostol 28, 82–83, 88, 90, 93, 95–98
COVID-19 pandemic 26, 56, 59, 75, 86, 93–94
criminalization of abortions
  impacts of 104, 159
  misoprostol restrictions and 49, 101–102
  as mode of governance 128–129, 130–131
  social criminalization 104–105, 163
  strategies for women, and 37–38
  see also abortion laws; *acompañantes*; black market; mobilities
Cuba 5, 6, 95
curettage 27, 147, 149, 150, 152
Cytotec 23, 25, 26, 32, 33, 86, 88, 97

D

Davis, A. 155, 156
De Zordo, S. 2, 28, 96
death *see* mortality
decolonial feminism 15–16
decriminalization of abortions
  abortion laws and 131, 164
  author's overview of 158–159
  marea verde (green wave/tide) 6, 51, 124, 164
  misoprostol access after 26
  responses to 108
  social decriminalization 109–110, 132, 156
de-medicalization of abortions 33, 41, 160–161
diclofenac 43, 144–145, 146
DKT International 150
doctors *see* medical professionals
Dominican Republic 6, 95, 103
Donda, Victoria 126

dosages
  acompañantes on 37–38
  clinical studies on 29
  experimentations with 24, 25, 40
  knowledge of, lack of 33, 41–42, 82, 100
  regimens, effective 35–37
  WHO guidelines 36–37, 39
  see also costs
doulas 164–165
Downie, W.W. 31
drones 94
drugstores *see* pharmacies

E

Ecuador 43, 44, 47, 51, 76, 95, 126
El Salvador
  abortions laws in 6–7, 103, 105, 164
  legal persecution in 123, 126
  misoprostol access in 95
embodied knowledge 39, 40, 41
emmenagogues 134–135
England 166
Erdman, J.N. 26, 49
ESAR (Education for Reproductive Health) 151

F

Facebook 60, 85, 111, 113, 120, 125–126
Facioli, L.R.R. 85
fake pills 85, 86, 143
fatality *see* mortality
FDA *see* Food and Drug Administration (FDA)
feminism
  decolonial 15–16
  science and technology studies (STS) 14–15
feminist movements
  abortion access activism 6, 51, 94, 130
  acompañante groups, activism by 54–55
  see also acompañantes
Fernández Vázquez, S. 2, 65
Florencia 161
Fonseca, W. 30, 31
Food and Drug Administration (FDA) 23, 27, 29, 32–33, 142, 144, 146, 166
Freeman, C. 127
Fundación ESAR (Education for Reproductive Health) 151

G

Gago, V. 19
G.D. Searle & Co 23
  see also Searle
gendered violence 8
generic misoprostol 23, 26, 34, 87–88
Gilmore, R.W. 156
Gomperts, R. 44, 90
González, C.H. 27

governance *see* abortion governance; criminalization of abortions; reproductive governance
green tide/wave *(marea verde)* 6, 51, 124, 164
Greene, J.A. 35
Guatemala 95, 112
Gutierrez, M. 151

H

Haiti 6
harassment 125–127, 132, 163
Hardon, A. 134, 154
Harrison-Woolrych, M. 163
healthcare professionals *see* medical professionals
herbs/plants 24, 71, 72, 133, 134–140
Hernandez, P.M. 8
Honduras
  abortion laws in 6, 103, 105, 164
  fake pills in 86
  manual vacuum aspiration (MVA) 150
  misoprostol access in 95, 111, 112
hotlines *see* abortion hotlines

I

ignorance *see* strategic ignorance
Indigenous communities
  abortion restrictions and 7, 104
  acompañante support for 55, 100, 101
  colonialism and 15
  healthcare access for 20, 51
  traditional knowledge 17, 133, 134, 136, 140
Indigenous feminist thought 16
information
  abortion hotlines 13, 43–45, 47, 57–58, 64, 80, 121, 137–138
  on abortion laws, lack of 107–108
  manuals 45–46, 47, 58–59, 67
  see also knowledge
International Projects Assistance Service (Ipas) 68, 150–151
interviewees
  on abortion experiences 42, 62, 70
  on abortion law navigation 118–123
  on abortions 2
  on access to abortions 7
  on access to information 44, 45–47, 57–58
  on access to misoprostol 34, 81–84, 85, 86–87, 87–88
  on *acompañante* collectives/groups 55, 73–74, 76
  on *acompañante* experiences 63–64
  on *acompañante* motivations 69–72
  on *acompañantes*' role 56–65
  author's overview of research 17–19
  on concealment strategies 111–117
  on costs of abortion pills 88, 95–98
  on dosages of misoprostol 37, 38
  on experimentations with misoprostol 35–36
  on feminist activism 54–55
  on harassment/persecution 124–127
  on herbs/plants 136–140
  on medical professionals 66, 67–68
  on mifepristone 142–143
  on misoprostol 2, 80, 119
  on movement of misoprostol 25–26, 92–94, 101–102
  on procedural abortions 149, 150, 152
  on scholarship on misoprostol 28
  on strategies for women 37–39
  on virtual accompaniment 58, 59–61
  on WHO guidelines 38, 39, 118–120, 121
Ipas *see* International Projects Assistance Service (Ipas)
Ireland 94, 159

J

Jane Collective 51, 152
Juarez, F. 107–108
justice *see* mobility justice; reproductive justice

K

knowledge
  knowledge building 38–40, 70, 73–77, 120, 160
  lack of 33, 41–42, 82, 100
  traditional knowledge 17, 133, 134, 136, 140
  types of 39, 40, 41
  see also information
Krauss, A. 105–106, 162
Kumar, A. 128

L

La Revuelta 50
laboratories 87–89
Larrea, S. 39
Latin America
  abortion laws in 5–7, 5n1, 103–104, 104–108, 118
  abortion liberation in 164–166
  abortion rates in 5, 129, 151
  anti-abortion movement in 124–127
  reproductive justice in 9–11
  science and technology studies (STS) scholarship 15
  strategic ignorance of states 127–131
  see also abortion laws; *acompañantes*; anti-abortion actors/movement; *specific countries (e.g. Argentina, Colombia)*
lawfare *see* abortion lawfare
laws *see* abortion laws
legalities *see* abortion laws

Lesbianas y Feministas por la
  Descriminalización del Aborto 45, 67
letrozole 133, 145–146, 153
liberation *see* abortion liberation
Liboiron, M. 41
Lockwood, C. 32
Lugones, M. 15

M

machismo 8
Macri, Mauricio 130–131
Maffeo, F. 74
magic
  herbal 136, 139–140
  of misoprostol 2–3, 101
Mahoney, M.J. 26–27
malformations in children 28, 30–31
manual vacuum aspiration (MVA) 149–153
manuals 45–46, 47, 58–59, 67
marea verde (green tide/wave) 6, 51, 124, 164
marianismo 8
Martin, P. 54
Martin, Z.C. 111
Mason-Deese, L. 19
McGoey, L. 103, 127
McMahon, B.D. 165
McMahon, H.V. 165
McReynolds-Pérez, J. 65, 123, 158
medical abortions
  author's overview of 4
  costs of 28
  medical professionals and 65–69
  medications for 144–146
  mobility of pills 13
  mortality, impact of on 88–89, 135, 142, 148, 163
  reproductive justice and 20, 54
  scholarship on 28–29, 159
  spaces for 98–101
  strategies for 37–39
  World Health Organization on 48–49, 119–120
  see also abortion liberation; dosages; mifepristone; misoprostol
medical professionals
  abortion access, blocking of 65
  in collectives 66
  obstetric violence 152
  pharmacies 81–84
  scripts to say to 115–116, 117
  support from 66–67, 121–123
  traditional medicine 136
medicalization of abortions 111, 135, 136, 152, 155, 159–160
medications *see* abortion pills; dosages; mifepristone; misoprostol
menstruation regulation 134–135, 136, 138
mercado negro see black market

methotrexatate 133, 145, 146, 153
Mexico
  abortion laws in 6, 103, 105–106, 107–108
  acompañantes in 37, 51–52, 60–61, 62, 63, 72, 74, 149
  feminist activism in 54, 120
  harassment in 125
  herbs/plants, use of in 136, 138, 139
  Indigenous communities in 55
  legal persecutions in 123–124
  mifepristone in 142–143
  misoprostol in 26, 81
  movement of misoprostol in 89, 91, 92, 93, 94
Mexico City 5, 26, 63, 94, 99, 107
mifepristone
  code words for 112
  cost of 143, 144
  as essential medicine (WHO) 36, 141, 147
  fake pills 143
  in medical abortions 4, 28–29, 119
  -misoprostol combination 33, 49, 50, 51, 52, 89–90, 133, 141–144
  restrictions on 133, 145, 146, 149
  studies of 142
Milei, Javier 107, 108, 131
Millar, E. 4
MisoChat 45
misoprostol
  author's overview of 1, 2
  author's summary of 153–154
  coagulation of 91–92, 102
  controversies 30–35
  cost of 28, 82–83, 88, 90, 93, 95–98
  experimentations with 24–25, 26, 28–29, 35, 144–146
  fake pills 85, 86
  generic misoprostol 23, 26, 34, 87–88
  information on, access to 41–42, 43–47, 165
  magic of 2–3, 101
  malformations in children 28, 30–31
  medication combos, and other 144–146
  -mifepristone combination 33, 49, 50, 51, 52, 89–90, 133, 141–144
  off-label uses of 29–30, 67, 134, 147–148
  restrictions on 31–32, 49, 79, 81, 148
  sales of 25, 31
  as stomach ulcer drug 23
  studies of as abortifacient 27, 28, 133
  see also abortion laws; black market; dosages; interviewees; laboratories; medical abortions; mobilities; pharmacies; self-managed abortions
mobilities
  author's overview of 12–14
  of knowledge 73–76
  of misoprostol 20, 80, 89–91, 99, 101–102
  strategies, anti-coagulation 91–94

INDEX

mobility justice 12–14, 79–80, 101–102
Mobility Justice (Sheller) 12
Monsanto 23
Morgan, L.M. 10, 11
mortality
  abortion laws and 129, 130, 159
  abortions, from 7–8, 24, 25, 42, 128, 163, 165–166
  maternal, sources of 33, 150
  medicalization on, impact of 88–89, 135, 142, 148, 163
Murphy, M. 149, 151, 154, 163
MVA *see* manual vacuum aspiration (MVA)

N

Necochea López, R. 115
Ni Una Menos (Not One [Woman] Less) movement 130
Nicaragua 6, 103, 105, 112
non-binary people 55
Norman, J.E. 28–29
Northern Ireland 94, 159

O

Oberman, M. 6–7
obstetric violence 152
obstetricians *see* medical professionals
off-label use of medications 29–30, 67, 147–148
Oxaprost 43, 144–145

P

pandemic *see* COVID-19 pandemic
Paraguay 8
patents 32, 33, 34, 87
patriarchy 8, 54, 69, 106, 151, 158
persecution 123–127
person-centred care 161
Peru
  abortion access in 7, 99–101, 164
  abortion laws in 105, 106, 119–123
  acompañante groups in 73, 75–76
  acompañantes in 2, 37, 38, 39, 56–58, 60, 62, 63–64, 69–71
  author's research in 17, 18
  Colectiva por la Libre Información para las Mujeres (CLIM) 44–45, 46, 120
  concealment strategies in 112–117
  feminist activism in 54
  harassment in 125–126
  herbs/plants, use of in 135–136, 137–138
  information access in 44, 47
  knowledge making in 39–40, 41
  legal persecution in 123
  marginalized populations in 55
  medical professionals in 2, 28, 34, 66
  mifepristone in 141, 143

misoprostol access in 34, 79, 81–82, 83–84, 85, 95–98, 101, 102
misoprostol production in 87–88
movement of misoprostol 25, 26, 80, 91, 92, 93
procedural abortions in 149, 150–151
punishment, culture of in 152
Pfizer 23, 33, 87, 88
pharmacies 81–84, 136
pills *see* abortion pills; medical abortions
plants *see* herbs/plants
political candidates 126, 130–131
post-abortion care 68, 122–123, 149, 150, 152, 160
pregnancy terminations *see* abortions
prison abolition 155, 156
pro-abortion actors/movement 54, 85, 94, 126, 127, 130–131
procedural abortions
  acompañante support for 63
  author's overview of 3–4, 149
  benefits of 134, 149
  manual vacuum aspiration (MVA) 149–153
  misoprostol use in 29, 34, 147–148
  obstetric violence during 152
  reproductive justice, and 20
  travel for 98, 102

R

rAborta 94
Reagan, Ronald 42, 142
re-criminalization of abortions 6, 131, 163
Red Compañera 75–76
religion 5, 7, 8, 11, 75, 105
reproductive governance 11, 52, 127, 158
reproductive health
  access to services 6
  herbs/plants, and 136, 138
  misoprostol access and 88, 89, 101, 148
  reproductive justice and 9, 10, 158
reproductive justice
  abortion liberation as 156, 157–159
  acompañantes and 51, 55, 74, 77–78, 102, 110
  author's overview of 9, 157
  doulas and 165
  Latin American context, in 9–11
  organizations 5
  scholarship 9–11, 19–20
reproductive mobilities *see* abortion mobilities; mobility justice
reproductive rights 9, 10, 105, 106, 157, 158
reproductive technologies
  abortion medications 3
  author's overview of 20
research by author 17–19 *see also* interviewees
rights
  abortion laws and 105–107, 128
  reproductive rights 9, 10, 105, 106, 157, 158

Roberts, E.F.S. 11
robots 79, 92, 94
Rodríguez, S. 17, 127
Ross, L. 9–10
Roussel Uclaf 28, 141–142
Rowlands, S. 163

S

Safe Abortion: Technical and Policy Guidance for Health Systems (WHO) 36
safe abortions
  access to 7
  acompañantes and 53, 68–69, 163
  misoprostol and 65
  mobility justice and 12–13
  reclassification of 48–49
  see also unsafe abortions
Sanabria, E. 134, 154
scholarship
  on abortifacient properties of misoprostol 27, 28
  geographies of 14–17
  on medical abortions 28–29, 159
  on misoprostol use 24–25, 26–29
  on mobilities 12–14
  on reproductive justice 9–11, 19–20
  science and technology studies (STS) 14–15
Schönhöfer, P.S. 27, 30
science and technology studies (STS) scholarship 14–15
scripts 115–116, 117
Searle 22, 23, 30, 31–33, 34
Segato, R. 8
self-managed abortions
  abortion laws and 118–119, 123–124, 143, 155–156
  abortion liberation and 160, 163, 165, 166
  access to information for 45–47, 108
  acompañantes support for 50, 51–52, 53, 61–63, 77
  author's overview of 4
  concealment strategies for 111–117
  experiences of 42–43, 70–71
  increase in 3, 156
  knowledge building 73, 160
  spaces for 99–100
  studies on 27
  virtual accompaniment 50, 58–61, 100
Sheller, M. 12–13, 79–80
Shepard, B. 127, 132
Signal 60, 100, 112–113
Singer, E.O. 52, 118
Sismondo, S. 35
social decriminalization of abortions 109–110, 132, 156
Socorristas en Red 39, 57, 67–68, 69, 74–75, 108, 124, 163
Sodero, S. 91

Solinger, R. 9
strategic ignorance 103, 127–128, 129–130
subversive epidemiology 123
Suh, S. 123, 148, 158
Suriname 6, 164
Sutton, B. 54
Szwarc, L. 2, 65, 67

T

tacit knowledge 39, 40, 41
Telegram 60, 100, 112–113
therapeutic abortions 6, 119
Thomsen, C. 157
Thong, K.J. 28
tinctures 140
traditional medicine 135–136 *see also* herbs/plants
trans men 9, 55

U

ulipristal acetate 133, 146, 153
ultrasounds 38–39, 61
United States
  abortion access in 51, 99, 111, 149, 166
  Food and Drug Administration (FDA) 23, 27, 29, 32–33, 142, 144, 146, 166
  International Projects Assistance Service (Ipas) 68, 150–151
  mifepristone in 142, 145, 146
  misoprostol studies in 28
  reproductive justice in 9–10, 158
unsafe abortions
  classification of 48–49
  experiences of 70–71
  herbs/plants, and 135, 137, 138
  mortality rates 7–8, 25, 163, 165–166
  reproductive justice and 158, 159
  see also safe abortions
Urry, J. 80
Uruguay 5, 6, 44, 47, 76, 90, 95
uterine contractions 2, 24, 27, 141, 142

V

Veldhuis, S. 53
Venezuela 80, 81, 85–86, 90, 96, 121, 137–138, 152
Vessey, M.P. 27
virtual accompaniment 50, 58–61, 100

W

WhatsApp 45, 64, 85–86, 112, 113
WHO *see* World Health Organization (WHO)
Whyte, S.R. 16
wilful blindness 103, 128, 132
Women Help Women 90
Women on Waves 13–14, 44, 94
Women on Web 87, 90, 94

World Health Organization (WHO)
　abortion safety, classification of 48–49
　on black market pharmaceuticals 85
　essential medications for abortions 4, 22, 29, 34, 36, 91, 141, 147
　interviewees on WHO guidelines 38, 39, 118–120, 121
　on letrozole 145
　regimen guidelines for misoprostol 36–37
　and traditional medicine 136

Z

Zurbriggen, R. 39–40

www.ingramcontent.com/pod-product-compliance
Lightning Source LLC
Chambersburg PA
CBHW051545020426
42333CB00016B/2105